GUARDIAN
OF THE
WILD

GUARDIAN
OF THE
WILD

THE STORY OF THE NATIONAL WILDLIFE FEDERATION, 1936–1986

Thomas B. Allen

Published in Association with the National Wildlife Federation

INDIANA UNIVERSITY PRESS
Bloomington & Indianapolis

Manufactured in the United States of America

Library of Congress Cataloging-in-Publication Data
Allen, Thomas B.
Guardian of the wild.
Includes index.
1. National Wildlife Federation—History.   2. Nature conservation—United States—History.   I. Title.
QH76.A43   1987   333.95′16′06073   87–45113
ISBN 0–253–32605–2

CONTENTS

7.

GETTING THE LAW ON OUR SIDE 138

Illustrations follow page 118.

FOREWORD

George Bernard Shaw once said, "This is the true joy in life: The being used for a purpose recognized by yourself as a mighty one."

Guardian of the Wild is the story of just such joy. On first reading, this book may appear to be a straightforward chronology of the formation and growth of a dynamic and effective conservation organization. *Guardian of the Wild* is that. But it is more.

Like any good history, it goes beyond a simple retelling of events. It focuses on individuals—millions of them—who for the past 50 years have devoted themselves to a mighty purpose, who have given their energies and their vigor to conserving the natural resources that nurtured their forebears in the hopes that those same resources would also nurture generations yet unborn.

It is, finally, the story of the environmental movement's tremendous—if somewhat unanticipated—success.

That success is directly attributable to the steadfast adherence to the first commandment of NWF's founders: Educate.

The Federation's educational effort has been laudatory: first-rate magazines for every age group, from preschoolers to retirees; teaching guides; youth camps; outdoor family vacations; and since 1938—without interruption—the annual celebration of National Wildlife Week. The result has been the transformation of the conservation credo into a national passion.

Public opinion polls today indicate that the vast majority of Americans value environmental quality on a par with free elections, freedom of worship, and freedom of expression. Conservation has become a banner under which people of divergent heritages and competing personal and political ideologies can unite.

Conservation education has changed the face of America. It has turned the national spotlight on environmental quality. It has made Americans understand that polluted rivers and streams, smog-filled air, abandoned hazardous waste pits, eroded soils, and degraded vistas need not be the price of the "good life."

Educated Americans have demanded—and won—a mosaic of landmark federal environmental legislation: the Clean Air Act, the Clean Water Act, the National Environmental Policy Act, the Endangered Species Act, the Safe Drinking Water Act, and a host of other mandates. These laws and others have saved wilderness areas and wildlife habitat; helped clean the air and water; spared the bald eagle, the whooping crane, and scores of other species from extinction; and awakened America's corporate leaders to their social responsibilities.

Yet, the battle for environmental quality is far from over. Society is still straining the limits of the biological systems that support all life. We are overtaxing the oceans, grasslands, croplands, wetlands, and forests that hold the key to our future. We are spending our biological capital at breakneck speed, but we are not reinvesting in our resources portfolio at the same pace.

The last generation—including the nearly 2000 individuals gathered at the first North American Wildlife Conference and the thousands more people that they represented—saw a world careening toward environmental self-destruction, and they applied the brakes. They created the foundation upon which a strong and benevolent organization has been built to guard the health of this fragile planet.

Their aspirations—their mantle—has fallen to us. For the generations of the 21st century—including our generation—may well be the last to save the best of that which remains of our natural resources heritage. In tribute to those who created the National Wildlife Federation and on behalf of the generations yet to follow, we pledge not to fail in our stewardship duty.

Jay D. Hair

Jay D. Hair, President
National Wildlife Federation

GUARDIAN
OF THE
WILD

1

Making a Difference

In a Wisconsin classroom, fourth graders are watching "We Can Save the Eagle," a National Wildlife Federation film that shows how the American bald eagle, once found throughout the nation it symbolizes, has become a bird in danger. "I think eagles make me feel good," one of the students later writes. "They look so pretty when they soar through the sky."

In Washington, an official of the Environmental Protection Agency reluctantly hands over a report on acid rain to the National Wildlife Federation. The Federation had filed a Freedom of Information Act request for the report, which shows that acid rain imperils aquatic life in more than 9,000 lakes in fifteen eastern states. Highlights of the report are quickly published in the Federation's *Conservation 86,* which will alert 25,000 conservationists throughout the country. Federation lobbyists begin making their visits to congressional offices on Capitol Hill.

Soon the requests begin coming into the Federation mailroom, from garden clubs, PTAs, and the Federation's state affiliates: *Send me the publication on acid rain.* Like the fourth graders in Wisconsin learning about eagles, adults all over the country begin learning about the problems that acid rain has created in parts of their nation. "The wood frog's chirp has been stilled," says the Federation publication. "Stands of beech, spruce, and tamarack show signs of disease. And in more than 200 of the shimmering lakes, the trout are gone. Ospreys, loons, and kingfishers no longer frequent these lakes. The otter, unable to find crayfish, has long since gone elsewhere."

The publication does more than inform people about acid rain. It also tells them how to get a message to their senators and congressmen. The message: No more stalling. Strengthen the Clean Air Act* to include acid-rain controls.

While the acid-rain crusade builds, the Federation continues its work on other issues. A conference call, laced with legal terms and talk about trees, links a Federation lawyer in Washington with another lawyer in the Federation's Northern Rockies Natural Resources Center, in Missoula, Montana. Also on the line are a Sierra Club lawyer in Washington and a Sierra Club official in California. The subject is oil and gas leases in the Lewis and Clark National Forest in Montana, and the question is: Which of us takes on the Forest Service this time?

Elsewhere, Federation regional executives range the country, working with leaders of NWF affiliate organizations to improve ways of tackling environmental problems. The problems range from long-standing concerns over wetlands to new worries about acid rain and other types of airborne pollution.

The teacher and the fourth graders, the regional executives and the affiliates, the lobbyists and the editors, the conference-call voices—overlapping, interrupting, arguing, supporting, questioning—were all part of the modern environmental chorus. Elsewhere, other voices in the chorus are talking to senators and governors and city council members about other environmental problems caused by, say, interstate highway construction or poor logging practices. Many of the voices belong to members of state affiliates of the National Wildlife Federation, and they can be heard throughout a state, a region, the nation.

Today, more than ever before in the nation's history, environmental problems are solved by people whose voices will not be stilled. The people in the neighborhood may be heard by local officials who can answer questions and stop projects that threaten the quality of neighborhood life. But, as issues grow beyond the neighborhood and into the air and the streams and the soil of states and nation, the chorus is needed. Sometimes the chorus belongs to the National Wildlife Federation or another conservation organization, and sometimes the anthem of the environment comes thundering from the mighty chorus of many of the nation's environmental organizations united as one.

The idea of strength through union is as old as our democracy. What Alexis de Tocqueville saw in nineteenth-century America, the

*For the formal name of an act, refer to appendix 8, "NWF Legislative Timeline."

founders of the Federation still saw in the Depression days of the 1930s. "As soon as several of the inhabitants of the United States have taken up an opinion or a feeling which they wish to promote in the world," de Tocqueville observed, "they look around for mutual assistance; and as soon as they have found each other out, they combine. From that moment they are no longer isolated men, but a power seen from afar, whose actions serve as an example, and whose language is listened to."

The voice of the National Wildlife Federation has been heard throughout the nation since the Federation's earliest days. What started in 1936 as a group of organizations concerned about the nation's wildlife habitats had become what Executive Vice President Thomas L. Kimball called in 1981 "the largest, the most influential, and the most effective grass-roots conservation organization in the world today." From those grass roots had come call after call for a national environmental conscience. The chorus of the Federation was heard often during Kimball's long tenure. And, in an awakening symbolized by Earth Day in 1970, the nation heard that chorus.

On Earth Day people gathered in cities and in meadows, in small groups and in great masses, to demand that national attention be paid to the task of redeeming their neglected land and air and water. During the decade that followed, the nation changed its ideas about how to make the United States and the world a better place to live in. Congress, pressed by an enlightened and aroused electorate, wrote landmark laws.

The National Environmental Policy Act required all federal agencies to prepare environmental impact statements for all proposed federal activities that would significantly disturb the environment. The Coastal Zone Management Act provided federal funding for states to develop and implement management plans for coastal habitats. (Today twenty-nine states and one territory protect coastal areas, and more are likely to follow, year by year.) The Clean Water Act resulted partly from a long, Federation-led crusade that still goes on. The Marine Mammal Protection Act and the Ocean Dumping Act gave federal protection to mammals and other creatures of the sea. The Federal Environmental Pesticide Control Act increased EPA control over pesticides. The Endangered Species Act held out the promise of life to species heading for extinction.

The Federal Land Policy and Management Act directed the Secretary of the Interior to develop and uphold land-use plans for public lands. The Toxic Substances Control Act of 1976 directed EPA to require testing of chemicals before they entered the environment. The

National Wildlife Federation not only backed the bill, but also made sure that it had within it provisions for detecting and controlling the especially dangerous polychlorinated biphenyls (PCBs). If PCBs are not kept out of the environment, they enter the food chain and, eventually, harm higher forms of life, including human beings.

The Surface Mining Control and Reclamation Act staked out lands that could not be mined and established standards for the reclamation and restoration of land that had been mined or was to be mined. The Alaska Lands Act, around which gathered a coalition of environmental organizations, set management standards for federal land in Alaska and put about 97 million acres of the 49th state into federal wildlife refuges and park systems.

During that same decade, environmental organizations grew in numbers and influence. The National Audubon Society of the 1960s was dominated by birdwatchers who occasionally involved themselves in issues. By the 1980s it had a membership of some 500,000 environmentalists. The Sierra Club, founded as a California organization, became a nationally recognized environmental force with over 400,000 members. The National Wildlife Federation in 1982 overshadowed all other conservation organizations, with more than four million members and supporters ranging from the young readers of *Ranger Rick* to the members of affiliates in every state and in Guam, Puerto Rico, and the Virgin Islands. In the Washington of the 1960s, the environmental lobby consisted of the Federation's few lobbyists and one or two more; by the early 1980s, more than eighty environmental lobbyists worked—with great success—for a host of organizations. About as many people worked for the environment in the Washington office of the Federation as were employed by the American Petroleum Institute. Environmental lobbying was no longer a job for just a few.

Together, the Federation and other organizations became the highly visible and highly vocal part of what is known loosely as the environmental movement. The movement is as varied as the problems it confronts. Some groups primarily engage in education, some in litigation, some in lobbying, some in research, and some, like the Federation, in all these activities and more.

The Federation moved aggressively in the 1970s and 1980s to take greater initiative in education. Already established *National Wildlife* magazine and *Ranger Rick* magazine were joined by *International Wildlife* magazine in 1971 and by *Your Big Backyard* in 1980. *NatureScope*, a unique series created especially for teachers, had its debut in 1984. The number of free teachers' kits distributed for National Wildlife

Week increased from 56,000 in 1973 to 580,000 in 1986. Audiovisual programs were created to supplement Wildlife Week materials. A full-fledged nature-book publishing program began in the 1970s, and in 1986 a nationwide radio program called Nature NewsBreak was first aired. Educational summer vacation programs were established for members of all ages, and specialized publications for professional wildlife managers and scholars were offered. The number of people reached by these means is in the millions—and, consequently, millions of Americans are better informed about wildlife, the environment, and the problems confronting them.

Educating Americans about the needs of nature is the most pervasive activity of the environmental movement, and it takes many forms—publishing magazines, books, and newsletters; making films; testifying before government committees; bringing lawsuits; lobbying; developing educational materials for use in schools; sponsoring nature camps; and more. Of these many activities, the ones that affect public policy usually capture the attention of the news media. From its earliest days, the movement has supported legislation that benefitted America's natural resources. More recently, it has also used the courts to ensure that environmental laws are respected. While these activities are only a small portion of the efforts NWF has expended on its various other educational activities, they have been featured in the limelight of the news.

After the Tax Reform Act of 1976, which established clear limits on the amount of money nonprofit charitable organizations can spend on lobbying (up to a maximum of $1 million), the efforts by the Federation and other conservation organizations to influence legislation became more overt and more publicized. At the same time, the Federation's conservation litigation program was increasing.

In the 1980s, one of the environmental movement's efforts that captured the nation's attention was the struggle to secure Superfund, officially known as the 1980 Comprehensive Environmental Response, Compensation and Liability Act—the first major federal law aimed at controlling the release of hazardous substances and other contaminants into the air, water, or land.

The Federation kept close watch over the Superfund from 1980 to 1984, when reauthorization of the trail-blazing law was due. Looking over congressional proposals for reauthorization, Executive Vice President Jay D. Hair and Patrick Parenteau, Vice President for Resources Conservation, saw that the Federation had to work not merely for reauthorization but for a stronger, more effective law. It would be a tough fight.

The original Superfund law authorized a five-year cleanup that would end in 1985. If Congress did not reauthorize Superfund in 1984, the law would remain in effect, but there would be no authority for appropriating money to enforce the law after 1985. NWF lobbyists agreed with Hair and Parenteau: reauthorization would not be enough. New measures had to be written into the law to force the Environmental Protection Agency to speed up the cleanup. As a Federation publication reported, "EPA's track record isn't very impressive."

In four years, only six sites had been cleaned up, the report said. Using EPA's own estimates, it would take nearly forty years to eliminate the nation's most polluted hazardous-waste sites. These "ticking time bombs" would explode before Superfund could defuse them. The only way to speed up the process, NWF said, was to reauthorize a Superfund law that was more effective and better financed.

The Federation's campaign for Superfund is a good case study of how issues of the 1980s are handled by the NWF of the 1980s. Factual descriptions of the campaign appeared in *Conservation 84,* a newsletter that functions as an early warning beacon on conservation issues. *Conservation* is mailed every two weeks to members of the Federation's Resource Conservation Alliance, which was founded in the early 1980s to give interested members a chance to become better informed on specific conservation issues. "Alliance members," says Jay Hair, "make sure their representatives in the nation's capital *hear from home* about cleaning up toxic waste sites, protecting our national parks and wildlife refuges, and keeping our air and water clean."

Concerning Superfund, *Conservation 84* warned that "thousands of hazardous waste sites may go uncleaned and uncontrolled all over the U.S. if stronger measures aren't adopted soon." As alliance members and other Federation supporters kept up a steady stream of pro-Superfund letters to their representatives, NWF stepped up its educational lobbying, spreading information through a Congress that was debating funding sources, citizen's rights, and pollution standards.

The Federation threw its support behind a bill that would raise the Superfund's size from $320 million a year to $1.8 billion a year for five years. After that, the fund would be permanently maintained through new fees to be collected if the Superfund dipped lower than $3 billion. The bill would give the lagging EPA only eighteen months to defuse *all* of the 546 time bombs on the agency's National Priorities List (NPL).

The bill would also provide victims of toxic wastes with emergency relief, such as safe water sources and expenses for relocation and medical care. In addition, victims would have the right to sue for injuries if they could show they were harmed by exposure to toxins from abandoned or inactive waste sites.

One aspect of the bill was particularly singled out by a Federation report urging support of the proposal: "It would also require EPA to revise the criteria now used for ranking sites for NPL listing, to take into account damage to natural resources which may affect the human food chain—a first for EPA." The agency had set high priorities for toxins released close to drinking water, but not for poisonous sites that contaminate rivers and introduce poisons into fish and shellfish that are eaten by people.

With Congress in a budget-paring mood, it became obvious that the original bill could not be passed. So the Federation supported a compromise that would pump a massive amount of money—$9 billion—into a new five-year Superfund but would not make the fund perpetual. By the time the House overwhelmingly passed the reauthorization legislation, the proposed fund had increased to $10.2 billion. NWF immediately shifted its campaign to the Senate, but to little avail, for the Senate failed to take action on a Superfund bill.

When the next session of Congress began in 1985, Ken Kamlet, director of NWF's Pollution and Toxics Program, called Superfund "the top environmental priority of the 99th Congress." He warned, however, that it "is not going to be renewed without bitter controversy." And bitter it was.

No fewer than five major bills were soon introduced to save Superfund from loss of its sources of funding in 1985. As the September 30 deadline neared, the Senate passed a bill that would give the EPA cleanup squads $7.5 billion for the next five years; the money would come from a new tax on manufactured goods. Later, the House passed a $10 billion bill. But 1985 ended without House and Senate agreement on a reauthorization bill.

With the two versions of a Superfund reauthorization bill tied up by struggles within a Senate-House conference committee and the deadline having passed, EPA officials talked of dismantling the cleanup program for lack of funds. President Reagan signed a stopgap measure in April 1986 to keep money trickling into the cleanup while the conference committee ground on, through June (the committee sets health standards and a cleanup timetable) . . . July (committee adds a community right-to-know provision, compelling companies to reveal releases of dangerous chemicals) . . . August (law is changed to aid victims of toxic waste) . . . September . . . October.

During the long, arduous process, NWF pushed hard for inclusion of two main provisions: recognition of food-chain contamination and explicit inclusion of federal sites—especially Department of Defense and Department of Energy waste dumps—under Superfund jurisdiction. NWF pointed out that the two departments, although implicitly included under the earlier Superfund law, had been disregarding it.

Not until October 1986, when President Reagan reluctantly signed a new five-year cleanup law, could NWF staff members hold their Superfund II party. They celebrated a law that authorized the EPA to collect and spend $8.5 billion to clean up toxic sites and targeted an additional $500 million specifically for leaking underground gasoline storage tanks. The money would come from taxes on petroleum products and feedstock chemicals, a special surtax on corporate income, general taxes, and an anticipated $300 million in penalties levied on waste-site offenders.

"We were able to get 80 percent of what we wanted in the bill," said NWF's Janet Hathaway, who led the legislative effort for the Federation. "It was because the public was with us on this issue and wasn't about to see health protection from hazardous wastes traded away. . . . This is a real testament to how public scrutiny and awareness can absolutely bar the Gucci-shoe lobbyist who represented industry on this issue. It was a rare case of the little guy winning because he was on the side of right."

Augmenting the new law was a new idea: Clean Sites, Inc., a nonprofit, independent organization founded by chemical and oil companies, the National Wildlife Federation, and the Conservation Foundation. NWF Executive Vice President Hair served on the steering committee that transformed the idea into reality. Soon after the founding of Clean Sites, Inc., in 1984, other industrial, academic, and environmental officials endorsed its philosophy: Privately sponsored cleanups of relatively small sites can release federal resources for use on large-scale toxic-waste sites.

Clean Sites will, in Hair's words, "encourage the companies that generate the dump wastes to clean up their sites voluntarily." He pointed out that in 1984, three years after the creation of the Superfund, as many as 15,000 hazardous sites still awaited even preliminary evaluation—"while the government's procedures grind slowly."

Clean Sites, Inc., he said, "breaks new ground. It supplements Superfund by enlisting the entrepreneurial zeal, the proven expertise, and the enlightened self-interest of America's private sector."

Here is how Clean Sites worked at one waste site in North Carolina. Two landowners had rented two warehouses to a waste-recycling company. One day in April 1985 the company's management unceremoniously ended the company's stay by handing the warehouse keys to the landowners and walking off. Inside the buildings were pieces of abandoned equipment containing oil that had been contaminated with PCBs. The warehouses had suddenly become a waste-disposal site that had to be cleaned up. But by whom?

The Environmental Protection Agency suggested that the landowners contact Clean Sites, Inc. (CSI), which set to work by first consulting the records of the waste-recycling company and then drawing up a list of some 180 customers who had shipped PCBs to the site. By July CSI had been able to bring together for a conference the warehouse owners, fifteen of the largest shippers, and a number of the smaller shippers.

One of the large shippers was the Duke Power Company of Charlotte, North Carolina. Austin C. Thies, executive vice president of Duke Power, said of the conference, "It was immediately clear that the discussion could either degenerate into a prolonged struggle over responsibility and liability or a concerted effort could set the stage for a prompt and effective cleanup."

The group chose the second course—and, under a CSI project manager, a cleanup began within weeks. The key to "this success story," Thies later wrote, was the early agreement by all parties to work together, relinquishing "their own 'rights' so that everyone could get on with the job."

The fight to save Superfund was one of the Federation's major lobbying campaigns of the 1980s. Other battles often involved NWF's shock troops, state-level conservation organizations that are affiliated with the Federation. Members of the Federation's shore-state affiliates, for example, worked hard for passage of the Coastal Barrier Resources Act, which preserves a system of undeveloped barrier islands and beaches along the Atlantic and Gulf coasts.

Federation teamwork with a single affiliate can also produce a local victory with national implications. During a Wyoming blizzard in 1983, a herd of pronghorn antelope struggled to reach Red Rim, their traditional wintering ground. Bluffs and gullies shelter them there, and winds on the high bluff whip away snow, giving the animals a chance to reach scant winter forage. But on this winter trek the herd was blocked from Red Rim by a woven-wire fence six feet high and twenty-eight miles long. Huddled at the fence, many pronghorn died of starvation and exposure.

The fence, put up by a rancher, ran across a checkerboard of public and private land. The Wyoming Wildlife Federation, an NWF affiliate, sued to get the fence removed. NWF, citing the 1885 Unlawful Inclosures Act, joined the local struggle. A federal judge ordered the fence removed, establishing a landmark principle regarding wildlife's access to public land. The decision was a victory for the pronghorn, which once again could reach their wintering grounds.

Around the time of the Red Rim case, the Federation was drawn into another much larger and longer-lived controversy over public and private lands in the West. Beneath the rolling plains and majestic mountains of much of the public land of the West lie vast reserves of oil, natural gas, and coal. Private developers wanted the rights to develop these resources, and the Reagan administration, thinking of the precarious dependence of the United States on foreign oil and of the burgeoning national debt, responded positively to these interests.

In 1981, the Bureau of Land Management (BLM), which has jurisdiction over most of these public lands, implemented, under the directive of the secretary of the interior, James Watt, a "land withdrawal review program." The ostensible purpose of the program was to review the status of federal land that over the years either had been classified by BLM in such a way that it could not be developed or had been withdrawn from settlement, sale, and development in order to reserve it for a particular public purpose or program. Federal land has been withdrawn, for example, to conserve important wildlife habitat, protect critical watersheds, and provide land for military reservations.

The real purpose of the land review program, as seen by NWF, was to open up public land for private commerce. The review of these withdrawals resulted in millions of acres of undeveloped land being opened up for mineral and mining leases. Consequently, more than 250 uranium claims were filed in a once-protected realm of elk and moose, deer and trout in Wyoming's Green Mountains. In southern Utah, the BLM opened up 136,000 acres for mining, thus endangering peregrine falcons. In other states, developers unrolled wilderness maps and began making plans for development. Between 1981 and 1984, the number of acres of formerly withdrawn public land leased for the purpose of energy exploration increased four fold.

The land withdrawal review program got off to a quick and unheralded start, but it soon tripped over legislative hurdles it had disregarded. The program had relaxed the standards for reviewing land withdrawals, and it had done so, according to NWF, in violation of three federal laws—the 1976 Federal Land Policy and Management Act (FLPMA), the National Environmental Policy Act (NEPA), and the Administrative Procedures Act.

FLPMA, landmark legislation supported by NWF, had instituted a national policy which required that the retention and management of public lands be guided by the principle of multiple use reflected in land-use plans developed with public participation. FLPMA further mandated that all withdrawals of public lands and all classifications BLM had given public lands under its management prior to 1976 be continued. FLPMA also established procedures for the review of public land status, requiring the Department of the Interior to submit any subsequent withdrawal recommendations to the president and Congress for review.

News of the extent of the land reclassification was slow to reach conservationists. In defiance of FLPMA, BLM gave no notices to the general public and made no withdrawal recommendations to Congress or the president. Diligent NWF interns reviewing the Federal Register began finding more and more notifications of previously withdrawn or classified land being opened up for leasing.

"Our review indicates that the Interior Department [under its land withdrawal review program] has lifted protective classification from approximately 185 million acres of land," said Kathleen Zimmerman, counsel for NWF's Public Lands and Energy Division in April 1985. "We estimate that the program has opened up at least 9.1 million acres of land to mining or mineral leasing."

The widely expanding leasing scheme portended revolutionary changes in the management of public lands. Federation reaction was swift and forceful.

In April 1985 NWF sent a detailed letter to Robert Burford, director of BLM, charging that BLM was revoking withdrawals and classifications of undeveloped lands in defiance of FLPMA, NEPA (no environmental impact statements had been prepared), and the Administrative Procedures Act (no regulations governing the land withdrawal program had been issued).

By July, as it became apparent that discussions would not halt the leasing, the Federation brought suit against BLM, making formal the charges outlined in its April letter. Filing for a preliminary injunction, NWF asked that the leasing be stopped and that protective status be restored to land that BLM had selected for leasing.

In December, U.S. District Court Judge John H. Pratt issued an injunction preventing the removal of the protective classification on more than 180 million acres of public lands. Mining and mineral development of these lands, Judge Pratt ruled, could "permanently destroy wildlife habitat, air and water quality, natural beauty, and other environmental values."

The injunction was a major victory in the Federation's battle to prevent improper and irrational uses of public land. Blatant disregard of federal land-management standards had ceased, at least temporarily.

Coincidental with the injunction that preserved public lands came a major victory for wetlands, a prime wildlife habitat that has always been of great interest to NWF. The Supreme Court, overturning the decision of a lower court, reaffirmed the intent of the Clean Water Act by ruling that protection provided by the act *does* extend to wetlands not directly connected to navigable waters. The decision concerned soggy grasslands in the arctic tundra, prairie potholes, and pocosins (landlocked shrub bogs of the Atlantic coastal plain, primarily in North Carolina), all of which sustain key populations of waterfowl.

The ruling provided a permanent answer to recurring claims by the U.S. Army Corps of Engineers that, though it is charged with overseeing dredge and fill operations that affect wetlands, its jurisdiction extends only to wetlands associated with navigable waters. "Without this ruling by the highest court in the land," said *Conservation 85*, "nearly half of our wetlands would have been vulnerable to commercial development."

A larger and more pervasive threat of development has been federal rather than commercial. The threat to wetlands and the waterways that nurture them comes in barrels. Pork barrels.

The term "pork barrel" goes so far back into American political history that no one knows for certain how a barrel full of pork became a symbol for government-financed projects that produce juicy patronage. But ever since the early twentieth century the term has been especially applied to legislation that establishes water-control projects to be built by the Corps of Engineers.

By the 1970s, with the dawning of the modern environmental movement, these Corps projects had become so destructive of wildlife habitat that Congress developed a schizoid attitude toward water proposals: They were attractive ways to please constituents who got patronage from them, but they were also nuisances that could infuriate conservation organizations and *their* constituents, who voted for the environment and against candidates who despoiled it.

As a result of this double-thinking, from 1976 until the middle of the 1980s, Congress resisted passing any omnibus water projects authorization bill. The legislative dam finally burst in 1983 when a flood of new water projects poured into a proposed omnibus water resources development bill. NWF saw merit in one particular provision: cost-sharing. This time finding itself on the same side as the Reagan administration, the Federation endorsed cost-sharing, which would bring about a gradual reduction of federal funds for the construction and maintenance of navigable inland waterways and flood control projects.

"Under cost-sharing," the Federation said, "worthwhile projects would be encouraged while those that are marginal and inequitable would be weeded out. We believe that if state and local governments are required to finance a share of the [planning and] construction costs [at the beginning] of new water projects, they will closely examine the benefit-cost analyses of such projects. As a result, state and local planners would be more likely to consider inexpensive and environmentally sound alternatives."

But, as the proposed legislation moved through the House and Senate, users of inland waterways—such as shippers and barge owners—put pressure on the administration. "It's going to be a tough battle for the National Wildlife Federation and other concerned groups," *Conservation 84* warned, noting that President Reagan had "muted his support for making non-Federal interests pick up more of the tab." In a tersely worded letter sent to the president, NWF's Jay Hair expressed his regret that the president had retreated from his previous support of strong cost-sharing and user-fee requirements. Then Hair and NWF moved to fill the gap left by the presidential retreat.

Congress passed, and the president signed, the Water Resources Development Act of 1986, the largest such bill enacted since 1970. The pork barrel was there, as always—the dredging and the flood-control projects, the dams and the port developments. But, thanks to the efforts of the Federation and allied conservationists, there was also something new: up-front cost-sharing had been included in the act.

The act also contained a new concept designed to give the Corps of Engineers an environmental conscience. The law compelled the Corps to alleviate damage done to the habitats of fish and wildlife. One way to do this is to compensate for a project's impact by purchasing land similar to that lost to the project and manage it to improve its wildlife value. In the past, the Corps had complained that it did not have enough money to buy additional land. The new law specified that authorization for funding was already available for that purpose. And the damage-control portion of the law stated that the Corps now had the authority to go back to its previous projects and remedy any damage previously done.

The Federation has devoted a great deal of its resources to the protection of wetlands. Landmark NWF cases dominate the history of environmental litigation. (See chapter 7.) Above all, the Federation has been the prime watchdog of the Corps of Engineers. Some memorable battles in which NWF or its affiliates have challenged the Corps:

• The Corps approved a proposal to change the definition of "wetlands" in such a way that more than 67 million acres of wetlands would be excluded from protection under the Clean Water Act. In response, NWF and its affiliates have spent considerable amounts of time and effort through lawsuits to reinstate many of the excluded wetlands.

• The Corps refused to issue an order to stop the draining of Texas ponds while trying to decide whether it was obliged to protect these "isolated" waters. NWF has filed a suit to force the Corps to assert jurisdiction over "all waters of the United States," including small Texas ponds.

• When the Corps pronounced that pocosins were "not wetlands" and therefore not subject to their regulatory authority, NWF and six other conservation organizations filed suit charging that the Corps' decision was based on a "cursory and incomplete" study. A U.S. District Court agreed with the plaintiffs, ordering the Corps to reconsider the issue.

• The Corps granted a permit to build a shopping mall on a forested wetland in Massachusetts. The Massachusetts Wildlife Federation and NWF strongly criticized this decision by the Corps because it violated the clause in the Clean Water Act stipulating that a wetlands project must be dependent on water to be granted a permit. The Federation and its affiliate actively lobbied EPA (which has veto power over Corps' wetlands permits) in an effort to stop the mall from being built. The veto was delivered, the developer brought suit against the government, and NWF intervened as a defendant. The lawsuit is in progress.

Not all the Federation's wetlands fights of the 1980s involved the Corps of Engineers. To stop one mammoth project, the Bureau of Reclamation's Garrison Diversion Project in North Dakota, NWF focused its resources against a wide range of powerful supporters in the state and on Capitol Hill.

For years the Federation and the National Audubon Society had tried to stop the Garrison Diversion head-on. But in 1986 the two conservation organizations took a negotiations route, putting together a compromise between federal and state government officials and conservation organizations. Ed Osann, director of the Federation's Division of Water Resources, led NWF's part in the negotiations. The compromise was incorporated into a congressional act. One of the most important elements of the compromise was an agreement that the Bureau of Reclamation would restore or protect one acre of wetland for every acre of wetland damaged by the project. The original irrigation plan was scaled down from a 250,000-acre project that would have harmed twelve wildlife refuges to a 130,940-acre project that created a new refuge.

Wildlife refuges—where an eagle can soar over a vast primeval marsh, a bobcat prowl in a dense forest—are what people usually imagine when they conjure up images of the National Wildlife Federation. But farming practices seriously affect wildlife and the quality of the environment, and the Federation's concerns include farmland as well as wilderness, perils to soil as well as perils to wildlife.

On farmland, perils sometimes are not as apparent as they are in the wilderness. An NWF specialist on soil conservation, for example, might be alarmed by the sight of a field of golden wheat growing on what had been rangeland the year before. Government subsidies and tax preferences had created a rising demand for agricultural fields and coaxed more and more farmers to plow fragile, highly erodible soil even though the nation is choking on excess agricultural production. Farming on these marginal lands means silt washing into streams and creeks and topsoil whipping away as winds whistle across the range. With our pervasive reliance on fertilizer and pesticides, it also means more man-made chemicals percolating into groundwater and draining into lakes and rivers, resulting in what is known as nonpoint pollution—a tainting of the water by sources that cannot be as readily pinpointed as, say, an industrial dump leaking toxins.

Erosion in the 1980s was carrying off six billion tons of soil a year—nearly twice the rate recorded during the Dust Bowl years of the 1930s. "The land is vanishing beneath our feet," *Conservation 85* said as the Federation urgently pressed for an improved soil-conservation law. "Nearly 40 percent of our farmlands are losing soil." The worst losses were in hilly areas such as western Tennessee or in dry areas on the high plains. Iowa's rich topsoil, once a foot deep, was reduced to half that depth.

The Federation urged legislators to add "swampbuster" and "sodbuster" provisos to farm legislation pending in 1985. The swampbuster provision would deny federal benefits to farmers who plowed, filled, or drained wetlands. The sodbuster stipulation similarly would withhold price supports and other benefits for crops grown on highly erodible soil.

The Farm Bill of 1985, which set the nation's agricultural policy for the next five years, did contain swampbuster and sodbuster measures. It also provided for a conservation reserve, which set aside millions of acres of land susceptible to erosion. Farmers would be paid to plant cover crops on these fragile reserve lands.

NWF's agricultural achievements have been important, and they continue. But that eagle soaring over the marsh is the enduring symbol of the National Wildlife Federation, which has never lost sight of its symbol and has never forgotten its middle name. The spirit of that symbol and that middle name is captured by the saga of the Federation's crusade on behalf of the Endangered Species Act.

Concern over endangered animals dates to the founding of the Federation. Interest in a law to cover all species traces back almost as far. The Federation helped to bring about the Endangered Species Act in 1973, and the Federation has been one of the rescuers every time the act has been threatened with extinction in Congress.

The first attempt on the life of the Endangered Species Act occurred when it came up for reauthorization in 1978. The act won renewal, but at a price: to correct what critics called its inflexibility, Congress added a Cabinet-level committee that, by a vote of no less than five to seven, could grant exemptions to the act. Some angry environmentalists dubbed it the "God Committee" because it might well decide whether a species would continue to live or become extinct. In 1979, the God Committee met to decide two issues: whether the Tellico Dam could be built in Tennessee despite its threat to a tiny, endangered fish called the snail darter; and whether the Grayrocks Dam in Wyoming could be built even though it threatened the endangered whooping crane.

Because the Federation had already initiated a lawsuit to protect whooping crane habitat that would be destroyed by the Grayrocks Dam, the God Committee granted an exemption to the Endangered Species Act on the condition that a unique settlement being negotiated between NWF and the proponents of the dam was achieved. (See chapter 7.) The committee denied an exemption for the Tellico Dam. In 1980 the Federation successfully fought off an attempt by a petroleum company to go before the committee for an exemption so it could build an oil refinery on the Maine coast. The Federation's argument was that the plant's location threatened bald eagles, which are on the Endangered Species List.

Powerful commercial foes, smarting from losses in encounters with the Endangered Species Act from Maine to Wyoming, confronted the Federation and some thirty other conservation and scientific groups when the act came up for reauthorization again in 1982. NWF told Congress that a survey showed 91 percent of all NWF members endorsed the concept of the act and 75 percent believed that endangered species should be protected even when such protection blocked some commercial activity.

Once again, the act managed to continue its own threatened life. And once again in 1985, commercial forces, this time centered in western dam-building country, united to gut or kill the act. The Federation argued that at least four species of fish native to the Colorado River system were threatened with extinction because of water development projects. Westerners also offered amendments to the act that would have increased hunting pressures on grizzly bears.

The House passed its version of a renewal act, but western senators placed a hold on the Senate's reauthorization bill, keeping it from a vote. Finally, breaking the stalemate came down to persuading only one more senator to vote for the bill.

In January 1987, Jay Hair spoke for the Federation. "For the first time since 1973," he said, "the nation has no Endangered Species Act on the books." He called on Congress not only to reauthorize the act but also to reform it. "For instance," he said, "we must put species on the threatened and endangered list in a more timely fashion. At the current rate of adding sixty species a year, it will take nearly a lifetime to list the 1,000 species certified as worthy by the U.S. Fish and Wildlife Service. Yet, 3,900 other candidates are awaiting federal evaluation. More tragic is the fact that recovery plans have been developed for only 58 percent of the species already listed as threatened or endangered in the United States."

The Federation's voice was not the only one speaking for reauthorization of the Endangered Species Act, which had not been approved before this book went to press. As had happened numerous times before, NWF stood with other environmental organizations. But it stood as a giant, the largest nonprofit conservation education organization in the world, with 4.6 million members and supporters.

To understand how the Federation reached this peak and that moment, you must go back fifty years to its beginning, a time not of peaks and world views, but of the Dust Bowl and fear, the Depression and despair, a time when people worried about their own fate and only a few gave thought to the fate of American wildlife.

2

The Beginnings

The cartoon in the *New York Herald Tribune* shows a ragtag army storming Washington. Men armed with guns and fishing rods have climbed a ladder and are plucking a frightened figure labeled *Congress* from the Capitol dome. "I've always been sympathetic to conservation," Congress is sputtering. "Sympathy is not enough," says a man with a shotgun. "What we want is *ACTION*." Below him, in ranks strung out as far as the eye can see, people march beneath signs proclaiming their cause: *14 Million Sportsmen Who Buy Hunting or Fishing Licenses* and *Federated Garden Clubs, Women's Clubs and Outdoor Girls* and *Federated Rod and Gun Clubs* and, in the midst of a platoon of children, *The Next Generation Who Want Some Thing Left for Their Enjoyment.*

Almost anyone who glanced at a newspaper editorial page in 1936 would have recognized the style of that cartoon. From the fat congressman on the dome to the government officials trembling before a hunting dog, the cartoon showed the irreverent touch of artist Ding Darling. His talent for lampooning the rich and powerful had won him a Pulitzer Prize and syndication in newspapers throughout the country. But Ding Darling was to do far more than draw cartoons. As an organizer, he was to bring his ragtag army cartoon to life, showing lawmakers and bureaucrats the reality of conservationists' political clout. He was one of the major organizers of a real army of conservationists that slogged through a snow storm in Washington, D.C., on February 3, 1936, to launch a crusade to save the nation's wildlife.

Most Americans in that winter of 1936 were not worrying about birds and beasts. They were simply trying to rebound from America's Great Depression, in which millions of people went hungry and lost jobs. Men, women, and children shuffled for hours in long lines to get handouts of free bread or cups of soup. There seemed to be little chance for getting federal money to help animals at a time when the unofficial national anthem was "Brother, Can You Spare a Dime?"

Beyond the city's bread lines and soup kitchens, the land was also down and out. Once-great forests had become bald wastelands and runways for rivers in flood. Prairies and farms turned to dust. "There were no fields, only sand drifting into mounds and eddies," said a report on a dust-covered South Dakota farm. In the farmyard, fences, machinery, and trees were gone, buried. . . . "

Darling once sketched a vivid word image of wild ducks he had seen dying during the long drought that parched the Midwest: "By midsummer, the cracked mud bottoms of dried up sloughs were splotched with thousands of clusters of little yellow legs, and here and there a few wisps of fuzzy down clinging to skeletons fluttered in the winds."

The black blizzards struck farms throughout the Midwest, bankrupting farmers, driving farm families on desperate treks to cities for jobs that were not there or to California for crop-picking work that usually was not there. They were leaving what people called the Dust Bowl, the conservationists' symbol of a nation heedlessly devouring its heritage. Birds, mammals, and fish were suffering and dying, and not many people seemed to care.

Those who did care did what they could. They tried to save patches of prairie wetlands. They wrote letters to their governors or to their state fish and game commissions. Most of them were hunters and fishermen, banded together in local or even statewide clubs. Others were birdwatchers or members of garden clubs. There were thousands—by some counts 36,000—of these organizations concerned with wildlife. They varied in size and energy. Joined together, they could be heard; they could help a wounded land. Some of these people wondered how to get together. One of them was Ding Darling. With words and cartoons, he tried to make policymakers see that there was a constituency for wildlife—the hunters and the fishermen, the gardeners, the kids Who Want Some Thing Left.

Jay Norwood Darling was a man of two American centuries, a man of the Midwest, a man who personified America's faith in being new, in organizing to get important things done. The nation was celebrating its hundredth birthday when he was born in the Michigan town that gave him his middle name. He knew many homes as his father, an itinerant minister, wandered from pulpit to pulpit. One move took the family to Sioux City, Iowa, where young Jay thrilled to the sight of great flocks of golden plovers and prairie chickens sweeping across the skies, filling his mind "with pictures which have never been erased." In later years, when those great flocks no longer appeared, Darling felt the first stirrings of his lifelong interest in conservation.

In 1906 his cartoons began appearing regularly in the *Des Moines Register and Leader.* He signed his editorial cartoons *Ding*, which had evolved from *D'ing*, an abbreviation of *Darling*. In 1916 the *New York Herald Tribune* began distributing his cartoons through its syndicate, which served about one hundred and thirty newspapers. Long before winning his first Pulitzer Prize in 1924, he was nationally known. (He won a second Pulitzer for a 1942 cartoon. Neither prize-winning cartoon was about conservation.)

In a steady stream of seven cartoons a week, he illustrated the issues of the day, from the odd behavior of politicians to the plight of wildlife in a nation on the move. Cities were filling up and spreading. Suburbs were being invented. Farms were becoming agricultural factories that exhausted the soil and threatened the future of water resources. Darling caught all this in a single image: the nation's natural resources being dumped into a hopper atop the "U.S. Natural Resources Rendering Work," which converts the animals and the trees, the beauty and the promise, into money and waste. Darling usually added a statement to his cartoons. On this one he asked, "How rich will we be when we have converted all our forests, all our soil, all our water resources, and all our minerals into cash?"

That was the vision: a land ravaged, a land with few stewards and few champions. Timberlands were clearcut, pastures overgrazed, croplands overplowed. Wildlife belonged to the hunters, the fishermen, and the farmers who shot or poisoned any animal that tradition labeled a predator.

Ever since colonial times, North America has been a battleground for wildlife issues. As the American civilization spread across North America, wildlife was part of the harvest. At first people hunted and fished for survival. For those who did not hunt, market hunters killed on a wholesale scale. Buffalo hunters, slaughtering great herds of bison for nineteenth-century railroad builders, almost wiped out the symbol of the American frontier. As towns and cities rose behind the frontier, market hunting increased. Game laws were nonexistent in many places and ignored in others.

Belief in conservation can be traced as far back as colonial America, when some colonies established closed seasons on deer hunting. But, as the frontier pushed westward, the idea of closed seasons did not. Nor did there seem to be much sense in establishing bag limits. The continent teemed with wildlife. By the early 1800s most states and a few territories had laws protecting some game species, but enforcement of these laws was spotty. And advocates of conservation were not heard, at least as individuals. So, in the American tradition, they organized.

One of the earliest conservation organizations to lobby successfully for stricter game laws was the New York Sportsmen's Club, founded in 1844. The club's members included many attorneys, some of whom brought suit against game-law violators previously untouched by law enforcement agents. Another organization of the same vintage, the New York Association for Protection of Game, lobbied successfully for an act to protect moose, deer, and several other game species. Sportsmen in Boston, Providence, and other eastern cities fought for similar laws.

The Boone and Crockett Club, co-founded in 1886 by Teddy Roosevelt and George Bird Grinnell, editor of *Forest and Stream,* kept watch over the preservation of big game. A candidate for membership did have to prove he had bagged at least three American big-game animals. But the club, looking past the trophies on the wall, used its considerable influence to help provide room for wildlife to roam. Members testified against a bill that would have removed a large chunk of Yellowstone National Park to satisfy the demands of western railroaders and mining interests. What Roosevelt called the "B and C" also backed the Park Protection Act and led the campaigns for the creation of the National Zoo in Washington and the New York Zoological Park, better known as the Bronx Zoo.

The West produced its own conservation organization in 1892 when John Muir founded the Sierra Club, which helped to create Yosemite National Park and dedicated itself to the preservation of the breathtaking California landscape that Muir had exalted. Around the same time, from one coast to the other, concern about the massacre of birds by market hunters grew. From this concern came the founding of the first of several individual Audubon Societies. All members promised they would not kill wild birds except for food, and women pledged they would not wear plumage from nongame birds. In 1902, working in conjunction with the American Ornithologist's Union, the National Committee of Audubon Societies united and expanded their concern toward mammals as well as birds.

Market hunters, plume merchants, and thoughtless gunners decimated species, as did loss of habitat to farms. So many passenger pigeons died in so short a time—more than a billion were slaughtered in a few weeks in 1878—that the species became extinct. The last passenger pigeon died in the Cincinnati Zoo in 1914, and there, four years later, died America's last Carolina parakeet.

Fears that the brown pelican would become a memory inspired President Theodore Roosevelt to establish the nation's first wildlife refuge in Florida in 1903. The refuge, which saved the pelican, spurred the development of what would become the system of more than four hundred wildlife refuges we have today.

Roosevelt also sought congressional and grass-roots support for a pioneer federal conservation law that had been enacted just before he became president. The Lacey Game and Wild Birds Preservation and Disposition Act of 1900—which bore the name of Congressman John F. Lacey, a member of B and C—prohibited the interstate shipment of wild birds and mammals that had been taken in violation of state laws. The act also laid down regulations for the importation of foreign species.

Support for the Lacey Act came from many of the new conservation organizations that had been founded around the turn of the century. The League of American Sportsmen and the Audubon Societies were especially active. The buffalo, championed by the president, got new assistance from the American Bison Society, formed in 1905 to restore the species. The society successfully lobbied for a law that established the National Bison Range near Missoula, Montana.

The first use of *conservation* in terms of nature also was recorded in this era that saved so much of America's wilderness heritage. Gifford Pinchot, first chief of what would be the U.S. Forest Service and the savior of American forests, said in his autobiography that he and another Forest Service official started using *conservation* when they were looking for one word that would offset *protection* and *preservation*, which, to them, implied keeping the wilderness without using it.

Roosevelt picked up the word and used it as the theme of the 1908 White House Conference of Governors. "Roosevelt and Pinchot," wrote wildlife historian James B. Trefethen, "used the Conference of Governors to hammer home their theme—that the states must join the federal government in inventorying, managing, and husbanding their respective natural resources."

Roosevelt created the National Conservation Commission with Pinchot as its chairman. Out of the commission arose the National Conservation Association, which set the pattern for national annual meetings of people who were, by Pinchot's definition, conservationists.

Although *conservation* was making its mark as a new way to define the saving of the wilderness, the word was ignored in 1911 by a group of sportsmen who, with conservation in mind, formed what they called the American Game Protective and Propagation Association. Despite the apparent semantic conflict, the new association was as dedicated to wise use of the wilderness as was any new-born conservationist. The association threw its support behind the 1913 Weeks-McLean Act, which gave federal protection to migratory birds. The original version of this bill had given protection only to migratory game birds. But, with the backing of the Game Protective and Propagation Association, the National Association of Audubon Societies, and the Boone and Crockett Club, all migratory birds were covered.

The Weeks-McLean Act was the precursor of the 1918 Migratory Bird Treaty Act, which the American Game Protective and Propagation Association helped to write. The 1916 treaty, signed by the United States, the British Empire, and later Mexico and Japan, abolished market hunting. And, being based on a scientific understanding of bird biology, the treaty took into consideration the breeding season of each species of game bird and abolished spring hunting. The treaty saved birds for generations to come. In the Supreme Court decision that upheld the constitutionality of the treaty, Justice Oliver Wendell Holmes appraised the extraordinary value of the legislation. "But for the treaty and the statute," he said, "there soon might be no birds."

But protection of the birds did not extend to their habitats. The birds were losing their North American breeding sites because of the steadily increasing, heedless draining of wetlands. Waterways that supported large bird populations were also endangered because of the pollution spewing from booming cities and towns. Wildlife refuges were few. States were not making up for the loss of habitat by acquiring land dedicated to wildlife.

Once again, an organization of sportsmen came to the rescue. They called themselves the Izaak Walton League, founded in 1922 to save birds, mammals, and fish indirectly by saving their realm—the nation's threatened wetlands, streams, and ponds. By 1927 the league had more than 100,000 members in 43 states.

If politicians were not impressed by the magnificent vistas of preserved wild lands, they were impressed by the voting strength of sportsmen's organizations. But, even in states where such organizations were politically powerful, pork-barrel politics, not sound conservation practices, frequently motivated much of the politicians' conservation work. State officials, as one commentator pointed out, "often knew a hell of a lot about local politics and worse than nothing about game management. If you voted for Governor Beeswax you received a clutch of pheasant eggs or a can of trout fingerlings regardless of whether you had proper cover for the birds or proper water for the fish."

When Ding Darling the cartoonist decided to do more than draw sketches of conservation problems, he took aim at the politics that was hampering the work of the Iowa State Fish and Game Commission. In 1931, he convinced the Iowa General Assembly to make the commission nonpolitical, and he was made a member of the state's first commission dedicated to wildlife rather than to politics.

Darling solved the problem of politics in game management with moves as quick and sure as the strokes of his pen. He got Iowa State College (later to become Iowa State University) and the fish and game commission to join together for an approach to conservation based upon scientific research. When the state asked where the money was going to come from, he pledged his own money toward the project— the nation's first Cooperative Wildlife Research Unit.

Iowa's research unit was an innovation that could and later would be expanded into a national network. But that expansion would come as a result of federal involvement in conservation. Times were changing. People began looking to the federal government for solutions to problems that states no longer were able to solve on their own. The greatest conservation crisis, the dwindling number of waterfowl, was far too large for a single state or even a group of states to handle. The Dust Bowl knew no state boundaries, and the black blizzard's victims were not only farmers. The draining of wetlands to expand prairie farmlands had dried up the potholes and marshes that had sustained the North American breeding grounds of many species of waterfowl.

Some far-sighted conservationists realized that the American wildlife crisis could be ended only by action taken on a national level. The first step toward that solution came in 1930 when the Senate established a special committee on wildlife—an idea brought forward by Senator Frederic C. Walcott, a founder of the American Game Protective and Propagation Association, and Senator Harry B. Hawes of Missouri, who had helped to create the Upper Mississippi Fish and Wildlife Refuge.

Out of the new committee came the Migratory Bird Hunting Stamp Act, whose early history would be entwined with that of the National Wildlife Federation.

During the election campaign between Franklin D. Roosevelt and President Herbert Hoover in 1932, Ding Darling, a Republican, vigorously supported Hoover, a fellow Iowan and a longtime friend. But it would be Roosevelt, the winner, who set in motion the series of events that propelled Darling into national politics, put him in Washington, and led to the creation of the National Wildlife Federation.

Conservation was a cornerstone of the Roosevelt administration. Among the measures swiftly enacted in a Congress entranced by FDR's New Deal were the Tennessee Valley Authority Act, which created the TVA to manage flood control, generate electricity, and bring irrigation to parched farmland; the Soil Erosion Service (later named the Soil Conservation Service); and the Civilian Conservation Corps, which put more than three million young men to work on America's neglected land, building flood-control dams, laying out fire trails, and planting some two billion trees.

In August of 1933, Roosevelt, near the end of his first summer as president, wrote to his secretary of agriculture, Henry A. Wallace, about maintaining "the good will of the fish and game clubs and associations," an interest dear to "our good friend, Thomas H. Beck." Beck, the editor of *Collier's*, an extremely popular magazine, was also an active conservationist. He was a member of the Connecticut State Board of Fisheries and Game and had been the first president of the American Wildlife Institute. Beck was also a member of the original board of directors of the More Game Birds in America Foundation, Inc., founded in 1930. (The foundation, whose lineage went back to the B and C, later became Ducks Unlimited.)

During the Hoover administration, the More Game Birds Foundation warred with the U.S. Bureau of Biological Survey, the government agency charged with enforcing federal game laws and the forerunner of the U.S. Fish and Wildlife Service. Beck, powerful both as a journalist and as an advocate of conservation, was the type of influential man Roosevelt wanted on his side.

While Wallace pondered how to stretch an already thin Agriculture budget in ways to please hunters and fishermen but not displease farmers, Beck wrote to Roosevelt and got an interview in which he laid out a plan for restoration "of one of our great natural resources—game birds." The plan, which focused on paying farmers to develop game birds as a cash crop, got a chilly rejection from the Biological Survey.

In a move that seemed to be aimed at soothing Beck and improving the work of the Biological Survey, Roosevelt told Wallace to appoint Beck chairman of a Wildlife Restoration Committee to study ways of restoring the dwindling flocks of migratory waterfowl. The other two members were Darling and Aldo Leopold, a professor of game management at the University of Wisconsin and a distinguished authority on what would become known as the science of ecology.

The committee began work on January 5, 1934, and completed the report on February 8, 1934, establishing what is probably an all-time speed record for government report writing. But the White House reacted with go-slow signals, especially since the report suggested that the restoration could cost as much as 75 million dollars. No one was going to advocate helping ducks while Americans were starving. As Beck bitterly remarked, "Ducks don't vote." Nor did the federal conservation bureaucracy, particularly the Biological Survey, enjoy the prospect of another recommendation: the appointment of a Restoration Commissioner, a new czar of the outdoors who would run national parks and forests, watch over fisheries and wildlife, and administer soil-erosion projects.

Yet, to ignore the work of Beck's committee meant the risk of offending an influential editor, an outspoken, anti-FDR cartoonist, and a well-connected professional conservationist. Each man was backed by a segment of a large constituency that, united, could bring forth a wellspring of resistance to New Deal plans. The problem called for a Rooseveltian solution—a sweeping, audacious decision that would silence critics and bring opponents into the FDR camp. In a single move, Roosevelt did just that: On March 1, 1934, Roosevelt named Ding Darling chief of the Biological Survey.

The Survey, founded in 1896 as part of the Department of Agriculture, was engaged primarily in research until it was given the task of enforcing the Weeks-McLean Migratory Bird Act of 1913 which, among other things, set bag limits and ordered closed seasons on specific birds. The Survey's scientific staff studied animals but did little research on the kind of wildlife problems presented to Beck's committee. As Roosevelt had put it to Wallace in a confidential memo, "I get from a good many sources suggestions that the Biological Survey spends too much time on scientific experimentalism, and that we ought to have a more practical spirit."

Darling intensified Survey law enforcement, sending federal game wardens after outlawed market hunters and out-of-season hunters from Maryland to California. For the first time in memory, lawbreakers were being caught, convicted, and put in jail. Darling tightened waterfowl regulations, and when "game hog" hunters complained to congressmen, Darling told them, "The regulations will stay as long as they are needed to bring back the ducks, and if tougher restrictions are needed, we will find some tougher regulations."

Just prior to Darling's appointment as head of the Survey, Roosevelt had signed the Duck Stamp Bill, which obliged waterfowl hunters to purchase each year a stamp for a dollar. The funds went toward the purchase and restoration of habitat for the birds. A drawing by Darling—two ducks about to land in a marsh—became the illustration for the first duck stamp.

Because no money had been appropriated to support the Duck Stamp Act, Darling began hunting for funds on Capitol Hill and, through some parliamentary legerdemain, managed to get $6 million. In a note to Roosevelt, Darling used both words and sketches to convince the president that wildlife needed even more money. "Redistribution of wealth, eh?" one ragged-looking duck at the bottom of the note says to another. "Where do we come in?"

Roosevelt responded with a letter saying that Darling was "the only man in history who got an appropriation through Congress, past the Budget and signed by the president without anybody realizing that the Treasury had been raided." Darling, the president said, had got the federal courts to "say that the United States Government has a perfect constitutional right to condemn millions of acres for the welfare, health and happiness of ducks, geese, sandpipers, owls and wrens. . . . " The president went on to remark that he had not been able to get the courts to issue similar condemnation orders on "a few old tenements in the slums."

When Darling attempted to broaden his Cooperative Wildlife Research Unit from an Iowa project to a national program, he again discovered a lack of funds and again searched for money. He arranged for a dinner with representatives of the leading suppliers of ammunition to hunters, the du Pont Company, the Hercules Powder Company, and the Remington Arms Company. "Out of this single meeting," Darling later wrote, "there emerged, either directly or indirectly, the Cooperative Wildlife Research Unit Program, the American Wildlife Institute, the National Wildlife Federation, and the North American Wildlife Conference. . . . "

Darling's idea for a North American Wildlife Conference stemmed from his belief in the need for wildlife groups to speak with one voice—a mighty chorus made up of individual voices. Many individuals, many local and state organizations, even a few national organizations were speaking out for wildlife. But they were too much like a group of soloists competing with each other in a practice hall. Their individual voices sometimes were heard, and sometimes not. They rarely joined together in one harmonious performance. Darling wanted to create an organization that would simultaneously be powerful on a national level while drawing strength from numerous organizations still rooted in a myriad of issues and goals on the local or state level. At his urging and with his assurance that he would do all the necessary work, President Roosevelt officially called the conference for February 3 to February 7, 1936, in Washington, D.C.

"My purpose," the president proclaimed, "is to bring together individuals, organizations, and agencies interested in the restoration and conservation of wildlife resources. My hope is that through this conference new cooperation between public and private interests, and between Canada, Mexico, and this country will be developed; that from it will come constructive proposals for concrete action; that through these proposals existing State and Federal governmental agencies and conservation groups can work cooperatively for the common good."

Darling's purpose was to establish a national conservation organization based on one he had seen in Indiana in 1933. Darling had first heard of the Indiana federation through a meeting with its creator, C. R. "Pink" Gutermuth, the Indiana Department of Conservation's director of education. Gutermuth, who would later become president of the Wildlife Management Institute, had set up more than 500 conservation clubs throughout the state. Each club sent delegates to a county conservation council. Each council elected a representative to carry its ideas to conservation-district meetings. The county delegates to the conservation district then elected a district representative to the State Conservation Committee.

Darling's plan adapted this structure to work on a national level. Soon after Roosevelt set the date for the conference, Darling began meeting with and writing to state officials, state officers of organizations like the Izaak Walton League, and officers in the fifteen states that already had conservationist or sportsmen's federations. He urged states that did not have such federations to organize them, so that state delegates could be selected to serve as delegates to the president's national conference. Within five months new federations of conservationist clubs formed in twenty-five states; four other states were organizing federations. The hectic activity guaranteed that the conference would host a large number of state federations.

Darling also worked to get representation from major conservation organizations. "It took a great deal of conferring and reasoning," he later recalled, "to quiet the fears of several prominent organizations, among them the Izaak Walton League and the representatives of the Audubon Society and the Ornithological Union particularly, that the new Federation would not be a competitor in the membership field."

The overwhelming response to Darling's invitation to the conference demonstrated that thousands of people shared his frustration over piecemeal state efforts to solve conservation problems.

The conference replaced the American Game Conference, which had been held every year since 1915. That conference drew state fish and game officials and representatives of sportsmen's organizations. There was a new look to the first North American Wildlife Conference, which united representatives of state and federal agencies, along with a wide array of people who cherished the outdoors—from fishermen and hunters to bird lovers and hikers, from nature photographers to gardeners.

More than 70,000 invitations had gone out in 1935 to people in the United States, Canada, and Mexico. Among the nearly two thousand delegates who arrived in Washington, D.C., were farmers, sportsmen, and representatives of Boy Scouts and Girl Scouts, 4-H Clubs, garden clubs, and women's clubs. One delegate from Wisconsin sold two dogs to pay for his trip. Texas sent about forty delegates, led by Mrs. Hal Peck, the state game commissioner. Representatives attended from every state, thanks to the formation of new federations in many states. Canada and Mexico also sent representatives.

The long lobby of the Mayflower Hotel, the conference center, was lined with exhibits that showed the diversity of the organizations and delegates represented. Mounted animals looked down from the walls. Live bass and trout swam about in aquariums. Divergent groups showed the joy of appreciating birds—with binoculars and with shotguns.

Shortly before the conference opened, Darling had quit as chief of the Biological Survey. In his resignation statement he said, "Wildlife interests remind me of an unorganized army, beaten in every battle, zealous and brave but unable to combat the trained legions who are organized to get what they want." He had transformed into words his cartoon of the ragtag army storming the Capitol. In his address to the conference, Darling picked up the theme of organized strength. Mentioning Beck's "ducks don't vote" remark, Darling said, "neither do conservationists." And, he added: "Our scattered and desultory organizations—36,000 of them—have never, to my certain knowledge, influenced so much as the election of a dog catcher. Thirty-six thousand clubs, leagues, and associations whose chief objective is wildlife conservation. . . . And yet, with all this potential voting strength, the wildlife conservationists together exert less influence on our governments, both state and national, than the Barrel-Rollers' Union in Pumpkin Center. . . . The problem resolves itself, therefore, into one of federation of the group interests to bring to bear their voting strength upon the men who are willing to serve when the demand is made by impressive numbers."

The conference's national significance was underlined by the appearance of two members of Roosevelt's Cabinet—Secretary of Agriculture Henry Wallace and Secretary of the Interior Harold Ickes, who took that occasion to announce that he would oppose any more building of roads in national parks. Wallace could not resist twitting Darling, the former bureaucrat who was always looking for more money for wildlife. "I think he is an awfully good cartoonist," Wallace said, but "I don't think much of him as an economist."

On the last day of the conference, the delegate from Mexico announced that his country had signed the Migratory Bird Treaty Act that had been in effect since 1918 between the United States and Canada. The announcement indicated how conservation leaders viewed the importance of the conference. By that last day it had become obvious the conference would be more than merely an annual event. This first conference would be the setting for the launching of a new organization.

From the delegates had come the first stirrings of support for a federation that would put wildlife on the national agenda. When Darling asked what the roomful of conservationists wanted, a man from Missouri stood and made a motion that "an organization be formed as outlined by Mr. Darling." Another motion set as a future objective the organizing of *all* "agencies, societies, clubs and individuals which are or should be interested in the restoration and conservation of wildlife."

An organization was created at the conference, and it was named the General Wildlife Federation. The name Darling had picked for the new organization was "Conservation Federation." But a name wanted by representatives of duck hunters—"Wildlife Federation"— won out. The debate over the name paralleled a general debate over the role of sportsmen's groups.

During a discussion of the constitution, Carl Shoemaker, who would become the Federation's secretary and conservation director, proposed that state representatives must be selected by a federation of wildlife interests "whose primary purpose is conservation of wildlife." Shoemaker wanted to restrict voting rights primarily to sportsmen's organizations—"to prevent the women's groups, the 4-H Clubs and the farm organizations, and particularly wool growers and cattlemen, from getting any representation within the state federation."

Shoemaker's belief that sportsmen should dominate the Federation was an article of faith he shared with Darling and most of the other leaders in the conservation movement. But Darling never wavered from his desire to include in the Federation unaffiliated individuals and nonsporting groups, such as the National Council of State Garden Clubs.

The final constitution reflected the reality of the sportsmen-first philosophy. The responsibility for decision-making was given to each state's "federation of wildlife interests"—essentially, organizations of sportsmen active in conservation. But the constitution also gave non-voting membership to any individuals or to any groups that wished to join and somewhat limited representation to unaffiliated national organizations.

The delegates elected Darling president and adopted the temporary constitution, which named the organization and set up a mechanism for ratification by affiliates in individual states. The constitution was to be formally ratified the following year. The delegates were to spend the year organizing themselves into a new champion for the nation's beleaguered wildlife. And, as they organized, they were to reach out to Americans who did not know about the plight of wildlife or the lack of an effective, national means to help wildlife.

F. A. Silcox, chief forester of the United States and chairman of the conference, ended it by saying, "Jay Darling, God bless you. The baby is yours now." That was the image: the new organization was Darling's to do with as he wished. At that moment, whatever had been formed was Darling's. Soon, though, it would become something more, and Darling would no longer be there.

The General Wildlife Federation—it would not be named the National Wildlife Federation until 1938—opened its first annual meeting in St. Louis, Missouri, on March 3, 1937, with delegates from the District of Columbia and forty-two states. The meeting, unlike the conservation conference that created it, focused solely on the creation of the new organization. The National Audubon Society, the Izaak Walton League, and other national groups that had attended the conference the year before were not present. In caucus, the delegates chose thirteen regional directors. This board of directors, drawn from a full geographical spectrum, was to be the guiding body of the Federation. Each state affiliate of the Federation would send a voting delegate to the annual meeting of the national organization. Policies of the Federation would be based upon resolutions passed at the annual meeting. These principles of organization would endure.

In his address to the delegates, Ding Darling stressed the need for political action. During his short career in the Biological Survey, he said, he had learned that people concerned about wildlife did not have what many other outdoor organizations had: a pressure group with a voice that was heard in the competition for federal funds.

Darling gave the delegates a look at what really happened inside the government: "If the National Park Service needed pressure to get additional appropriations to carry out a sound policy, to further the interests of the people themselves, and called for help, the National Parks Association, a popular group with no official capacity . . . came to the rescue and supported the Park Department in its request.

"If the Forest Service felt that for the good of the nation they needed more forest land, if they needed more appropriations to plant more trees . . . if they needed legislation to give them more authority, the American Forestry Association came out of hiding and bombarded Congress. . . . If there was a bridge or a series of bridges or power dams planned across the major rivers of the United States, perhaps choking one of our main arteries of fishways and fish production, making an inert desert out of what had been productive waterways, if those dams and power plants were set up and introduced into Congress, all the Chambers of Commerce and the real estate associations and the Congressmen who represented them were active. If I chose to oppose that and sent out word for help, only an echo of my own voice came back; there was no cohesive group in the United States which represented the conservation, the saving of the balance of nature. . . . "

Darling then raised an issue that became a dominant Federation theme for the next fifty years: clean water. He spoke of the Connecticut River, "once a broad, clear stream with bottom vegetation that nurtured all the biological elements of the sustaining resources; now a sewer in which nothing can exist. A million-dollar industry in salmon went up and down the Connecticut River, and now a crayfish can't live in it. Is it so expensive to build a sewer to do the job, that we have to ruin a million-dollar salmon industry?"

Darling underlined his belief in the need for political pressure by showing the results of a little politicking he had already done—a telegram from Congressman Willis Robertson, chairman of the House Conservation Committee. In his message, the influential congressman said he hoped that this first annual meeting would forge a permanent national organization "that will give shape and direction to the national conservation policies." He promised that "such an organization can confidently depend upon sympathetic cooperation from the House Conservation Committee."

Another message sent to the delegates sounded merely like an endorsement of the Federation. But Darling thought something was being said between the lines. The note, assuring the Federation of continued cooperation, came from Mrs. Kimball White, who held the Conservation Chair for the National Council of State Garden Clubs.

After reading the note to the crowd, Darling said, "I think the women's organizations can give you men cards in spades and lick you on any ground. They . . . mean business." Darling's comment was a warning to those delegates who might have continued to see the Federation as an organization devoted solely to hunting and fishing interests.

The delegates ratified the temporary constitution and unanimously elected Darling as president of the Federation. With organizational matters smoothly taken care of, Darling immediately turned to telling the Federation what needed to be done. He called on the new Federation to press for the creation of congressional committees that would "further the interests and . . . guard [against] the bills which may be contradictory to the interests of conservation."

"Fisheries and Biological Survey," he continued, "are the two bureaus which are first cut when an economy wave sweeps through the government, and the last to be restored when prosperity returns. That also is a job for the Federation. You know the reason they are neglected is because of popular demand. There is a memorandum in the files of the Secretary of the Treasury saying that if conservation and wildlife are to receive appropriations, the voice must come from the people through Congress. . . .

"If you want adequate appropriations for wildlife, the request must come from you. . . . Three and a half million dollars of excise tax which comes out of the outdoor pocket, that is what we commonly call nuisance taxes, are collected by the federal government from the men who go out and enjoy environmental conditions in the open— three and a half million dollars that goes into the general treasury and never comes out for wildlife or conservation. That belongs to conservation. A bill should be introduced in Congress earmarking that money for conservation purposes. I think we could do an awful lot of good with that if we didn't do any more than set up our cooperative research and demonstration activity."

One of the seven resolutions the convention passed—extension of federal aid to the states through the distribution of funds collected from the excise tax on arms and ammunition—carried out Darling's recommendation. This resolution would lead to the Federation's first important accomplishment, passage of hallmark conservation legislation, the Pittman-Robertson Act.

Other resolutions established the Federation as an organization with a wide spectrum of concerns. The resolutions were:

- A call for extension of the Civilian Conservation Corps, with emphasis on activities benefiting wildlife.

- Maintenance and expansion of the Quetico-Superior Wilderness, as recommended by the Minnesota Wildlife Federation. Preservation of the wilderness was not a new idea, but the move was bold in an era when economic pressure groups encouraged intensive land use for agriculture, industry, mining, and electrical power.

- No relaxation of regulations controlling the importation of foreign livestock, especially those restrictions relating to the potential spread of hoof-and-mouth disease. This often fatal disease chiefly spreads among cattle, swine, sheep, and goats.

- Expansion of wildlife research through the use of federal and state funds, as was being done for farming through the Agricultural Extension Service.

- Federal action to curb water pollution. The resolution called for the establishment of a federal water agency, for more federal research on the problem of water pollution, and the granting of loans to municipalities and industry for the building of sewage-treatment plants.

- Restrictions on the trapping of furbearing animals. At that time, many states paid bounties on supposedly undesirable animals, such as cougars, bobcats, foxes, raccoons, skunks, and weasels.

The delegates, many of them hunters and fishermen from ranching or farming country, vigorously debated that last resolution. Ranchers saw cougars and bobcats as threats to herds and flocks. Farmers hated foxes and raccoons. Fishermen despised the fish-eating otter and mink. Hunters treated all predators, from skunks and weasels to foxes, coyotes, and bobcats, as competitors for waterfowl, ground-nesting upland birds, and small furred game. The fact that the delegates managed to pass such a resolution helped prove that the new Federation was not a self-serving organization of sportsmen merely looking for ways to get more game, but one that would restore and conserve the nation's wildlife heritage.

The delegates also endorsed a plan to create an annual National Wildlife Restoration Week. The week helped to launch the Federation, bringing to public attention not only the needs of wildlife but also the existence of a new force working all the weeks of the year to preserve the nation's most fragile natural treasures. Conceived as a fund-raiser and as a public education program, the week did not bring any money into the financially endangered Federation. But in that first year, and for years to come, the week reminded Americans about their wildlife heritage. And in that mission the week became a perennial success.

Lack of funds would plague the Federation for years. Payment for some of the day-to-day expenses came out of Darling's own pocket. Other supporters probably also anted up contributions, though the records of that era are so haphazard that no one will ever know who paid what bill. The Federation had no money to pay postage, let alone open an office.

During the Federation's first year, the American Wildlife Institute allowed the Federation to use the Institute's Washington offices. The Institute, founded in 1935, later became the North American Wildlife Foundation, which gave "moral support and financial assistance to wildlife restoration efforts and conservation." In 1946, most of the work of the American Wildlife Institute was assumed by the Wildlife Management Institute, headquartered in Washington.

Shoemaker, secretary of the Senate Wildlife Committee and now also secretary of the General Wildlife Federation, operated out of an office in the Senate Office Building and the one provided by the Wildlife Institute. He and Darling and a few other Federation leaders, as Shoemaker put it, managed "to carry on a very sketchy and, at times, a very humble effort to keep the loosely organized Federation functioning."

The probability of imminent bankruptcy haunted the Federation's early years. Rumors often spread that a formal declaration of bankruptcy was drawn up and ready to be filed. Not until 1941 did income exceed expenses, and even then the net surplus was only a little more than $6,300. The perilous financial state is shown in a report on income and expenses over the Federation's first decade. There was a net loss of more than $11,000 in 1937; the loss for the next year was only $1,700, though earlier debts remained unpaid. In 1939 the gross income was $109,700, but the total expense was $159,290. In 1940, both income and expense were diminished, and the annual net loss was reduced to $13,200. In 1941 came the first net surplus.

The first cash contribution, a $750 check, came to the Federation shortly after the first annual meeting. Hartley Dodge, Chairman of the Board of Remington Arms Company and an enthusiastic conservationist, presented the check. Remington was the nation's major supplier of ammunition for sport hunters.

Soon after the Remington donation to the Federation, the American Wildlife Institute agreed to lend the Federation $26,000 for organizational work and $25,000 toward the expenses of Wildlife Restoration Week. Without this money the Federation might well have gone under and the Pittman-Robertson Act, the first great lobbying accomplishment in the Federation's history, might never have been passed. The act reflected the Federation's resolution calling for the federal government to distribute to the states the wildlife funds collected from the federal excise tax on arms and ammunition.

A federal excise tax of ten percent already was levied on sporting arms and ammunition. By 1937 the government was collecting about $3 million a year, but the money went into the government's general fund. The Federation wanted the money earmarked for wildlife.

Shoemaker, former state game director in Oregon and an old Washington hand, took on the job of transforming the Federation resolution into law. He talked to officials in the Biological Survey and to hundreds of others—state fish and game officials, arms and ammunition manufacturers, sportsmen's groups, garden clubs, and women's organizations. After having written thirteen drafts, he felt he could show the proposed bill to the Sporting Arms and Ammunition Institute, the trade organization whose approval was vital to the proposal.

Shoemaker's next session was with Congressman (later Senator) A. Willis Robertson, who had been chairman of the Virginia Fish and Game Commission. Robertson inserted a provision prohibiting "the diversion of license fees paid by hunters for any other purpose than the administration of the state fish and game department" and offered to introduce the bill in the House. Key Pittman of Nevada, chairman of the Senate's Wildlife Committee, introduced the bill in the Senate, which passed it and sent it to the House. A snag developed in the House, where the bill had to be referred to the Agriculture Committee. Shoemaker was concerned about this because he wanted to bypass unsympathetic bureaucrats in the Department of Agriculture, which usually was asked to comment on bills before the House Agriculture Committee.

Congressman (later Senator) Scott Lucas of Illinois, a duck hunter, a sportsman, and a supporter of the Federation, was supposed to steer the bill through the Agriculture Committee. When Darling and Shoemaker heard that Lucas was not moving fast on the bill, they sent telegrams (paid for by Darling) to all the garden clubs and women's organizations in Illinois urging them to write, wire, or phone their congressmen.

"The good ladies responded," Shoemaker recalled. "A flood of wires reached the office of Lucas." A few days later, Shoemaker encountered

Lucas outside his office in Washington, and Lucas exclaimed, "For God's sake, Carl, take the women off my back and I'll report the bill at once!" He did, saying in his report to the House that one of the major objectives of the General Wildlife Federation "is the passage of legislation to authorize federal grants-in-aid to the states for conservation purposes. This bill carries out that objective and its provisions have been endorsed by virtually every conservation agency, public and private, in the United States."

On September 2, 1937, President Roosevelt signed the Pittman-Robertson Federal Aid in Wildlife Restoration Act. The law enabled the states, using federal funds, to undertake an enormous expansion of conservation activities, including surveys and research, habitat acquisition, and coordination of activities on wildlife projects. Ira N. Gabrielson, Darling's successor as chief of the Biological Survey (which became the U.S. Fish and Wildlife Service), said the law "produced the first semblance of a national wildlife program in history" and was "the most significant conservation legislation that has passed the Congress in many years."

From its borrowed Washington office, the Federation kept close watch on the administration of the act and passed along information through bulletins and weekly newsletters. A typical example of this watch-and-warn network came in a March 1939 newsletter:

"Your national headquarters received word about two weeks ago that drastic cuts had been made by the subcommittee considering the appropriations for not only the Biological Survey, but the Forest Service as well. This information was verified. $1,000,000 only had been recommended for carrying on the projects under the Pittman-Robertson Act. Your national headquarters became immediately active in the matter. Instead of decreases or drastic cuts being made, every item of the Biological Survey received this year what it had last year or was given an increase. The campaign that was conducted by your National Federation to restore these cuts and provide increase was all in a day's work and we simply record it here as having been accomplished. Many of you who receive this letter helped."

Such activity by the Federation proved that Darling's dream had indeed come true: diversified conservation groups had joined together; the federational structure was working. But the Pittman-Robertson triumph and the obvious effectiveness of the Federation's first campaign on Capitol Hill were not enough for Ding Darling. He was always looking for something more, and looking from his vantage point, for the Federation was, after all, his baby. Although he was reelected president of the Federation in 1937 and 1938, he seethed over what he saw as the failure of his idea to go where he wanted it to go and do the things he wanted done.

His anger focused on the failure of the Federation to finance itself. He had expected more fund-raising efforts on the national organization's behalf from the state affiliates, ignoring the fact that many of them were struggling with financial problems of their own. The political strength of the Federation came from its structure of affiliates in every state. But that same structure did not produce a fund-raising system. Darling failed to see this, and he railed at the system without analyzing its weaknesses. And he much preferred to wail over what he saw as shortcomings rather than hail accomplishments like the Pittman-Robertson Act.

Darling, a man of metaphors, dramatized his disillusionment with the Federation and his contempt for its ability to go its way without him by disowning the new baby and calling it a bastard. He moved from the metaphor of birth to the metaphor of death in 1939, when he turned down reelection. The Federation, *his* Federation, he said, was dead, and so in 1939 he wrote "The Coroner's Verdict."

Darling was especially upset about the way the early fund-raising wildlife stamps had been handled. The first stamps, which he himself drew, had been distributed to members of the Federation who were expected to hand them out in hopes of receiving a contribution for them and send the proceeds to Federation headquarters. According to Darling's "verdict," the Federation was paralyzed. "So complete is the demonstration of disinterest [among the state affiliates] that at this August date no state representative of the Federation, with one possible exception, has completed this report or sent in the money for stamps sold last March. . . . So good-bye, Federation, good-bye. . . . Gone is the prospect of a nationwide pressure to introduce the teaching of conservation in the public schools and a coordinated method of teaching the teachers what and how to teach conservation."

Shoemaker and others who knew Darling well saw the "verdict" more as a challenge than as a bitter document of despair. They pointed out that he had accepted the title of honorary president and continued to help the Federation. His friends also explained away his disillusionment as a temporary depression brought about by a personal tragedy. In January of 1939, his twenty-nine-year-old son John, a physician at the Mayo Clinic in Rochester, Minnesota, had suffered brain damage in an automobile accident and had become an invalid.

Although Darling declined to work on any committees, he did take a deep interest in the educational activities of the Federation. But his writings for the Federation bristle with hyperbole and bitterness about the efforts of conservationists to unify their power. He irrationally attacked the generally praised Civilian Conservation Corps, claiming that one-half "of the CCC camps has cut away more vegetation than the other half of the CCC camps has planted." As for his dream, he wrote, "Voluntary organizations which sought to unite the conservationists into powerful nationwide movements have failed dismally. Conservation is a sissy with ruffled pantalettes, a May basket in her hand and a yellow ribbon in her hair."

By the early 1950s, when the Federation was in financially good health, Darling had all but broken with the organization he had brought into the world. In correspondence with Shoemaker, Darling acknowledged the "mounting figure of money in the Federation treasury," but said the organization was wrongly named—"We have no more federation than a bunch of wild rabbits"—and was being run by "a damned incompetent bunch of chowderheads." In 1954, he resigned as honorary president and forbade the use of his name in any way by the Federation.

Darling's departure from the Federation produced no drastic changes in its operation. Ironically, his walkout confirmed that the Federation had progressed from being the creation of a man with a dream to a mature organization no longer dependent upon the dreams—or whims—of just one individual. Darling had been something of a cult figure in the early days, a man of national prominence whose name and efforts helped to establish the young, struggling Federation. By the 1950s, the Federation had proved itself to be a self-sustaining organization.

But, as the Federation grew and the generation of founders gave way to the generation of managers and administrators, old-timers did not want Darling to be a bitter memory. He represented a matter of history, a matter of putting things to right. This became a special mission of Thomas L. Kimball, a former state game official who was named executive director of the Federation in 1960. When Kimball was only four months on the job, he wrote to Darling and began a slow process of reconciliation. "One can scarcely have been associated with the National Wildlife Federation for even so short a time as I have," Kimball soothingly wrote, "and not feel the impact of your tremendous pioneering influence."

One of Darling's persistent complaints down the years had been that the Federation had failed to act as "a conservation clearinghouse." Yet, from the beginning, Federation publications, especially newsletters, reflected the belief of Federation officers that the organization was a source for national, regional, and state information—and an advocate for action on every level, from forming local conservation groups to alerting congressmen to conservation issues.

Concentrating on Darling's obsession with the idea of a conservation clearinghouse, Kimball, in warm and patient letters, tried to convince Darling that his idea had not been ignored and his work as founder had not been forgotten. Darling, it turned out, had had an extremely detailed plan for his conservation clearinghouse, a plan that called for an organizational structure far different from that of the Federation as it existed in the 1960s. Kimball could not restructure the Federation to please Darling. But he could—and did—bring Darling up to date on Federation matters. And he assured Darling that the concept of the clearinghouse would be incorporated into the planning of the new Federation library.

Finally, Ding Darling was asked to be co-chairman of the 1962 National Wildlife Week, along with Walt Disney. He accepted the offer as "a nice compliment." The long siege of bitterness had ended.

On February 13, 1962, a month before National Wildlife Week, the *Des Moines Register* published a cartoon that Darling had drawn some time before. It was entitled "Ding's Farewell." The cartoon showed Ding's office, with an unfinished work on his drawing board and some of his most famous cartoons on the wall. Cobwebs entwined duck decoys, fishing rods, hunting gear, a shotgun case, a pile of manuscripts. The door to the office was ajar, and a spectral figure was vanishing into the darkness beyond. "'Bye now," the cartoon says, "—It's been wonderful knowing you." This was Ding Darling's epitaph. He had died the day before. He was eighty-five years old.

Ding's baby had become a major force in American conservation by the time Ding said farewell, and it would become even stronger. As in the beginning, the Federation kept watch over America's wildlife and wild lands. And now there was an International Division and a global watch.

Some things, though, never changed, even after half a century. The voices of many still blended in a chorus, the ranks were still filled with people who knew what they wanted. The people still knew that, marching together, they had strength, as had Ding's first army back in 1936.

3

One for All, All for One

When Ding Darling explained how he expected the Federation to work, naturally he spoke in cartoons. One cartoon shows several individuals crouched at separate campfires, each solitary cook trying to light a single log. The logs are labeled Soil Conservation, Wild Life Conservation, Sportsmen's Leagues, Saving the Song Birds, Parks, Horticulture, Independent Clubs, and Water Conservation. "It is hard to start a fire with one stick of wood," the cartoon says. A second cartoon shows all the logs piled under a big, bubbling pot labeled Conservation Clearing House. The cooks, now united, stand shoulder to shoulder, smiling happily, and the headline says, "But if you ever get the fire wood together in one pile—"

Darling's idea of a national federation went back at least to 1934, when, as chief of the Biological Survey, he attended a conference where he learned about Indiana's state-level federation, with representation from 508 conservation clubs. Each club elected its own slate of officers and a delegate to the state federation. The federation was the work of the educational division of the Indiana Department of Conservation. "It seems to me," Darling wrote to C. R. "Pink" Gutermuth, chief organizer of the Indiana federation, "you are getting control of conservation in the hands of real sportsmen and conservationists. . . . I would like to see this same plan tried in many other states."

Darling proposed his notion of a federational organization at the 1936 conference, and it was accepted and used even before official adoption of the General Wildlife Federation's bylaws in 1937. Each state that wanted to join the Federation was required to have its own state federation, which would select a representative to the national Federation. Thirty-three states had no such organization prior to the formation of the national Federation, but leaders within the states set out immediately to rectify the shortcoming. Within a year after the Washington conference, fourteen states began forming federations. One of the earliest federations inspired by the conference was the Massachusetts Conservation Council, whose ranks included sportsmen, scientists, farmers, women's clubs, and members known simply as nature lovers. By 1938, only four states (California, Louisiana, Maine, and North Carolina) did not have an affiliate connected to the Federation.

Arkansas not only started a federation but also launched its own conservation week, which was independent of the Federation's nationwide observance of National Wildlife Restoration Week. Such state activities reflected the Federation's attitude of allowing, even encouraging, local activities that demonstrated a kind of "state's rights," a sensitive political issue in many states. From the beginning, the Federation's policy has been that each state affiliate, while contributing to and receiving benefits from the national Federation, is autonomous.

When the idea of the Federation was first formalized at the 1936 North American Wildlife Conference in Washington, much discussion was given to the structure of its governing body. The nation, the founders decided, was to be divided into thirteen regions, each region electing its own representative to sit on the board of directors. The western states, fearing that the East might gain control of the board of directors, pressed for directors at large in addition to the thirteen regional directors. So the original by-laws provided for nineteen directors, six of whom were to be directors at large. Further, no fewer than three of the directors at large had to reside west of the Mississippi River.

Year after year, delegates tinkered with mechanisms for giving affiliates an equitable representation on the national level. The directors-at-large idea, for example, was scrapped in 1949 and later restored. Essentially, though, the structure has remained unchanged from the way it was set up at the first national meeting of the Federation.

Today's National Wildlife Federation includes in its membership fifty-one state* affiliate organizations, each of which sends a voting

---

*"State" includes other U.S. possessions, such as Puerto Rico and the Virgin Islands, each of which has an affiliate. For a list of all affiliates and associate member organizations, see appendix 1.

delegate to the Federation's annual meeting. The delegates propose and vote on the resolutions that set NWF's policies. They also elect the officers and thirteen of the board of directors, who in turn elect up to nine at-large directors. The national officers include the president and three vice presidents, one from the East, one from the central United States, and one from the West. These elected officials are unpaid. NWF also includes in its membership nine associate member organizations (such as the Caribbean Conservation Association) and, since 1963, individual, nonvoting associate members.

The structure—affiliates joined in a federation—is as old as the Union and has been used before by groups with simultaneous national and local interests. The American Federation of Labor had such a relationship, with several unions sending representatives to a national governing board that set broad policy but left local matters alone. The American Legion similarly has a national organization tied to state organizations of Legion posts. Commenting on the 1936 wildlife conference's adoption of this structure, an observer noted that the new organization had set up a "delicate balance of cooperation" between "highly organized groups of sportsmen" and "'posey-pickers' and other sentimentalists."

Delicate though this balance may have been, the affiliates of the young Federation were zealous in spreading the conservation message through their states. At a National Wildlife Federation board meeting in 1938, a vice president, Dr. Walter B. Jones of Alabama, spoke of his trials and triumphs in the Deep South states. Like a missionary in a pagan land, he preached the conservation gospel to many groups, telling the members of the Knife and Fork Club, for example, that the Federation had "taken the viewpoint that if you want to preserve your upland game, don't burn—give life, food, and cover there. If you want fish, don't pollute streams, and let us not take the little ones."

He told of "game hogs" in Alabama, and what he preached to them: "You have killed your songbirds with slingshots and air rifles and .22 rifles, and you have killed the quail to the last bird in the covey, and burned your woods in order to grow more tough beef for me to eat in restaurants, and the white-fringed weevil comes, and this is what you can expect, exactly, and now you [must] do something about it. It is your weevil and he will eat your beans and corn and tear up your tomatoes. The thing that you can do is to restore your birds [so they can help control the weevil]." The sermon "made them all mad," he said, but not long afterward he received a few letters apologizing and saying, "We are going to work."

Colin M. Reed, a regional director, recalled the results of his visit to a country school in New Jersey. He had recited Joyce Kilmer's poem

"Trees" and said to the pupils, "Of course, you can't make a tree. 'Only God can make a tree,' but you can plant a tree." About two weeks later, he met a friend who said, "You got me in a hell of a fix. My boy has made me buy twenty trees to plant down on our place. . . . And I don't think I am nearly through yet."

By such sometimes grudging acceptance, the Federation and its affiliates continued their missionary work among clubs and schools. The spread of education about conservation issues was relatively easy compared to the attempts to bring some long-established organizations into the Federation fold. A board member who had been recruiting outdoor groups said the organizations he had been talking to "are scared." He singled out the Izaak Walton League as especially fearful because it looked upon itself as "a competing organization."

Mrs. H. G. Bogert, a director at large and the only woman in the Federation hierarchy, told of working "just as hard as I could" with women's clubs, the national Parent-Teachers Association, university women's organizations, the auxiliary of the American Legion, and the Daughters of the American Revolution. "But not a single women's organization will give a list of names." Women's groups, she said, were suspicious of a male-dominated organization. The Federation, she told her male colleagues, needed more women in its leadership before it could expect to attract more women to become affiliates—and to get women's organizations to trust the Federation.

Not all organizations saw themselves as endangered competitors. The head of the Massachusetts Audubon Societies directed the 1938 National Wildlife Restoration Week in his state. The same year, in Maine, where the Federation did not even then have an affiliate, a garden club official organized the state's observance of the first Wildlife Week. The week became a success in many ways, not the least of which was the cooperation it had elicited from conservation organizations, which, by helping out on Wildlife Week, had also helped welcome the newcomer Federation to the conservation realm.

The proposal to create a national wildlife week had come from Frederick Jordan, a New York advertising executive and chairman of the Federation's first Finance Committee. At the annual meeting in 1937, Jordan raised and eloquently answered the question of how to pay future bills. In his address he cited the meeting's "many splendid reports . . . on how we can broaden the range for game, how we can populate the hills with wild flowers, how we can fill the air with song birds, how we can rid the streams of pollution and give abundant fish to those to whom they rightfully belong." All of this, he said, would cost a considerable amount of money and "I don't know where you expect to get it." Actually, he did, for he proposed an annual "Wildlife Restoration Week," to be proclaimed by the president of the United States. "And all during the proposed week," he said, "sportsmen's groups, luncheon clubs, the Granges, the Boy and Girl Scout troops, the 4-H Clubs, every Parent-Teacher Association, and the rural and city schools can hold Wildlife Restoration meetings. . . .

"You can name week after week that has been held throughout the United States in the past twenty-five years to raise funds, and there has not been one of them that has had such a broad appeal. . . . I don't think there is a man or a woman or a child old enough to know what it is all about that doesn't love at least one bird, one animal, or one flower. . . . It would be a pretty base man, or a pretty base woman or a pretty ignorant child, that couldn't find some one thing in nature to interest him or her sufficiently to at least want to give a dime for wildlife restoration.

"How are we going to get this money? How are we going to organize to do it? Who is going to do it?" Jordan named the National Federation of Women's Clubs, garden clubs, Parent-Teacher Associations, and "the only body of human beings that has ever put over anything without a catastrophe following it—the women of America."

"When we get this money," he asked his audience, "what are we going to do with it?" Again, he answered himself: "You spend it where you raise it. . . . in your own states." Jordan's speech brought the assembly to its feet cheering. The meeting immediately passed a motion to sponsor an annual National Wildlife Restoration Week.

Carl Shoemaker, because of his many connections in Washington, was asked to arrange for President Roosevelt to proclaim a wildlife week. Shoemaker began his assignment by forming a distinguished committee to call on the president. He also wrote to Roosevelt's secretary, Marvin McIntyre, naming the members of the committee and pointing out that Roosevelt himself had issued the call for the North American Wildlife Conference. A few days later, McIntyre phoned Shoemaker to tell him the president would see the committee on August 12, 1937.

Shoemaker, aided by the Federation's favorite legislator, Senator Key Pittman, had recruited Secretary of Agriculture Henry A. Wallace, former Senator Harry B. Hawes, and Congressman A. Willis Robertson. Other members of the committee were Jordan, Tom Beck, the editor of *Collier's* and a longtime supporter of conservation, and Henry P. Davis of the American Wildlife Institute.

Hawes began the meeting with Roosevelt by telling a story about his favorite retriever. The president responded with a hunting story of his own. He had spent most of a beautiful day and not bagged anything when he saw two geese coming in high over the decoys. He fired at one and hit it, then swung around and fired at the second one—but couldn't tell if he hit it because, at that instant, the first goose landed on his head, knocking him down in the blind. The goose he had killed had almost killed him, he said. After a laugh and some more small talk, Hawes formally asked Roosevelt to issue the proclamation for a National Wildlife Restoration Week.

Roosevelt nodded benevolently and simply asked, "When do you want it?" Surprised by the alacrity of the president's acceptance, no one answered, and Roosevelt asked again, "What dates do you suggest?" According to Shoemaker, "That was something neither Hawes nor any of the rest of us had thought about. There were blank stares on all of our faces, and everyone looked at me." Shoemaker had not given the date any thought, but he suddenly blurted out, "The first week of spring."

"All right," Roosevelt replied, "I'll have Mac fix it up." And so the first National Wildlife Restoration Week was scheduled for March 20 to 26, 1938. The date was accepted by all—except for religious members of some affiliates who wondered about celebrating anything during Lent. (There were to be dances, barbecues, and fish fries.) When news of this religious concern reached Ding Darling, he shrugged it off, saying, "This is God's creation that we are working with."

Darling, Shoemaker, Jordan, and the rest of the Federation had hoped that National Wildlife Restoration Week would bring in money for the financially strapped organization. The week did win new public support for wildlife restoration and did introduce the Federation as a new and potentially powerful force for conservation. But it did not raise much money, and shortly afterwards it became purely a program to bring national attention to wildlife problems.

In September of 1937, as soon as the Pittman-Robertson Act was signed, workers at the Federation's temporary headquarters in Washington mailed a questionnaire to all state affiliate officers and to others who had attended the first convention. The questionnaire asked for suggestions on how to finance the work of the Federation.

More than a hundred and fifty replies came in. One is said to have come from a man in Kansas, who wrote, "Why don't you paint some wildlife pictures and have them printed on paper with glue on the back and sell them to lovers of wildlife all over the country? I'm sure they will be well received." According to this version of the genesis of wildlife stamps, Ding Darling instantly responded by making sketches for use on stamps.

Soon afterward, Shoemaker and Darling, together with Fred Jordan, "were on a train out of Des Moines headed for Cheyenne, Wyoming, to attend the state meeting," as Shoemaker recalled. "He [Darling] had a table brought to us and out came his cardboards and watercolors, and before we had reached our destination he had finished eight of the paintings. In the hotel at Cheyenne he painted the other nine. Beautiful, they were! The next project was to find a lithographer and some money. . . ."

Each of the historic "first issue" stamp sheets consisted of one hundred stamps. A stamp portraying a miniature version of the first National Wildlife Restoration Week poster was printed once in the top row, and sixteen of the portraits of birds and animals painted by Darling were duplicated at least six times on the sheet. For some years afterward, all the stamps were called "Wildlife Poster Stamps." The first National Wildlife Restoration Week poster depicted a Canada goose high above a desolate landscape. Near the top left corner, the poster—and stamp—bore the legend *Where To Now?* Across the bottom was printed, *National Wildlife Restoration Week March 20–26, 1938.* All the other 1938 stamps bore a slogan printed across the bottom: *Help Restore Our Wildlife.* Across the top of each full sheet of stamps was the headline, *National Wildlife Restoration Week,* and a brief statement of purpose: "For uniting the efforts of all friends of Outdoor America to the end that future generations shall have their rightful heritage of Wildlife." The 1938 stamps, singly and in sheets, have become collector's items, and the original paintings reside in the Smithsonian Institution.

The stamps were not exactly sold. They were distributed in the hopes that recipients would make a suggested $1-a-sheet contribution. Distribution of the stamps was tied to National Wildlife Restoration Week. On the eve of the first observance of that week, newspapers throughout the nation published a photograph of President Roosevelt, the world's most famous stamp collector, admiring the first set of wildlife stamps.

Leading firms in the sporting arms industry made some of the first contributions for stamps. Remington Arms, a major account handled by Fred Jordan for the advertising firm by which he was employed, contributed $5,000; Winchester, $1,000; du Pont, $1,100; Hercules Powder Company, $400; Savage Arms, $500. Distributors of the stamps included chapters of the Junior Chambers of Commerce, garden clubs, the General Federation of Women's Clubs, and the state affiliates of the Federation. The distributing organization retained a percentage of the contributions—sometimes 35 percent, sometimes

40 percent, depending upon the deal made with the Federation—and remitted the remainder to the Federation, which paid the cost of printing and distribution.

This distribution plan seemed sound, but, in fact, the handling of the stamps inadvertently aggravated Federation-affiliate problems. Disputes over the stamps threatened to kill off the Federation before it reached its third birthday.

"State affiliates had been asked about how many [stamps] they could use," Shoemaker recalled. "Their estimates were in many cases excessive. Their requisitions were cut at times to take care of our limited print order. But they wired or phoned and pleaded for more of the stamp sheets. We asked for periodic reports on sales. It soon became evident that their enthusiasm had not been justified. . . . The campaign which started off with such great zeal promised to become a flop—a dismal failure."

A few affiliates earned contributions on respectable numbers of stamps, but other affiliates got rid of few, kept sloppy records, and haggled about how to split the contributions. One affiliate set up an office and distributed several thousand dollars' worth of stamps, but remitted only $31 to the Federation. Volunteers in many affiliates failed to distribute or even return the stamps. As late as the 1970s the Federation heard from people who had just found a box of undistributed stamps that a forebear had stored in the attic in 1938. The Federation's own inventory of 1938 stamps, which numbered about 50,000, was not cleared until they were burned in a warehouse fire in 1960.

Faced with potential disaster in this first effort, desperate Federation officials in Washington quickly started renting address lists from public-relations firms and mail-order agencies and distributing the stamps directly. The Federation sent out about half a million sheets of stamps in 1938, along with solicitations asking the public to help wildlife by sending the Federation a dollar. "The money," Shoemaker said, "began to roll in."

But when the affiliates heard about the mail campaign, they deluged the Washington office with protests that the national organization was—in Shoemaker's words—"undercutting their efforts . . . taking the cream of their prospects and . . . if we didn't do something about it, there would be mutiny." Further, some people whose names appeared on several mailing lists complained that they had been solicited as many as four times.

The Federation agreed to credit the affiliates with a percentage of all the mail-solicited income received from within their respective states. Instead of having the affiliates send revenues to the Federation, the Federation said it would send revenues to the affiliates. The arrangement produced complicated and costly accounting procedures, creating new problems instead of solving the original one.

"The 1938 stamp sale," Shoemaker said, "was distressingly inadequate to finance the Federation. But we knew that we could not rely on the affiliates to do the job. There were too many cross currents to chart a safe course in this sea of uncertainty. Yet we knew the idea was sound. And we decided to go forward with it again in 1939."

That decision inspired Darling's "Coroner's Verdict" on the death of the Federation, added to his reasons for refusing to accept reelection as president, and eventually brought about a bitter defection from the organization he had founded. But the persistence demonstrated in 1939 eventually paid off, for in future years the stamps became both a successful fund-raising device and an effective method for spreading the word about the Federation.

Whatever damage may have been caused by the early stamp debacle, the Federation was able to keep its affiliate structure intact through communications between Washington and the states. From the beginning, the Federation had used publications issued from headquarters to inform affiliates about legislative issues in the nation's capital—and about what the affiliates were doing on their own. The primary source of information was Carl Shoemaker's steady stream of news bulletins, which managed to be informative, authoritative, and chatty. He said he wanted what he sent to the affiliates to be as informal as a story told around a campfire.

The affiliates also had stories to tell around the Federation campfire. In a typical 1938 issue of *The National Wildlife Federation Bulletin*, reports from state affiliates showed a rich variety of interests and issues. Alabama had questioned the Tennessee Valley Authority's mosquito-control program, "which apparently is destined to have a seriously adverse effect on the fish, animal, bird, and plant life of the lakes impounded by TVA. . . ." Arkansas reported that CCC workers were fencing off a wildlife preserve to keep out cattle. Florida's affiliate, the Florida State Fish and Game Association, had brought the Future Farmers of America into the state's conservation battles.

In Indiana, 182 conservation clubs were earning money by breeding fish for state fish-stocking projects and another 160 clubs were earning 75 cents a bird raising pheasants. The Iowa Wildlife Federation reported that its garden club members had taken over the planting of trees and shrubs in a state park. The Nebraska Wildlife Federation was campaigning to raise the license fees for hunting and fishing to provide more funds for state conservation work.

The Tennessee Wildlife Federation won a legal fight when the state supreme court ruled that state conservation laws could not be bypassed by obstructive county laws. The Texas federation's Wildlife Planning Board drummed up grass-roots support for conservation by drawing members from each of the state's 254 counties. The federation then successfully campaigned for the creation of a Department of Wildlife at A & M College. Vermont clubs were raising fish and buying land near fish hatcheries to protect the water supply. Wyoming enlisted 4-H boys and girls to raise pheasants.

The Utah affiliate contributed $4,000 to the state for conservation work as Utah tried qualifying for a project under the Pittman-Robertson Act, which had become a unifying force for the fledgling Federation—and set a course for the congressional lobbying it would do in the future.

On a national level, the Federation rightfully claimed that it had almost singlehandedly gotten the Pittman-Robertson Act passed, and, on the state level, affiliates used the act as a way to transform conservation rhetoric into real projects. "Remember," the state affiliates were told through a Federation newsletter, "the Pittman-Robertson Act is a Federation measure, no matter who else claims it." Affiliates were urged "to tell the world you belong to the National Wildlife Federation. If you are affiliated, say so whenever and wherever the opportunity presents itself. And if it doesn't present itself—say it anyway."

By early 1939, more than twenty Pittman-Robertson projects had been approved in eighteen states. Most of the early projects involved studies on managing wildlife: beavers in Utah, bighorn sheep in Wyoming, waterfowl in Massachusetts, turkeys in Virginia. The ever-growing list of projects proved that the Federation had been right in deciding to venture into national-level conservation politics. The Pittman-Robertson Act was on its way to becoming the most important legislation ever devoted to aiding wildlife restoration.

The Federation was still struggling to survive when the United States went to war in 1941. A nation at war had little time or energy to spare for conservation. But the Federation did not become a casualty of the war, primarily because of its affiliate structure, which became a network both for spreading the news and for bonding Washington headquarters to widely dispersed organizations throughout the country.

States began to appreciate a voice in Washington—a voice that, for instance, recommended to the War Production Board that it "release sufficient ammunition to provide for such harvests as would be consistent with the defense program." As Federation president David A. Aylward pointed out, hunting "has a real value as an additional food source, and the down, feathers, fats, etc., go directly into the war effort." The Federation did not, however, support war-factory workers who asked for extensions of shooting seasons so they could have time to hunt.

While giving attention—but not unquestioning allegiance—to its constituency of hunters, the Federation also kept watch on the way the war effort hurt the environment. Little could be done during the war, but soon after V-J Day, the Federation called for a cleanup of waters sullied by factories that had worked night and day in an all-out national-defense effort.

The report singled out as a special problem the synthetic rubber industry, which had filled the wartime vacuum created by a lack of natural rubber. The new—and apparently permanent—industry "produced a type of water pollution which, scientists say, has for the most part failed to respond to treatment. Cities have had to increase the chlorine content of their domestic water supply to make it safe for use." The "heavily polluted Ohio River watershed," *Conservation News* reported, had become "one of the foulest, filthiest in the world. From the environs of Pittsburgh on down stream below Louisville these waters bear noxious materials which have made them practically a biological desert." The *News* then analyzed water-pollution bills that were before Congress and explained why the Federation was supporting a particular one.

This dual service—providing information on wildlife issues and keeping a watch on Washington—set the pattern for the Federation's relationship with affiliates. The relationship was strengthened by another factor: the continued reliance on the regional system.

In the early years, it was the regional director who, while serving on the board of directors, also gave close attention to the activities of affiliates in his region and kept headquarters apprised. One of his responsibilities was to offer assistance to affiliates in membership drives and conservation projects. He also relayed information from Washington back to the affiliates.

As the Federation and its affiliates grew and became more active, the job of regional director became too much for volunteers. In 1948 a field program was begun with the hiring of Bud Jackson. He regularly called on affiliates to stimulate greater cooperation between the

Federation and its affiliates; to lend them assistance in such areas as leadership development, fund raising, and strategy for supporting legislation; and to get local suggestions that could be folded into national activities. Later, the field services program expanded so that each of the Federation's thirteen regions was served by a field representative from that area. Eventually, the title *field man* changed to *regional executive*.

Today, regional directors, still volunteers, continue to work closely with the state affiliates they represent, participating in some activities, counseling on others. Their main function, however, is to represent their region on the NWF board of directors.

Reports from affiliates, given at NWF annual meetings, have always helped spread information among the states. At the meeting in 1946, for example, the delegate from Rhode Island was describing the pollution that was hurting the state's clam industry when the Alabama delegate asked for an exchange of water pollution data. The Rhode Island representative, right on the floor, began a cooperative effort to find out "the good thinking in other communities," and other states began, at that moment, to attack water pollution problems together. At the same meeting, Minnesota shared its experience in how to shelve plans for an undesirable dam.

Each region had its own special issues. A 1951 report showed the breadth of those issues. Water pollution problems concerned Region 11 (Washington, Oregon, Alaska). Recruitment dominated activities in Region 9 (North Dakota, South Dakota, Nebraska, Iowa, Kansas), where relatively few fishermen and hunters belonged to any conservation organizations. Region 13 (Idaho, Wyoming, Montana) reported "our major problem is high dams."

In Region 1 (New England), Connecticut had asked the state legislature to prohibit "the drawing down of reservoirs to such an extent that aquatic life is impaired," while Rhode Island was pushing the state to declare an official "statement of policy on wildlife conservation," and New Hampshire was focusing on conservation legislation—urging on the good proposals and stopping the bad ones. In Massachusetts, a covered wagon rolled from one summer camp to another, carrying people who set up a workshop to teach campers about conservation. The Vermont affiliate had its eye on "legislation desired by power interests that would be harmful to conservation." Maine was concentrating on finding new member clubs and developing its own publication.

To foster the affiliate system, the National Wildlife Federation once awarded financial grants to state affiliates for carrying on local projects, especially those having to do with legislation and education. (One grant request that was turned down: $250 for the purchase of buffalo meat to be served at a banquet for state senators. The Federation's board of directors considered the request "of questionable appropriateness.") Direct financial aid to state affiliates gradually ended because national officials believed it introduced a kind of paternalism into the delicate relationship.

The Federation had been offering advice and services to affiliates ever since 1936, but in 1979 it created an Affiliate Services Department to provide more backup to the regional executives and to offer directly to the affiliates a wide array of support services, including help in developing fund-raising strategies and technical assistance on such matters as promoting conservation issues and improving lobbying skills.

Affiliate Services Department staffers, a Kentucky affiliate officer said, "are as close as your phone. Their expertise and knowledge on national issues is unequaled." Sometimes staffers go to affiliate meetings to clarify issues. Affiliate Services also offers training through a leadership development program designed around the special challenges of effectively running a state-wide volunteer organization. The Federation keeps in touch through the *Leader*, a monthly newspaper sent to affiliate leaders.

Lynn Greenwalt, a former Mid-Atlantic Regional Executive who served affiliates in Virginia, West Virginia, Delaware, and Maryland, once described his position as being a route for people in his region who want help to get "the support . . . and the expertise of the National Wildlife Federation without my doing it for them." The Federation's affiliates, he said, "are not like chapters of the Audubon Society and the Sierra Club. They are separate, autonomous organizations which, by and large, share the same objectives—some closely, some less closely—as the National Wildlife Federation, but are not beholden to it. . . . They can do as they please, but what they 'please do' almost invariably coincides with the National Wildlife Federation and makes for an excellent relationship."

Even an excellent relationship has its ups and downs, however. Affiliates have not always seen the world of wildlife exactly as national headquarters has. The two parties have lived, as a Federation staff member put it, in "dynamic equilibrium."

Examples of sometimes amiable, sometimes acrimonious give-and-take appear again and again at board of directors' meetings and at NWF's annual meetings, where affiliates, through the passage of state-crafted resolutions, determine National Wildlife Federation policy.

An affiliate does not necessarily wait for a resolution at the annual meeting to get a point across. At a board meeting in 1968, the Washington State Sportsmen's Council (that state's affiliate organization) complained that the National Wildlife Federation had supported the creation of another national park in Washington. "We now have two national parks in this state, both of which are woefully underfinanced and underdeveloped," the affiliate said. "We can ill afford a third." Executive Director Tom Kimball said in response, "I cannot see the wisdom of accepting at complete face value the position of our affiliates on controversial matters at all times. . . ."

Two years later, during a board of directors discussion of the old issue of hunters and fishermen versus nature lovers, Kimball defended the National Wildlife Federation's national-affiliate structure. He was responding to Vice President Ray Arnett, who had said, "I think we should make up our minds whether we are going to be an affiliate type of organization or an associate type, leaning toward the Audubon Society, the Izaak Walton League, and others. . . ."

"On the other hand," Kimball asked, "why cannot we be both?"

"First of all," Arnett answered, "because I think we have not succeeded in being an affiliate organization. We have not succeeded there."

"I think," Kimball said, "that this is a broad statement—that you are painting fifty affiliates with a broad statement that really is not correct. I would say that we have a substantial number of affiliates who are cooperative and effective and who work well with the National Wildlife Federation. On the other hand, there are others who are weak and yet are willing, and we are concentrating on those states where they will accept this type of assistance."

Down the years, the Federation has tried to strengthen affiliates by showing them ways to develop leadership and financial stability. The national organization has also helped affiliates by joining with them in lawsuits. The first such cooperation came in 1969, when NWF and the Idaho Wildlife Federation confronted the federal bureaucracy to stop a mining operation that threatened a proposed national recreation area within the White Clouds mountains in Idaho. The National Wildlife Federation, by entering what appeared at first glance to be a local controversy, took its first step down the legal activist road.* Ever since then NWF has joined with affiliates in legal battles, supporting, for example, the Michigan affiliate when it filed suit under the Clean Water Act, and the Oregon Wildlife Federation in a suit

*For a full account of the confrontation, see chapter 7.

claiming unwarranted destruction of spawning streams by the U.S. Forest Service.

Washington headquarters and state affiliates have also tangled in court, as when the National Wildlife Federation and the Virginia Wildlife Federation found themselves on opposite sides in a legal fight over the use of off-the-road vehicles (ORVs) on a Virginia wildlife refuge. (The National Wildlife Federation won, holding the line on the ORVs.)

The affiliate structure does not promise all parties a life free of conflict. But the structure works.

Just as a state organization can become affiliated, it can also become unaffiliated, and even reaffiliated. The affiliate in New York, for one, left NWF in 1956 and rejoined again four years later. When an affiliate is ousted or disaffiliates itself from the Federation, the regional directors and regional executives work to replace it as quickly as possible so that the state continues to be represented. The Massachusetts Conservation Council, formed and affiliated in 1936, was replaced by the Massachusetts Wildlife Federation in 1965. In 1975 the California Wildlife Federation withdrew from NWF after the Federation informed it that NWF could not provide the financial support it had requested. Within a year, a new affiliate, the California Natural Resources Federation, had been formed. Alaska lost its affiliate status in 1983 because it had simply ceased to function and would not cooperate with the National Wildlife Federation in any way. The Wildlife Federation of Alaska was organized as a replacement, and it was accepted as an affiliate in 1986.

The National Wildlife Federation limits affiliate membership to one organization in any state, and a state affiliate must meet standards set by the board of directors to qualify. These standards include a broad membership base throughout the state; a good leadership system (including a way to remove leaders who fail to perform their duties); stable and adequate finances; knowledge of state and national conservation problems—and active participation in solving those problems; good internal and external communications, such as statewide publications; sound business management; a good public image and a good reputation; and support of the objectives and policies of the National Wildlife Federation.

A state affiliate, which often has the word *Federation* in its name, frequently reflects the two-tier structure of the National Wildlife Federation by having a state-level organization made up of representatives from affiliated local garden clubs, local wildlife groups, and other environmental organizations. A few affiliates have as many as four tiers in their structure. Affiliate officers are volunteers, but many affiliates have paid workers. A 1984 survey showed that thirty-nine affiliates employed a total of more than one hundred full-time staffers. They and the other affiliates were spending nearly $7 million a year on publications, education, and work on state and regional conservation issues.

More than 250,000 state affiliate members receive newspapers and newsletters published by affiliates. A sampler:

The Nevada Wildlife Federation's *Great Basin Reporter* reveals that the Department of Defense is trying to gain control of two wildlife refuges in the region. Wyoming's *Pronghorn* warns that acidic pollution from two plants threatens fishing in high-altitude lakes. Wisconsin's *Wisconservation* urges homeowners to create backyard habitats for animals. The West Virginia Wildlife Federation's *Wildlife Notes* looks at the problems that come with extensive spraying for gypsy moths.

South Carolina's *Out-of-Doors* warns that a North Carolina law limiting land disposal of chemical waste could mean that South Carolina will get the waste. New Mexico's *Outdoor Reporter* tells how members of the state's congressional delegation voted on a clean-air bill. *New Hampshire Wildlife* reports new research about bobcats.

Montana Wildlife explains that game animals are causing more damage to agricultural crops. *Iowa Wildlife* backs a program to plant switchgrass, which provides cover to nesting game and song birds. *Colorado Wildlife* says pollution from mines is poisoning the Arkansas River. *Mississippi Out-of-Doors* focuses on soil problems, *Maryland Out-of-Doors* on eagles, *Arkansas Out-of-Doors* on outdoor photography.

Each affiliate holds an annual meeting during which state resolutions are passed, setting the conservation policy for the affiliate. Also on the agenda of the state annual meetings are two actions linking the affiliate directly to the National Wildlife Federation: proposing national resolutions and selecting national delegates. Resolutions passed at these affiliate meetings are presented to the annual national meeting of the NWF, along with any resolutions proposed by the staff at national headquarters. The delegates attend the annual meeting and vote on the proposed resolutions which, if passed, become the bedrock of Federation policy. The delegates bring to the annual NWF meeting their knowledge of grass-roots conservation activities and problems—and the power to take action to solve problems.

One such problem was once widespread and seemingly insoluble: politicians in many states treated fish and game programs like patronage preserves. The political appointees selected to manage these programs often were woefully amateurish. From the 1930s into the

1960s, Federation affiliates, in state after state, led the way in transforming state fish and game commissions into professional organizations that use scientific principles in their work for wildlife.

In 1936—the founding year of NWF—the Conservation Federation of Missouri worked on drafting a constitutional amendment that led to the creation of the nonpolitical Missouri Department of Conservation. The amendment made the department an independent wildlife and forestry agency. Similarly, in Kentucky, the affiliate worked to take the State Fish and Game Division out of politics by involving sportsmen from each of the nine wildlife districts in the selection of district commissioners.

The Florida Wildlife Federation led a drive to amend the state constitution to require that the Florida Game and Fish Commission be nonpolitical. The Louisiana Wildlife Federation helped to establish a bipartisan commission that developed policy and set regulations governing the management of state fish and wildlife resources. The Kansas affiliate, Kansas Wildlife Federation, Inc., in the 1960s was at the forefront in upgrading the Kansas Fish and Game Commission into what an affiliate spokesman calls "a modern and progressive wildlife management agency staffed by professionals."

The hunters and fishermen who founded the North Carolina Wildlife Federation in 1945 did not like the way fish, wildlife, and habitat problems were being managed in their state. They worked to change the situation, and in two years the North Carolina General Assembly formed the Wildlife Resources Commission. The Federation's Oklahoma affiliate lists as a major accomplishment the establishment of a similarly independent wildlife commission in 1956.

The South Carolina affiliate was responsible for passage of legislation that established the South Carolina Wildlife Resources Commission in 1952. The commission directs the Wildlife Department policy in management and law enforcement and appoints its chief executive. This legislation helped to make state wildlife management a professional activity.

Federation affiliates also act as local guardians of nationally known ecological treasures. The North Carolina Wildlife Federation, for example, keeps special watch over the state's estuarine waters. Action by the affiliate garnered 120,000 acres of wetland habitat that became the Alligator River National Wildlife Refuge. The Oklahoma Wildlife Federation worked with a major paper manufacturer to initiate wildlife management programs on timbered tracts. The Maine affiliate, the Natural Resources Council of Maine (NRCM), long has been a watchdog and defender of Maine's north woods. NRCM helped to create the Land Use Regulation Commission and has consistently worked to stop the use of chemical sprays to control spruce budworm infestation.

Besides keeping its general watch over the north woods, NRCM has concentrated its local efforts on preserving Maine's wild rivers and coasts. Beginning in 1960 with the fight to establish the Allagash Wilderness Waterway, the campaign broadened to include lobbying for a Maine river law that forever protects Maine's finest rivers from development. The Maine affiliate won a twenty-year battle to save the St. John River from an Army Corps of Engineers plan to dam it. Another proposal, to dam the West Branch of the Penobscot River, was also successfully stopped. NRCM based its case on sound economic and energy alternatives to the dam.

NRCM has fought numerous proposals to put industrial facilities along Maine's coastline and has been a leading advocate for the protection of Maine's fragile coastal dune system. It also keeps watch over Maine's lakes and tamed rivers. After the affiliate filed an intent to sue under the Clean Water Act, two firms signed a consent decree and paid $100,000 in fines.

In Michigan, the Michigan United Conservation Clubs (MUCC) headed the Porcupine Mountains Wilderness Association, a coalition of conservation and environmental organizations formed in the late 1950s to fight attempts by a mining company to develop a copper mine and smelter within Michigan's largest state park. MUCC raised funds for the campaign by taking a page from Federation experience: printing and selling "Save the Porkies" stamps. The coalition's efforts paid off in 1959 when the mining company abruptly withdrew its request for a mining lease.

MUCC led a campaign that convinced voters to overwhelmingly approve a "bottle bill," making Michigan the first industrial state in the nation to ban nonreturnable bottles and cans. It also conceived a plan to earmark revenues from oil, gas, and mineral production on state-owned lands for purchase of public recreation lands. Through the land trust fund that was established, thousands of acres of prime recreation property and environmentally fragile land have come under public ownership.

Commercial gill netting once indiscriminately killed an alarming number of lake trout in the Great Lakes. A campaign by MUCC ended with the Michigan legislature banning large-mesh gill nets. When Indian commercial fishermen continued to use gill nets, claiming treaty fishing rights, MUCC joined with the Department of Natural Resources in litigation that led to an historic agreement in 1985 controlling tribal fishing in the Great Lakes.

Minnesota's affiliate, the Minnesota Conservation Federation, worked with the RIM Coalition to pass the Reinvest In Minnesota (RIM) Resources Act, a complex fish and wildlife habitat program that coordinated and helped to pay for habitat-saving actions on farms and in commercial forests.

Many of the activities of affiliates are local, but each state's work contributes to the strong environmental network that is the National Wildlife Federation. The activities range from conservation awards that recognize local leaders in conservation to legal actions that have national repercussions.

The Mississippi Wildlife Federation made law history when it joined with NWF in a case to save a crane habitat from an interstate highway. The case established that the Endangered Species Act of 1973 applied to federal activities that imperiled an endangered species. (See chapter 7.)

The Mississippi Federation, with the support and cooperation of statewide sportsmen's organizations and state conservation agencies, initiated SMART (Sportsmen of Mississippi Acting Responsibly Together). The program was established to improve the image of hunting and hunters, to stress ethical outdoor behavior, and to strengthen relations between landowners and sportsmen. A hotline for reporting wildlife and fisheries violations (1-800-BE SMART) was installed at the Mississippi Department of Wildlife Conservation. Contributions from sportsmen and member organizations of the SMART Council finance the hotline.

The Mississippi Federation led the drive for passage of a hunter education bill that requires anyone sixteen years old or over to have completed a hunter education program before being able to purchase a license.

The Minnesota Conservation Federation sued both the Environmental Protection Agency and the Army Corps of Engineers to stop engineers from dumping into open water the contaminated dredge spoils from the Duluth Superior Harbor in Lake Superior. A hunter safety campaign organized by the affiliate included the first comprehensive study of every hunter accident, including the physical and psychological condition of the shooter. The study inspired passage of the State Youth Firearms Safety Training Program.

The Arkansas Wildlife Federation lead the efforts to form a coalition of other wildlife and conservation clubs in the state. The coalition has worked at stopping herbicide spraying in Ouachita National Forest and supported an unsuccessful effort to enact a sales tax to be used exclusively by the Arkansas Game and Fish Commission.

The Arizona Wildlife Federation has worked to ban uranium mining on the Grand Canyon Game Preserve and North Kaibab Forest. The preserve is home to the famed Kaibab mule deer and the unique, tassle-eared Kaibab squirrel.

The Colorado Wildlife Federation one day might be leading a study on black bears and the next day working to stop a proposed ski resort expansion that would have destroyed elk and deer habitat. At a state park, affiliate members built special blinds for handicapped hunters. Other members worked with Western State College in sponsoring the first acid rain workshop in the West.

Work by the Florida Wildlife Federation led to the state's appropriating $240 million for the purchase of endangered wildlife habitat and $20 million each year for additional areas. The Florida affiliate also led a campaign that produced the Florida endangered species act.

The Louisiana Wildlife Federation worked alongside NWF for years in an effort to find a compromise that would satisfy the needs for flood control, habitat preservation, and public use in the huge Atchafalaya Basin Swamp. (See chapter 7.) The Louisiana affiliate is particularly concerned about habitat protection in refuges and wildlife management areas. Joining with other conservation groups, the affiliate helped to acquire about 140,000 acres of prime wildlife habitat for public ownership.

The Conservation Federation of Missouri led the drive for a special conservation sales tax for wildlife habitat acquisition and other programs run by the Missouri Department of Conservation. Missouri thus became the first and, so far, the only state to earmark, in its constitution, a general sales tax specifically for wildlife and forestry programs.

Back in the early 1930s, members of the New Mexico Wildlife Federation introduced the first pheasants into the state. That organization sponsors a hunter safety program for hundreds of boys and girls each year. The New York affiliate, the New York State Conservation Council, is proud of its Conservation Education Workshop for teachers, which received the Gulf Oil Conservation Award in 1983. The affiliate awards scholarships to state-operated camps that specialize in conservation education.

When the U.S. Forest Service suddenly tried to change the direction of national forest management in North Carolina in 1985, the North

Carolina Wildlife Federation joined with the North Carolina chapter of the Sierra Club to hire a consultant and set up a panel of experts from North Carolina colleges to prepare an alternative. The Forest Service's plans would have greatly increased timber harvest and road building in more than two million acres of National Forest land in North Carolina, threatening nearly all wildlife populations. The affiliate also asked thousands of its members to write to the Forest Service to protest the plans. As a result, the Forest Service rewrote the draft to protect wildlife and wildlife habitats and to significantly reduce timber harvest and road building.

When the U.S. Department of Agriculture's Soil Conservation Service began channelizing thousands of miles of streams in North Carolina, ostensibly for flood control, the North Carolina Wildlife Federation asserted that the channelizing was actually draining more bottomlands for farming and timber harvest, devastating fish and wildlife habitats. The NCWF joined with NWF, Friends of the Earth, the Natural Resources Defense Council, and others to file suit to stop proposed channelization in two counties. After an extended legal battle, NCWF and its cohorts prevailed: the Soil Conservation Service was ordered to develop ways to minimize habitat destruction.

The Pennsylvania Wildlife Federation, allied with the Pennsylvania Federation of Sportsmen's Clubs—PFSC/PWF in shorthand—is affiliated with the Pennsylvania Conservation Network, which consists of many conservation-oriented organizations. The PFSC/PWF publishes the only conservation oriented magazine in the state—the *Pennsylvania Wildlife and Outdoor Digest*—and was instrumental in bringing about a constitutional amendment that guaranteed every Pennsylvanian the right to clean air and clean water.

The Pennsylvanians have developed a network of Conservation Leadership Schools in more than twenty counties. The state federation also sponsors annual Conservation Education Conferences; recent topics have included acid rain, solid waste, problems of the Chesapeake Bay, and wildlife habitats. Under the sportsmen's leadership, the state legislature established an oil-and-gas-lease fund for conservation projects, parks, and flood-control projects.

The Pennsylvania affiliate's work on ballot-box issues convinced voters to back a $100 million sewage plant construction plan and, in another vote, to approve the spending of $70 million for land acquisition that benefited not only hunters and fishermen but also town and city dwellers, who received a substantial amount for local parks. Conservationists' endorsements helped gain the passage of a strip mining bill that was later used as a model for the federal act.

"Our most important achievement," says a spokesman for the Natural History Society of Puerto Rico, Inc., "was collaborating in the preparation of an environmental impact statement on a proposed nuclear plant. As a result, the plant was not built." In other work, the affiliate organized a team of scientists to study the ecology of Mona Island and then organized a successful international effort to stop plans to turn the island into a superport. The Puerto Rican conservationists also were successful in a court fight to save an ecologically significant stand of mangroves imperiled by a proposed tourism complex.

South Carolina's affiliate, the South Carolina Wildlife Federation, played a vital role in setting up a consortium of environmental organizations that successfully campaigned for the Congaree Swamp National Monument. Congaree protects the last significant tract of virgin southern bottomland hardwoods in the southeastern United States. The affiliate also led the successful fight against the building of an oil refinery in Georgetown, South Carolina, on the Winyah Bay.

In the twenty-three years between 1986 and 1963, the year the South Dakota Wildlife Federation founded its conservation camp, nearly 2,500 teenage boys and girls have learned about the wild world in the Black Hills of South Dakota. Many of the graduates of the outdoor seminar are now becoming leaders in the South Dakota conservation movement. Through grass-roots legislative work, the SDWF helped provide for public access to public lands throughout South Dakota.

Sportsmen's Clubs of Texas, known as SCOT, is in the leading ranks of a clean water crusade. SCOT, the Sierra Club, and the Environmental Defense Fund sued the Environmental Protection Agency because it accepted Texas water-quality standards the conservation groups believed were not strict enough. While the court case was pending, the EPA ordered the state to rectify some of the problems pointed out in the suit. As a result, the state has fined polluters, including cities that were dumping raw or poorly treated sewage.

SCOT was a major supporter of the Wildlife Conservation Act, which gave the Texas Parks and Wildlife Department statewide regulatory authority over wildlife and wiped out a maze of county-level game laws. The Nueces Bay Coalition, whose members included SCOT, convinced the Army Corps of Engineers to rewrite its plan for filling more than 1,200 acres of Nueces Bay—a valuable and productive estuary classified as a nursery area by the State of Texas. The new plan called for no filling of the bay.

The Wyoming Wildlife Federation, the state's oldest and largest conservation organization, has the highest per-capita membership based on state population of any affiliate in NWF. The WWF, whose motto is "Winning for Wildlife," feels especially responsible for conserving Wyoming's free-ranging wildlife—large herds of elk, bighorn sheep, moose, mule deer, and whitetail deer. River otters, beaver, and muskrat live in the Upper Greene, North Platte, and Yellowstone headwaters country of the "Wildlife State." These streams are home to one of the greatest trout fisheries in the Lower 48.

The endangered black-footed ferret, believed by many to be North America's rarest mammal, is making its last stand in Wyoming, and the endangered whooping crane graces Wyoming's North Platte and Green River region.

WWF teamed up with NWF to protect a critical antelope winter range in the Red Rim. The controversy involved a dispute over whether the range could be mined and then returned to a condition that still supported the antelope. The WWF and NWF succeeded in negotiating a compromise in which the antelope were protected while a mining company demonstrated the feasibility of full reclamation. The decision was a major breakthrough in wildlife conservation, for it required industry to be fully accountable for adverse effects on wildlife. (See chapter 1.)

For fourteen years, WWF campaigned for a law to protect stream-flow from dams and other developments that would spoil Wyoming's esthetic landscape—and economically important sport fishing. The campaign culminated in Wyoming's first citizen initiative: a demand for a stream-flow law. Victory came in 1986 with the passage of the law by a legislature that had to follow the voters' will.

WWF has one of the most active and effective lobbying forces in Wyoming. Much of its effectiveness stems from the fact that its grass roots go deep. WWF has twenty-five affiliates of its own throughout the state. Such extensive membership typifies the character and structure of many affiliates. But affiliates vary greatly, and it is difficult to generalize about them. Just like the states they represent, no two are exactly alike.

"The strength of the National Wildlife Federation is in the grass roots of America," the Federation guide for affiliates says. "It is the . . . affiliated state organizations who produce the . . . volunteer activity that educates children, legislators, and others to the necessity for conservation of natural resources."

But to reach even more children and the solitary nature lover who does not belong to any state organization, something new had to be added to the affiliate formula. The search for the new ingredient is a campfire story in itself.

4

Casting a Wider Net

The director of the Arizona Fish and Game Department wanted to make a deal with Tom Kimball, one of his newest employees. If Kimball would do the driving, the director would bring him along to the 1941 North American Wildlife Conference in Memphis, Tennessee. Kimball readily agreed. He had heard enough about the annual conference to know that it would give him a rare opportunity to meet the leaders in his new profession.

The National Wildlife Federation, by custom, held its annual meeting during the conference. Kimball, eager to talk about game management and soil conservation with his colleagues at the conference, had never heard of the Federation and showed little interest in its doings. After the conference, he returned to Arizona, enlisted in the Army Air Corps a short while later, and gave no further thought to the National Wildlife Federation.

In those days, the tottering Federation could easily fade from someone's memory. Even its most dedicated supporters were giving up on it. Delegates at the 1941 meeting questioned everything from the worthiness of the board of directors to the point of running another money-losing Wildlife Week and trying to distribute another edition of money-losing wildlife stamps. And critics had a new target: an ambitious educational program that had turned into a financial catastrophe.

Leaders of the Federation, who were operating out of offices in both Washington and Boston, had envisioned the educational program as a revenue-producing activity that would also help spread the word about conservation. The program had started off full of promise. Distinguished educators and conservationists had agreed to help. Such prominent radio broadcasters as Fulton Lewis, Jr., John Kieran, Raymond Gram Swing, and Lowell Thomas publicized the program. Sets of pamphlets called "educational units" were written and distribution was planned so that tens of thousands of pupils from the third to the eighth grade could study conservation.

The funding scheme for the education program resembled the foundering one to distribute wildlife stamps. But instead of using the existing national-affiliates organization, the architects of the educational program set up a complex structure to sell the pamphlets. They were to be sold for a dollar each, with twenty-five cents to go to specially formed local conservation councils, ten cents to state councils, and sixty-five cents to the National Wildlife Federation. Publicity was channeled through a new, ad hoc publication that also cost money.

By 1942, a total of 150,000 pamphlets had been produced and only 30,000 had been sold. The educational program's expenses totaled anywhere from $110,000 to $197,000 (the records were vague and the program was, in one board member's words, "a fiasco and a mess"). The revenue amounted to about $13,000. To keep the Federation from going bankrupt, newly hired business manager Louis Wendt went from creditor to creditor—by one count, there were fourteen— and got pledges not to press their claims for a year. The move saved the Federation, which in 1943 somehow managed to show a small income over expenses.

Despite the dismal sales of the pamphlets, year after year, thanks to such leaders as Wendt, who later became treasurer of the Federation, the organization grew financially more stable. In 1949 the Federation hired its first fulltime executive director, Richard Borden. The move was a sign of hope. As the organization entered the 1950s, the early worries about financial survival changed to anticipations of sustained success. The turning point came in 1950. The affiliates now represented 4,000 clubs. And in that year David Aylward, who had been president for ten years and maintained a Federation office in Boston, stepped down because of ill health. The way was clear for the money-saving consolidation of the Boston and Washington offices. Washington now served as both the center of legislative work under Carl Shoemaker and the headquarters of the Federation itself.

Claude Kelley of Alabama had become the Federation's new president in 1950 and Ernest Fremont Swift—Ernie Swift, as he was better known—became its executive director in 1955.

The former head of the Wisconsin Conservation Department, Swift had a reputation for being tough and knowledgeable about the ways of environmental bureaucracies. As a young Wisconsin game warden in the Roaring Twenties he had ended the vacation of four notorious Chicago gangsters by arresting three of them for fishing in a no-fishing stream and then, at gun-point, taking in the gang leader for poaching. When he was appointed assistant director of the U.S. Fish and Wildlife Service in 1953, he quickly learned that such direct action was not expected of high officials. In the bureaucratic woods of Washington, officials walked cautiously and did not carry big sticks.

Swift had endured eighteen stifling months of bureaucratic infighting when Kelley, searching for an executive director, passed the word to President Eisenhower that the Federation wanted Swift. "Well, Eisenhower didn't want to give him up," Kelley recalled, "but I told him what an opportunity we had to use such a man and what he could contribute to the conservation program." Eisenhower, Kelley says, "was very pleased that it was an opportunity for Ernie to render a very valuable service."

As executive director of the Federation, Swift once again served in the front lines of the conservation movement. One of his battles took him to the Pentagon, where he successfully urged officials to practice better conservation practices on military reservations. And he worked with Congress in the creation of the first U.S. Wilderness Act.

Swift is remembered best as the man who teamed up with business manager J. A. "Ash" Brownridge to build a strong financial foundation for the Federation. In 1952 Brownridge had launched a Christmas card and gift promotion that sent Federation income soaring to $943,000. The promotion brought in about the same amount the following year. But then, for a variety of reasons, revenues dropped off. When Swift arrived as executive director, Brownridge was ready with a new idea.

"Up to that time," Brownridge said in an interview, "the Federation had mailed one sheet of stamps all year long and made one mailing to its master list. I had suggested on many occasions that we try to get another sheet of stamps and try more mailings. But I was always told the cost was prohibitive and contributor resentment would be overwhelming."

In July 1956 Brownridge went to Swift with his idea: a special sheet of Christmas stamps derived from existing stamp art featuring winter settings. Swift's response was characteristically direct: "If you think it'll work, go to it." It did work. The Christmas stamps helped to make 1956 the first year the National Wildlife Federation's gross annual income exceeded $1 million. By then the Federation had more than one million members and supporters.

By the end of 1956 Brownridge was ready with another idea. "Ernie," he said, "I think we've now shown what we can do with an extra sheet of stamps. Why don't we promote a school sheet, showing the youngsters birds and flowers and so on?" Again Swift approved and again there was financial success.

This prosperity coupled with a sizable bequest made it possible for the Federation to construct a headquarters building on Sixteenth Street in downtown Washington. Construction began in January 1959, and the staff began moving into the nearly completed building over the weekend of April 8, 1960. President John F. Kennedy dedicated the building on March 3, 1961.

By then, the National Wildlife Federation was no longer struggling, no longer new and unknown. And by then Tom Kimball, who once had wondered what the Federation was, no longer wondered. He was running it.

Kimball's trail to the Federation went back to the end of World War II, when, mustered out of the Army Air Corps, he returned to the Arizona Fish and Game Department. He spent about a year as assistant director, and then, at the age of twenty-nine, he became the youngest fish and game director in the United States. He remained in Arizona until 1952, when he became director of the Colorado Fish and Game Department.

The principal conservation organization in Colorado then was the Izaak Walton League, which successfully lobbied for what fishermen wanted. But, in a state with large deer, elk, and antelope populations, hunters had no strong voice. And, according to Kimball, "We had problems with the legislature. We had differences with the stockmen, the cattlemen. We were having difficulty getting public support for sound wildlife programs. And so that's when I got interested in the Federation. It was organized in many states, but not in Colorado."

Kimball became the founder and first official member of the Colorado Wildlife Federation. "We organized a good group of sportsmen there, sportsmen who were primarily game people—game hunters interested in using their influence to better their sport," he recalled. "Along with the Izaak Walton League, they gave political support to me as director of the Colorado Fish and Game Department. And so I was able to carry out an effective reorganization of the department and get some scientific management into wildlife."

In 1959, Kimball traveled to another North American Wildlife Con-

ference, this time in Dallas. He was approached there by representatives looking for a successor to Ernie Swift, who planned to retire
in 1960. Kimball did not immediately accept the offer. He spent
months negotiating exactly what his role would be as the Federation's
executive director.

When he began his long tenure in 1960, Kimball was already familiar with a broad spectrum of conservation problems. He had graduated from Brigham Young University in 1939 with a degree in
agronomy and an emphasis on soil conservation. His first assignment
as an employee in the Arizona Fish and Game Department was to
help farmers whose crops were being gobbled up by jack rabbits and
quail. After that, he became Arizona's first professional employee to
work on a Pittman-Robertson project—a statewide wildlife survey. In
both Arizona and Colorado he had seen the interplay of conservation
needs with budgetary reality, the clash of conservation interests in
state legislatures.

He had learned one important lesson in two state capitals—the more
people you had on your side, the more the politicians listen to you.
Now he looked for ways to apply that lesson in the nation's capital.
"From the standpoint of producing revenue and influence," he said
of his first days at NWF, "we needed two things. We needed money
in order to hire competent people and we needed numbers to back
us up."

Kimball had reservations about the Federation's financial successes
in the previous decade. Despite the Federation's hard-won solvency,
Kimball saw the Federation as "a fairly weak and ineffective organization in terms of its two main purposes: education and support for
wildlife resources at the federal level, where a lot of decisions were
being made that affected the welfare of wildlife."

As Kimball described it, the Federation "needed both money and
ranks of individual members if the organization was going to influence
the wildlife and environmental policies of the executive branch and
the laws enacted by Congress." So Kimball sought ways to raise additional revenue. The Federation's principal sources of income were
the donations received in response to wildlife stamps and the sale of
Christmas cards and other merchandise, which Kimball believed produced "far too little to employ the scientists and resource specialists
necessary to give NWF credibility and clout among Washington power
brokers."

As Kimball saw the present, the Federation needed to go beyond
influencing the passage of legislation. As he saw the future, a broader
support base was needed to make the Federation a powerful force in

the battles looming over the environmental horizon. "You've got to have troops if you're going to be the commanding general of an army," he said. "If you don't have anybody behind you, why, you lead a charge—and nothing happens. And so we recognized early on that we had to have [additional] membership and we had to have money. And the way to do it was with the individual membership."

By suggesting an expansion of the Federation so that it included both state affiliates and individual members, Kimball, in effect, called for the creation of a new Federation. To the existing aggregation of traditional conservation and sportsmen's organizations would be added a new pool of people, each of whom would have his or her own idea of just what "conservation" was supposed to mean.

Membership dues would be a far more dependable income source than merchandise sales and small, sporadic donations from individuals. Whatever the success of the stamp promotions and merchandise program, income from them fluctuated from year to year. They did not have the sustained, predictable nature of dues. If NWF had a membership program of its own, budgets could be drawn up not with hope for another successful year in distributing stamps and selling Christmas cards, but with the expectation that last year's membership would at least hold steady and might even increase next year.

A large membership organization would improve the stature of the Federation. Legislators, state and federal agencies, and the public would realize that the Federation spoke for a constituency that included more than sportsmen.

When board members and affiliates heard Kimball's idea, they envisioned hordes of unaffiliated garden club members and birders attempting to seize control of an organization dominated by affiliates full of hunters and fishermen. But Kimball had another view. He believed the prospective newcomers could bring a new force to the Federation. "America," he said, "was suddenly awakening to the fact that something was rotten in the environment. Recreation areas were smelling and so were the rivers. You couldn't fish in them or swim in them. Air pollution was so bad it was just like fog, particularly in our larger cities."

Kimball believed that people would join a conservation organization if it offered them a chance to get together and clean up the environment. As he later put it, "People should belong to NWF because it would express the members' views in the nation's capital, and it would protect and defend wildlife and other natural resource values from predator-like special interests."

To transform his vision into reality, Kimball first had to recruit troops from the board of directors and the state affiliates. It was not easy. He also had to plan a campaign for subtle but substantial changes in the constitution and bylaws of the Federation—changes that would alter the structure without hurting the purpose.

Kimball's recruiting work among affiliates was quiet and, surprisingly, produced no outbursts of significant opposition. Under his plan, the affiliates would retain control of the Federation as an organization, while the individual members would give the organization new strength. Tradition was served: Each state affiliate would still send a voting delegate to the annual meeting; the one-affiliate-per-state rule remained. Affiliates, through resolutions and the election of the board of directors, would still be the guiding force of the Federation. The affiliates were not asked to change their ways.

In 1961, the proposed change was translated into a short new section in the bylaws: "In addition to state affiliates who shall make up the Federation, nonvoting associate memberships may be obtained by persons and groups. Such nonvoting associate memberships may be obtained under rules and regulations promulgated from time to time by the Federation Board of Directors." ("Groups" refers to another associate status: nonvoting associate membership for organizations. These groups are independent of state affiliates but want a connection with the Federation. Such groups include the Eagle Valley Environmentalists of Wisconsin, which is especially concerned about eagles, and the Arctic International Wildlife Range Society, which has a special interest in arctic wildlife.)

The change made in the bylaws was at the same time subtle and revolutionary. In the beginning, sportsmen-dominated affiliates had voted for objectives that included "securing adequate public recognition of the needs and values of wildlife resources." When the organization added associate members, the phrase "other natural resources" was added to "wildlife resources."

To the four original objectives of the Federation (organize conservation groups, develop a comprehensive conservation program, educate the public, cooperate with other conservation organizations) was added a fifth: "To stimulate a proper public attitude and appreciation regarding the use and management of all natural resources, enabling our people to appraise the aesthetic value and importance of all resources." Here was the heart of the change. In the added objective, "aesthetic value," the birder's and nature lover's abstraction appears—and "wildlife," traditionally the interest of sportsmen, does not appear. Both the concept of conserving wildlife and the concept of wildlife management for sportsmen, however, would remain.

The idea of opening the Federation to individual members was soon linked to the idea of publishing a magazine, which had been talked about for years. For their dues, associate members would get not only a way to join the conservation movement, but also a subscription to a magazine. The magazine would educate the readers, making them more effective as crusaders for wildlife. The associate members, in their role as magazine readers, would become informed and would inform. They would be asked their opinions through questionnaires and through surveys conducted by professional polling organizations.

The planning for a magazine began with practical questions about how to publish one. Kimball got some answers from a man named LeRoy Preudhomme, who had learned the hard way: He had published a magazine, *American Camper,* which had failed. Preudhomme was now working with the W. A. Krueger Company of Milwaukee, a printer interested in getting another magazine to print.

After some negotiations, Bob Klaus, president of Krueger, suggested a plan to Brownridge: Krueger would be responsible for editing, designing, printing, and distributing the magazine. The Federation would be responsible for the magazine's editorial content and for selling it to subscribers. The Federation would own all materials and keep all the income. The proposal solved the question of how the Federation could produce a magazine without having its own editorial staff and facilities. Kimball endorsed the plan and added his vision of it: "A four-color magazine, with the best editors, a sound editorial policy, and the best pictures money could buy."

Board members were as skeptical of the magazine proposal as they had been of the associate member idea. Some cited statistics showing that more than ninety percent of new magazines failed. Others noted that the wildlife magazine field was already occupied by the publications of the Audubon Society, Sierra Club, and Wilderness Society. Nearly everyone warned that publishing a magazine could endanger the National Wildlife Federation's nonprofit status.

Kimball merged the idea of creating an associate membership program and publishing a magazine and gambled that each would help the other. Kimball's gamble was not quite as risky as it may have appeared. Like a good stud poker player, he made his bet after a peek at his hole card. The ace was the Federation's mailing lists, compiled by Ash Brownridge.

Brownridge, who had already made the wildlife stamps into year-round fund-raisers, had a flair for promotion and mail-order selling. He also was selling stationery, Christmas cards, and wildlife games to raise money for the Federation's work in conservation. By the time

Kimball launched the membership campaign, Brownridge had assembled mailing lists containing about 1.5 million names.

Kimball knew that an outdoor magazine could be beautiful because he was familiar with *Arizona Highways*—a magazine that published stunning photographs of the natural world in a state he knew and loved. He and Brownridge also knew what they wanted in the magazine—an emphasis on conservation issues, accurate articles about wildlife—and what they did not want: fiction, puffery, articles that merely made the magazine a National Wildlife Federation house organ. Both men also knew they had to turn to outside help to produce such a magazine.

A simple reason underlies the failure of a majority of magazine ventures: lack of editorial and publishing talent. An organization that wants to publish a magazine often lets whoever is on the premises give it a try. Disaster almost invariably results, because administrators good at administering usually do not have the ability to visualize, invent, and produce a magazine. By turning to the outside, Kimball and Brownridge took the best first step they could. And Kimball had a reason to expect a beautiful magazine from the Krueger company. It printed *Arizona Highways*.

Krueger obviously could *print* a beautiful outdoor magazine. But could the company *produce* one, guiding a magazine from editorial concept to editorial realization? Krueger president Robert Klaus knew he had to find an editor capable of transforming Kimball's and Brownridge's inner vision into type and photographs. Klaus began and ended his search with one phone call. Back in Milwaukee, he dialed the number of John Strohm, owner of a small company called Publications, Inc.

Strohm, a self-described farm boy who had run a trap line on his family's Illinois land, had been editor of *Prairie Farmer* and *Country Gentleman*. He had also done much more than live down on the farm.

He had graduated *cum laude* from the University of Illinois in 1935 and had gone to work to earn enough money to finance a trip around the world. He started off with $600. "I did a lot of crazy things on that trip," he remembered. "I climbed Mount Fuji in the winter time, when they said it couldn't be done. I pulled a rickshaw in China. I went by outrigger canoe across Borneo. I spent a day with Mahatma Gandhi in India. I saw Hitler make a speech in Berlin. I ended up in the Spanish Civil War living three doors down the hall from Ernest Hemingway, who was writing *For Whom the Bell Tolls*."

Like Kimball years before, Strohm knew little about the Federation. But the idea of a wildlife magazine appealed to him. He went to work putting together a magazine dummy and soon was in Washington, showing the dummy to Kimball and Brownridge.

In March 1962, Kimball and Brownridge took the dummy to the annual meeting in Denver and presented it to the board. Brownridge well remembered what happened. "There was a lot of resistance to it," he said. "There were a lot of magazines going out of business at that time, and I was told there wasn't any way we could succeed. They said probably the most people we could get would be 100,000 people who would be interested in that kind of magazine—and 40,000 of them were at that time on the list for the Audubon Society."

The board finally staked Kimball's gamble by agreeing that both the attempt to get individual members and the production of the bimonthly magazine would be scrapped if he and Brownridge did not sign up 35,000 associate members, at $5 each, by the end of the year. Meanwhile, Strohm was to begin working on the production of Volume I, Number 1, knowing that it might never be published.

Brownridge and Krueger prepared a full-color brochure on the phantom magazine. The brochure was mailed to names on the Federation's own lists and on lists of people believed to be interested in conservation and wildlife. "On November 15," Brownridge happily recalled, "we had 67,000 members." At the end of the month, Volume I, Number 1 of *National Wildlife* was published.

The cover of this first issue, dated December-January 1962–63, was a photograph of a red-jacketed person walking back to his rural home through woods laden with fresh snow. Articles ranged from "There's a World of Beauty in Your Backyard" to "Should We Feed the Birds?" and "Bold Action Saves Land for Tomorrow's Outdoor Fun."

The question of how to edit and publish the magazine had been settled when the publication was only an idea. When Strohm had first shown the dummy, Kimball had said, "Well, we like it. But we'll do this down here. We'll edit it in-house because, after all, you don't know anything about conservation. And we do."

"You know," John Strohm recalled replying, "I think that's great. If you want 50,000 members—if you want 50,000 readers of this magazine—and if you want to preach to the converted, fine. You ought to do that yourself. But if you want to reach 500,000, then you need a publisher, you need an editor, you need someone who understands people and readers and how to put things together."

Strohm got his way this time, but not always. He remembered table-pounding encounters with Kimball in the early days. "Now, Tom, look," Strohm would say, "I think this is the way to do it. But you're the boss, if you want to change it. But I'm telling you I think you'd be wrong." About forty-five out of forty-six or forty-seven times, Strohm said, he, as editor, would get his way. Others from those days recall that the Federation gave Strohm lists of mandatory stories and kept track of all issues from early in the planning stage to page proofs. And there was never any doubt about one matter: Kimball had absolute veto power over magazine contents.

It was a delicate balance between Federation control and editorial independence. "It's the most natural thing in the world for everybody to want a story in the magazine," Strohm said, looking back through nearly a quarter of a century of editorship. "The education guy wants one. The lobbyist wants one. And so forth. And I said, 'Now, look, the thing that has made this magazine is its *independence*. It is not a *house organ*. It belongs to the Federation, but it is not a house organ. You make it a house organ and you're going to kill it.' And I think that what I said has held up."

From the first issue through the issue celebrating the National Wildlife Federation's half century, and then beyond into the issues of the second half of the century, Strohm has had a ritual when the magazine comes off the press: "We go over it with the staff, and I say, 'We could have done better.'"

By 1968, the print order for *National Wildlife* was 340,000. Competing magazines, which had been in existence longer, had circulations far below that figure. *Natural History* was then reporting a circulation of just over 100,000, and the Audubon Society's magazine was slightly over 50,000.

National Wildlife, like the Federation itself, served two constituencies. "The affiliates that make up the governing ownership of the Federation are primarily hunters and fishermen," Strohm has observed. "But Ash Brownridge said early in the game, 'These aren't the people who make donations for the stamps and these are not the people who became our associate members.' Associate members were not anti-hunters. But many of them were non-hunters.

"So right off the bat we had two groups of people here. You had the hunters and the fishermen who were in the minority in terms of readership and in terms of numbers, in the majority in terms of control. You have the associate members who were contributors, who were the ones interested [in conservation] more on a broader basis.

"Now how do you produce a magazine for both groups—and keep them happy? I think we've been successful. It is a kind of sensitive tightrope between not offending the hunters and putting out a magazine that is broad enough and interesting enough and has enough variety to cover all groups."

Strohm's success in walking this tightrope is partly the result of extraordinarily good nature photography displayed with breathtaking fidelity through fine printing and engraving. The photographs at first accompanied such articles as "There's a World of Beauty in Your Backyard" and "Bird Feeders You Can Build" (December-January 1963 issue). But by the 1970s, *National Wildlife* was developing an authoritative voice, one that spoke its mind. It reported the results of national conservation polls (Americans say . . . "more tax dollars should go for natural resource programs . . . less for space, defense and foreign aid") and printed articles on environmental issues ("Energy Crisis: How Big? How Bad? How Soon?" and "It's Time to Stop Killing the Ocean"). From an article on the horrors of a rattlesnake roundup came this summary: "It's not easy to feel sorry for poisonous snakes. But . . . by the time the last skin had been stripped from the last writhing carcass, my sympathies were entirely with the reptiles."

Clay Schoenfeld, Joint Professor of Journalism and Wildlife Ecology at the University of Wisconsin and Chairman of the Center for Environmental Communications and Education Studies, analyzed *National Wildlife*'s evolution through the 1960s and 1970s and found the magazine to be a case study of how America's view of nature shifted from conservation to environmentalism. "Conservation," Schoenfeld wrote, "was a collection of special interests, each of them narrow in *scope:* wildlife husbandry, water development, land conservation, forest protection, park management, and so on. The environmentalists began to realize that everything is connected to everything else. The *focus* of conservation was on disappearing redwoods and raptors. Environmentalism says the most endangered species is humankind itself." Conservationism, he said, quoting Aldo Leopold, had confined itself to "letterhead pieties and convention oratory," while environmentalism "has brought a sense of urgency and a set of brass-knuckles *tactics* to match."

The evolution from conservationism to environmentalism, Schoenfeld wrote, "is typified in the changing contents of a representative environmental magazine, *National Wildlife.* To follow that changing voice is to gain insight into the environment of environmentalism education today."

Schoenfeld then traced the changes, beginning with the December-January 1965–66 issue, which contained an inspirational message from Dr. Norman Vincent Peale: "One morning in New York between two appointments I stood for a long moment watching the ripples of the East River sparkling in the sunshine. The scene gave me such a lift that it affected the whole course of the day." Schoenfeld comments:

"No hint here that the river at the time was one of the most polluted in the world."

But the magazine's tone was changing, and there would be more than hints about a world gone wrong. In the lead article in the April-May 1966 issue, Executive Director Tom Kimball wrote, "Air pollution may be our biggest pollution problem today. Two-thirds of the population of the United States lives in 7,000 urban areas afflicted with polluted air. Their lungs are gray instead of a healthy pink, and some of them will die, or have their lives shortened, from breathing the polluted air." Of this article Schoenfeld comments: "No bucolic bird-watching here. The new conservation problem was urban and it threatened the human species itself."

Schoenfeld continues:

> In the same issue the redoubtable Ernie Swift, in his brief "Short Talk" column, saw the inexorable relationship between battle in Indochina and conservation in Indiana: "With an undeclared war on our hands, will the resources of our forests, mines, and farms once again be strewn and left to rot on every atoll in the Pacific?" Ernie did not live to see a new generation of college kids take to the streets against both the Vietnam war overseas and environmental degradation at home. [Swift died in 1968.] But his words were prophetic. A couple of issues later Swift was inveighing against "certain public officials who, after a token effort [at preserving wildlands], wash their hands of their responsibilities and let the commercializers have their way." Again, Ernie was ahead of his time in foreseeing outdoor buffs loving parks and wilderness areas to death in the absence of the crowd controls he knew would be needed. The same December-January 1966-67 *National Wildlife* had a sleeper article about how a little old Wisconsin lady in tennis shoes took on a county board and a state conservation commission single-handed—and saved 4,800 acres of forest from axe and plow. Success stories of grass-roots action like this were to come to characterize environmental coverage. What was to come was perhaps best foreshadowed by a report in the June-July 1967 *National Wildlife* from the 31st annual National Wildlife Federation meeting at San Francisco, where hundreds of old-line conservationists declared "contamination of our environment" to be the most pressing problem of our time. . . . Conservation had come a long way from the day when the most pressing problem was the plume hunter.
>
> The environmental storm broke in 1969, and *National Wildlife* was on top of the story. "Are We Teaching Johnny Conservation?" was the question posed in the December-January issue to Martin W. Schein, director of the prestigious National Science Foundation Committee on Undergraduate Education in the Biological Sciences. His answer was a resounding "No!" With perhaps more prescience than he knew, he said what was needed was "a new concept to give the whole natural resource field a new lift," and that "it may come from our urban ecologists." The same issue of *National Wildlife* told the story of how a new

breed of environmentalist, the birdwatcher turned activist, had saved Delaware's wildlands by "raising money, buying up, setting aside, restoring." The money came largely from du Pont executives via their Wilmington Garden Club wives. . . . "A Call to Battle!" was the headline of an April-May story about NWF's annual meeting, accompanying a Gallup poll indicating "73 percent of Americans will pay more taxes to fight conservation problems." The June-July 1969 *National Wildlife* issue picked up the tempo with a feature on the "Outward Bound Adventures" of a new generation of Americans forsaking affluence for the boondocks, and a photo-editorial inspired by the Santa Barbara oil spill, asking "Can man afford to foul his environment?" Even more diagnostic of the changing wind were that year's "Awards for Conservation Achievement": to a radio personality for encouraging citizen action against environmental degradation, to a cabinet member for conspicuous contributions to environmental quality, to a women's league president for fomenting environmental action programs, to a U.S. senator for an aggressive fight against water pollution.
. . . In the February-March 1970 issue the editors took off their gloves for a haymaker at water polluters: "The politician who permits pollution to be legal, the farmer whose land drains off chemicals and silt, the industrialist whose plant discharges waste, the alderman whose city discharges untreated sewage." This was no mellow voice from Walden Pond; it was a call to arms.

A few words on the cover of the April-May 1970 issue of *National Wildlife* signaled the shift to what Schoenfeld called environmentalism. The old cover slogan, "Dedicated to the Wise Use of Our Natural Resources," was changed to "Dedicated to Improving the Quality of Our Environment." Articles that year spotlighted mining abuses in Idaho, questioned the doings of the Bureau of Reclamation in North Dakota, and carried an open letter from Kimball to President Nixon in which Kimball wrote, "$75.5 billion for national defense and only $1 billion for environmental quality means our national priorities are out of whack."

According to Schoenfeld's thesis, the year 1971 marked the end of *National Wildlife*'s role as a sounding board of old-style conservation. By 1971, the magazine—and the organization behind it—had gone down the environmentalist road and there would be no turning back. In that year, Schoenfeld pointed out, Kimball took on the Public Land Law Review Commission for "putting one-third of the U.S. up for grabs"; Ralph Nader wrote, "Students shouting obscenities aren't tearing down America. It's chemical plants, steel mills, coal operations, paper and pulp mills, and utilities that are tearing down the natural resources of the country."

From the beginning, the magazine had carried information about natural-resources issues being discussed in the halls of Congress and in federal agencies. The "Watch on Washington," begun by Carl Shoe-maker in his newsletters of the 1930s, was taken over in the new magazine by the "Washington Report," written by Louis Clapper, then the Federation's conservation director and later a vice president. Clapper continued to cover the nation's capital for the Federation until his retirement in 1981. In "Washington Report," Clapper might fume about wasteful "pork-barrel" water projects in one issue and in another analyze attempts to control development of lands in flood plains or on steep slopes. The "Washington Report," once confined to a single column, is now called "Washington Digest" and has blossomed into a four-page spread full of reports on what officials are and are not doing about the environment.

As the word *environment* appeared with ever increasing frequency in *National Wildlife*, Kimball pushed for a new annual feature in the magazine, an Environmental Quality Index. The EQ Index, as it soon was called, would become one of the best known and most influential features of the magazine and was a harbinger of the annual reports of the president's new Council on Environmental Quality.

The idea grew from conversations between Strohm and Kimball in the mid 1960s to a multi-color, multi-paged annual feature in 1969, when it first appeared. "It had to be a report card," Strohm recalled saying, a report card that showed "how we think the environment is going" and asked, "Are we gaining or losing over last year? Where are our big problems?" The magazine describes the EQ Index as "a subjective analysis of the state of the nation's natural resources." The score—*worse, same,* or *better*—is determined through interviews with government, private, and academic researchers, news reports, and scientific studies.

When the EQ Index appeared in 1969, whale hunters threatened some species of whales with extinction, chemical pollution on land and in sea and river and pond imperiled the future of many bird species, including eagles, brown pelicans, and peregrine falcons. "Wildlife often shows the effects of pollution first," said the first index, which gave a low score to the EQ of American wildlife. "Dirty water kills millions of fish every year. Increased use of pesticides is having a harmful effect on the breeding potential of our birds of prey and possibly other forms of life—including humans."

The 1969 EQ Index cited air pollution as "probably the most serious threat to our environment. . . . It is a frightening kind of pollution that colors our skies, burns our eyes and blackens our lung tissues." Other subjects in this EQ Index were soil, water, minerals (including oil, gas, and coal), forests, and living space (later changed to "quality of life").

Copies of the EQ Index were sent to members of Congress, key governmental officials, and writers on conservation. The demand for the index overwhelmed the Federation. Some 100,000 copies of the first index had been distributed by the time the second appeared a year later. In the years that followed, the EQ Index became an important weapon in the fight for improving the environment.

The year that saw the creation of the EQ Index also saw the birth of the National Environmental Policy Act and ushered in what came to be called the Environmental Decade. Well before that decade ended, the EQ Index had become an institution.

According to Strohm, the new Environmental Protective Agency, intrigued by the EQ Index but not satisfied by its report-card simplicity, gave a substantial grant to a research firm to develop a more "scientific" index. But the scientific index had so many diagrams and formulas that the agency later gave another grant to simplify it.

National Wildlife has kept the EQ Index substantially unchanged through the years. Newspapers, magazines, and television use the index as a standard for judging environmental problems and accomplishments. The issuing of the report is thoroughly covered by all media. In 1985, besides the usual distribution of the report to newspapers across the country, the Federation sent a video version of the index to 420 commercial television stations, and the report appeared on every major network.

When the seventeenth annual EQ Index was issued in 1986, many newspapers played it as a factual counterpoint to the rhetoric-filled report on the state of the environment issued by the President's Council on Environmental Quality.

The success of *National Wildlife* led in 1970 to a proposal to publish the magazine monthly. A poll was designed to determine which would receive more support from members: increasing membership dues so *National Wildlife* would be received each month, or starting a new bimonthly magazine to be published alternately with *National Wildlife* and featuring wildlife and environmental issues beyond U.S. shores. The poll showed that fewer members would be lost by leaving *National Wildlife* alone and adding a new magazine, *International Wildlife*. "Wildlife and environment are both a national and international crisis," wrote one member in support of the publication of *International Wildlife*. "We are all citizens of the United States and the planet earth. The astronauts have made us all realize that mother earth is not as large as we once envisioned."

The poll's percentage figures were as supportive as the members' words. Without requiring the kind of test that preceded the arrival of *National Wildlife,* the board decided to publish the new bimonthly

International Wildlife—and to create two variations on associate membership. Members who received only *National Wildlife* would be national associate members, those choosing to receive only *International Wildlife* would become international associate members, and those who paid dues to receive both magazines would be designated world associate members. (The dues were increased from $5 to $6.50 for national and international members; world members paid $11.)

International Wildlife quickly took its place alongside *National Wildlife* as a publication that gave its readers important stories on environmental issues as well as beautiful photographs. *International Wildlife* was the first popular publication to report on the "nuclear winter" a nuclear war could spawn. It also reported about international efforts to save the polar bear, about the effects of drought on African animals, about ethnobotanists' search for plants with medicinal potential, and about fears that the increased use of fossil fuels was producing a warming trend that would profoundly change the world's climate.

Just as *National Wildlife*'s regular feature, "Wildlife Digest," covers North American environmental issues, the same feature in *International Wildlife* keeps watch on the world. *National Wildlife* in its October 1985 digest, for example, reported on the contamination of American tap water by lead pipes, the effects of the population increase in the Sun Belt, and a Federation call for a halt to the Forest Service's "road building spree." The following month, the digest in *International Wildlife* reported that China's massive hydroelectric project on the Yangtze River would destroy nearly 100,000 acres of farmland and threaten such endangered species as the Yangtze crocodile and the Chinese sturgeon. The digest also noted that the United States Fish and Wildlife Service was hiring inspectors to intercept illegal shipments of rare wildlife, such as ocelot pelts.

International Wildlife also provided a way to help the cause of conservation in foreign countries. Since 1974, the National Wildlife Federation has allowed the Canadian Wildlife Federation to use *International Wildlife* as a membership publication. The Canadians also were given financial assistance for a membership recruitment drive using NWF stamps and mail-order materials and techniques. Today the Canadians are self-sufficient and exert a strong influence on conservation issues in Canada.

In the late 1970s and early 1980s, NWF experimented with distributing *International Wildlife* in foreign countries. In an arrangement made with a Japanese philanthropist and the Japan Science Society in 1978, a special edition of the magazine was printed and distributed in Japan. Unfortunately, the distribution did not meet expectations and the project was stopped in 1981. An Irish conservation organization tried a similar program, but failed, and NWF discussions with another European country never came to fruition.

With a constantly growing associate membership, the Federation became a more powerful force in U.S. environmental issues. A "suggestion" from the Federation—with implied pressure from millions of American voters—could make politicians react. And often there was more than implied pressure, for thousands of members would write and phone their support.

At the annual meeting in 1975, Kimball examined what the Federation's membership increase—from a club and state affiliate membership of 1.4 million in 1960 to 3.5 million members and supporters in 1975—meant to the environmental movement. Taken separately, he said, "the hiker, the bird watcher, the ecologist, the conservationist, and the environmentalist" each represented a small minority. Taken together, they represented a substantial cross-section of the American population. The participation of this "grass-roots America," he said, "has given us the preeminent position in the conservation movement."

The Federation maintained that position by focusing much of its energies on legislative and agency activity in Washington—though Strohm, a stubborn midwesterner, kept producing *National Wildlife* and *International Wildlife* in Milwaukee. For decades, NWF and Strohm discussed moving the magazines to Washington, D.C. And for decades, Strohm resisted the idea. But in 1982, Federation officials insisted, and Strohm moved his editorial offices to the Federation's Laurel Ridge Conservation Education Center in the Washington suburb of Vienna, Virginia. Similarly, another renowned Federation publication, *Ranger Rick,* started its life outside the home office and years later migrated to Vienna.

Ranger Rick himself was born in *The Adventures of Rick Raccoon,* a book published by the Federation in 1959. The idea for appealing to youngsters had come from Ash Brownridge, who watched over the creation of the talkative little raccoon and wrote the book, using the pseudonym John A. Morris. Edward Bradford illustrated the book.

"It was a bright, clear wonderful spring morning as Master Rick Raccoon came to the door of his home," the book begins. Rick and his animal friends are starting off for a swim in Shady Pond when Rick spots Wally Wolf "waiting for his breakfast to walk up the trail." Rick suggests that the animals all shriek at Wally—who jumps in fright and then jumps in pain when he sits down on Pudgy Porcupine.

Rick gets "angrier and angrier" when he sees what has happened to the animals' Shady Pond and Clear Creek. "Their beautiful stream was filled with bottles and cans, the pool was choked with old tires, bedsprings and other trash. And there was Benny Bass looking very unhappy and gasping for breath in his cluttered-up home. There was hardly enough room to swim, and by the looks of Benny's thin sides, not very much to eat."

With Rick leading them on, the animals pitch in and clean up the creek and pond. Then Rick leads everyone in a song. The book was designed so that a small plastic figure of Rick nestled inside. The young reader could make Rick wiggle or dance (as Rick often did in the story) by turning a crank.

The Federation sold 50,000 copies of the book and followed it up the next year with *Ranger Rick and the Great Forest Fire* by "John Morris," with illustrations by Lorin Thompson. A board game accompanied the book, which vividly described a forest fire threatening the animals' woodland home. "Up the trees went the flames licking hungrily at the dry leaves and branches. . . . Fear tugged at Rick's heart, but he knew he must stay and fight this terrible enemy." Rick and his animal friends manage to stop the fire from totally destroying their forest. Tired and singed, "they all trooped off down the trail toward their homes that the day before they almost lost because someone was careless—Was it you?"

Brownridge had raised the idea of starting Ranger Rick's Nature Club in 1960. Membership in the club would include a subscription to a children's magazine. So much energy was pouring into *National Wildlife*, however, that Ranger Rick was put aside. Not until March 1966 did the board give conditional approval to Brownridge's proposal for a monthly magazine for children. As the board had done when *National Wildlife* had been proposed, the approval was tied to Brownridge's finding a specific number of subscribers. This time the goal was 60,000, although the board said it would approve the project if it reached the break-even point of 32,500 memberships. The deadline was October.

"By this time," Brownridge remembered, "I had long since decided that much of the adult population had been brought up with the firm conviction that our resources were inexhaustible and that those who were warning of future problems were alarmists and eco-freaks. It was very difficult to change this attitude. So I decided that the best place to go was to the children and develop a future generation of conservationists who would understand the problems and be willing to work toward the solution."

The crucial environmental force of the future consisted of the children of the present. And *Ranger Rick* was to be a way of reaching them, educating them, making them aware of their world. When *Ranger Rick* was first published, there were few four-color, high-quality magazines aimed at children and no children's publication devoted exclusively to conservation.

As with *National Wildlife* and *International Wildlife*, the Federation worked closely with the Krueger Printing Company to find editorial help. Gordon Elliott put Brownridge in touch with Trudy Farrand, who, with her husband, Bob, was operating a public-relations agency in Philadelphia. Trudy Farrand had worked at Curtis Publications, which published the *Saturday Evening Post* and other magazines. As assistant editor of a popular children's magazine, *Jack and Jill*, she had assumed both editorial and publishing responsibilities for nine years. She had shown that she knew how to produce a magazine that captured children's interest, educating them while entertaining them.

Volume I Number 1 of *Ranger Rick's Nature Magazine* had to be prepared for the printer while the promotional literature was being mailed. If the members turned down *Ranger Rick*, Volume I Number 1 would be nothing more than an expensive souvenir of a magazine that might have been. Farrand, in fact, prepared three issues, on the theory that if the Federation did decide to publish *Ranger Rick* there would be no time after the market test to set up a monthly magazine production line. With two temporary assistants and a design studio, Farrand put together an impromptu staff.

"We literally worked sixteen hours a day," Farrand remembered, "and I lay awake all night after I did get home because we had photographs coming in from everywhere and we didn't really have the knowledge and the facilities to take proper care of them. They were piled up on the table and we were scared to death, knowing that nature photographs are hard to come by.

"The art studio caused a lot of difficulties because they didn't know one animal from another—or one end of an animal from another— and they had to be led by the hand. They would come over and I would give them a group of photographs and tell them approximately what I thought I wanted to do with the layout, and they would disappear and come back two days later with something totally different. It was a very difficult time but an exciting time."

Ranger Rick was also giving Brownridge a difficult time. When the deadline came, instead of the required 32,500 subscribers, there were only about 30,000. But, according to Brownridge, "the board never even flinched." He was told to go ahead. *Ranger Rick's Nature Magazine* lost more than $300,000 during its first year and more than $200,000 in its second year. By the third year it began to break even.

Ash Brownridge's career, incidentally, provides an index for the Federation's spectacular growth. When he joined the Federation in 1949, gross receipts totaled $440,000. In 1983, on the eve of his retirement, gross receipts were $38 million. By then, with over four million members and supporters, the Federation had become the largest conservation organization in the world.

The *Ranger Rick* magazine that Brownridge had guided through red ink into black came out ten times a year at first, to coincide with the school year. But editors soon learned that summer is precisely when parents look around desperately for things for their children to do. And so *Ranger Rick's Nature Magazine*—the name was shortened to *Ranger Rick* in 1983—became a monthly magazine.

The objectives of the magazine were stated in the first issue, published in January 1967: "To give boys and girls a year-round program of activities, adventure and knowledge which will help them appreciate and enjoy nature. To help them know and respect all things that grow and creatures that move, that all may desire to conserve and wisely use the vital natural resources of the world." Leavening these earnest words were riddles, games, photographs worthy of *National Wildlife,* and the "Adventures of Ranger Rick" and his friends in Deep Green Wood.

Ranger Rick soon became a symbol of the Federation's awareness that the future of the environment lay in the hands of educators and the children they taught. Speaking in New Delhi in 1969 before the International Union for the Conservation of Nature, Kimball devoted much of his talk to the new Federation venture, *Ranger Rick's Nature Magazine.* "One teacher put it this way," he said: " 'I don't *teach* Ranger Rick; I simply announce its arrival.' In a day when there is so much talk about children being bored with education, this is extremely encouraging to an organization whose aim is indeed to educate in the broadest of fields, namely: how all living things affect each other and the world they live in.

"If there is fun and excitement along the way—so much the better! For we know that this generation of children must understand in their very bones the delicate balance between living things and their environment. . . . Teachers and parents both tell us they have found that *Ranger Rick's Nature Magazine* provides children with two-way motivation. One impels them from the home, club meeting or classroom to the library for more knowledge—even the reluctant readers. The other sends them to the outdoors to explore the natural world with heightened wonder and a keener understanding of what they are seeing."

Children with this understanding, Kimball concluded, can become the New Conservationists who would enact laws "that support wise choices about the environment and its resources." Subscribers to the magazine became members of Ranger Rick's Nature Club, and each member was asked to take a pledge, in which Kimball's thesis was spelled out: "To use my eyes to see the beauty of all outdoors. To train my mind to learn the importance of nature. To use my hands to help protect our soil, water, woods and wildlife. And, by my good example, to show others how to respect, properly use and enjoy our natural resources."

The first issue of *Ranger Rick* featured stories on bears, animal tracks, avalanches, wood ducks, and the feeding of birds in winter. Ranger Rick's first adventure in the new magazine was a shortened form of the saving of Benny Bass from his polluted pond, complete with song:

Keep our streams and rivers clean,
Keep our forests fresh and green,
We'll be happy. So will you,
These are all your playgrounds, too.

In its early issues, the magazine told boys and girls about the wonders of the Okefenokee National Wildlife Refuge, about octopuses and spider webs, about muskrats and hawks, llamas and bats ("Don't shiver and say 'Ugh, bats!' when you see shadowy creatures flutter across the evening sky. Be glad they are there. They are like tiny super-mice patrolling the air for gnats and mosquitoes").

Soon *Ranger Rick* began changing, just as *National Wildlife* did. And, while the grownups' magazine warned its readers about our worsening environment, *Ranger Rick* told his fellow creatures (and young readers): "Did you notice those dead fish in the stream near here? Well, I think I know what killed them. All the people in this neighborhood put too much fertilizer, weed killer, and insect killer on their lawns, shrubs, and gardens. When it rains, some of the stuff runs off into the stream and pollutes it. The fish and everything else there are being killed by all those chemicals! . . . All this run-off is called *nonpoint* pollution—"

The story ends with a note to Ranger Rick's Rangers, who are told where they can learn how "your family can take good care of your lawn and garden without causing nonpoint pollution." Ranger Rick had a direct line from his Rangers to their parents and teachers. They also had a direct line back to him.

Dear Ranger Rick, they all begin . . .

I have desided to learn all about natur. Please sent it to me at onse.

I have been geting your magazine and I like it alot. I like the Adventures of Ranger Rick best of all in the magazines. In the march 1986 magazine I liked the story about halleys comet. I think it is funny how some people in 1910 hid in barrels to get away from it's harmfull rays. I like the pitcher on page 6 of halleys comot.

. . .your magazines are wicked awesome. Next time your freinds take a picture of a racoon, please have them tell the racoon to brush its hair.

you know how you said loons where rare in the August 1985 issue? Well not in Damarescotta, Maine. Out there there is a lot of them. My father and I watched one for 20 mins. we even herd it call it sounded like this oooooooooo

At first, sportsmen-dominated affiliates feared that Ranger Rick and his cute little pals would foster what had become known as the "Bambi syndrome," described by a veteran outdoorsman as "the anthropomorphic tendency to regard wild animals as saintly, babylike creatures to be cuddled and shielded from vicious hunters—usually meaning hunters and fishermen—as well as the 'villains' in their own ranks, the wolves, lions, and other predators."

Ranger Rick's early adventures often portrayed Wally Wolf and Red Fox as just that sort of villain. Soon, though, they both became part of Rick's talkative, good-natured gang and not big, bad animals always preparing to dine on Rick or his pals. The "Bambi" fear also faded as sportsmen saw that Rick was a sound wildlife manager at heart.

Eventually, as in the real world, Ranger Rick's predominantly male realm became more sensitive to sexist ways. Scarlett Fox became Rick's deputy, Becky Hare appeared, and Rick's niece, Rita Raccoon, added a feisty new character to Ranger Rick's never-ending adventures in Deep Green Wood. (The Federation itself traditionally has displayed a curious male-female disparity in its membership. Among associates, male and female members are about equally represented. Membership in affiliates, however, usually runs to about ninety percent male.)

The Federation's next step in expanding its educational effectiveness came in the 1980s, when it launched *Your Big Backyard,* a publication for readers who could not read—and the result was extraordinary.

Your Big Backyard's roots can be traced to the discovery by educators that children achieve fifty percent of their general adult intelligence by age four and seventy percent by age seven. The typical reader of *Ranger Rick* was a nine-year-old.

How could the Federation hope to pour environmental knowledge into three- and four-year-olds? This was the kind of question that appealed to James D. Davis, now senior vice president for publications. Davis had come to work in 1966 as Lou Clapper's assistant in the Conservation Division. Later, as director of another division, he saw a new challenge for the Federation. Thinking back several years, he recalled efforts to build on the success of *Ranger Rick* by creating a publication that appealed to kids after they outgrew *Rick*. But the teen-age market had always been a difficult one to deal with editorially.

If you can't get kids after they outgrow *Ranger Rick,* Davis thought, why not try to get them *before* they reach the *Ranger Rick* reading age—at a time when values are first being established and when a fascination for nature subjects would be high? From this line of reasoning came *Your Big Backyard,* an educational product with a conservation focus. It met with immediate success and has become one of the major preschool serial publications in the nation.

The first issue of *Your Big Backyard* was mailed in January 1980 to more than 60,000 subscribers. Like all subsequent issues, this one displayed large photographs of animals, some common and some not. The type was large, the sentences short, the words basic and easy. Art helped the children to understand colors, numbers, and space relationships and to acquire "reading readiness" skills. The non-reader recipients also got help from adult readers, who were supplied with a four-page tip sheet about how to help children get the most out of the issue's contents.

The contents certainly did not seem to be typical fare for three-year-olds. "These birds are called willow ptarmigans," says a caption for one photograph showing three beautiful white birds in the snow. "How does the color of these three birds help them to hide?" The editors of *Your Big Backyard* did not hesitate to use the photographs and names of animals Ranger Rick never met in Deep Green Wood— koalas and gazelles, wildebeests and toucans. The predator-prey relationship is explained. A complex notion like recycling is explained with a reference a youngster can grasp: hand-me-down clothes going from a big kid to a little kid.

The photographs themselves have all been recycled from other Federation publications, and the three twelve-issue sets of *Your Big Backyard* can be recycled to a constantly changing set of new subscribers. Typically, a subscriber to *Your Big Backyard* gets set number one, set number two, set number three, and then is recruited for *Ranger Rick.*

Meanwhile, a new generation of subscribers comes of age and receives set number one, set number two, set number three.

"What we are doing," Davis said in an interview, "is building a future generation of conservationists by starting with three-year-olds. We are going out with materials for three-year-olds and beginning to sensitize them to be responsible for their surroundings, sensitize them to the fact that one animal interacts with another animal, and that is good. . . . [And] we are getting the message across."

With the success of *National Wildlife, International Wildlife, Ranger Rick,* and *Your Big Backyard,* the Federation had gone from a conservation organization made up of sportsmen's clubs to an environmental organization with a membership that spanned the American spectrum, from front-porch nature lover to mountain-climbing adventurer, from bird watcher to quail hunter, from school child to senior citizen.

The grand total of members and supporters was 4.6 million.

These numbers give the Federation power. That power is wielded in legislatures and in courtrooms. And it is used quietly, channeled into classroom and living room to teach and, without apology and without dogma, to preach the environmental ethic.

5

Spreading the Conservation Message

The National Wildlife Federation has always made education its chief mission, but finding the best ways of carrying out this mission hasn't been easy or without controversy. The founders of the Federation were divided between two approaches to conservation education: an immediate, intense classroom-level campaign and a longer-term effort starting with a careful exploration of the philosophy of a new educational subject: conservation.

Ding Darling championed the first approach. He was highly critical of the way conservation was taught in textbooks. "A botanist," he said, "still teaches the children that trees are to make lumber; they teach nothing about the roots of the trees carrying the water [up from] our subterranean earth; they teach nothing about the diffusion of moisture to the atmosphere."

Darling immediately set up an education committee with four major missions: to find out what state and federal agencies were doing to teach conservation, to find ways of coordinating the best of these programs, to outline plans for educational work by the Federation, and to begin developing a national educational policy aimed at teaching the necessity of conserving the nation's natural resources.

The committee concluded that conservation education would have to start with the educators. "You cannot go on merely repeating your crusade year after year, decade after decade," warned Eliot Benner, a member of the committee and Dean of the College of Education of the University of Illinois. "You might consider well ways and means of stimulating . . . faculty members in teachers colleges and teacher-training institutions."

The pioneering conservation educators did not have an easy time carrying out their ambitious tasks. There was, to begin with, the resistance of the educational establishment. In a confidential 1940 report, the Federation's education committee said that educators "generally are inclined to consider the conservationists as one of the numerous pressure groups seeking to force a way into an already overloaded curriculum. They often regard the subject as a fad, or at best, only interesting and of minor ethical significance."

The initial resistance from professional educators was tame compared to the emphatically negative reaction of Darling. A zealot who often had trouble translating his intense personal visions into realities other people could understand, he was especially outraged by what he considered the overly "philosophical" outpourings of the education committee. Darling wanted a fast and, by his lights, practical solution to what he saw as an urgent problem.

The committee certainly moved at a majestically slow pace. From its first meeting in 1939 had come a pamphlet by Benner. A year later came a second pamphlet reporting on a "round-table discussion" the committee had held. Then in 1942 came a 254-page book, *The Foundations of Conservation Education*, which set forth the problems of teaching conservation and, in effect, said that much had to be learned before anything could be taught.

That was too much for Darling, who had been waiting impatiently for action. When he received five copies of the book, he later wrote, "I hit the ceiling. . . . I swear I don't know five people whom I could or would willingly advise taking the time to read it." His indignation flowed in a letter to a man who had reviewed the book. "I would not have proved so generous," he said of the review. "I have felt, since I first learned of its preparation, that it was a waste of time, talent and money and in the name of all that is good and holy we haven't any time, talent or money to spare on misdirected efforts."

Many educators thought highly of the book. One reviewer especially agreed with the book's criticism of the way high-school biology courses concentrated on the dissection of animals rather than on the study of wildlife in natural surroundings. Teachers who were asked to endorse the book, however, gave relatively timid commendations, perhaps because the book intimidated them, with its heavy emphasis on philosophy and its disinterest in classroom teaching techniques.

Darling tried his hand at educational pamphleteering with *Poverty or Conservation, Your National Problem,* which was published during World War II. To Darling, the war was not what just about everyone else thought it was—a crusade against evil. He saw the war as an inevitability, with good and evil not the issue. "Whatever the pretexts may be by which Japan, Italy and Germany attempt to justify the slaughter of their neighbors and the seizure of their territory," Darling wrote, "the undisputed facts are plain that Japan could no longer sustain her bulging population on the decreasing resources within her island boundaries. Italy had to have expansion of both territory and food supplies or suffer ever-increasing national poverty. Germany must have land, food and a place to send her surplus of people or accept a gradual decline in living standards and face eventual national disintegration."

Exaggeration and bad taste peppered the pamphlet, which offered this odious judgment of Americans who disagreed with Darling: "Congressmen, army engineers, most Governors, state legislators and all known Mayors and County Supervisors are as oblivious to the import of Conservation principles as Adolf Hitler is to truth and human justice."

When Darling finally got around to education, his rhetoric was more subdued and his arguments more reasoned. He called for a new generation of students aware of their threatened environmental inheritance. In his vision he anticipated the age of environmentalism, when youthful activists marched to save the whale and the sequoia: "[U]ntil in fact we have a majority of the American public schooled in the fundamental principles of conservation, criminal waste will continue to reduce our heritage of natural resources. . . . To me, Education has become the only pathway that can lead us out of the doldrums."

The Federation shared Darling's vision that education was the pathway to solutions for environmental problems, and it continued its varied efforts to bring that vision to life. The board authorized a publishing group—working independently of the committee on education—to produce a series of children's booklets designed for use in the classroom. The booklets were published in 1941. Known collectively as the My Land and Your Land Conservation Series, they alienated the illustrious members of the education committee. Yet, at the same time, the books were invaluable, for they led the Federation to a lasting educational philosophy: Show children the natural world in an enjoyable, exciting way, and they will understand and cherish it for the rest of their lives.

One book, *Would You Like to Have Lived When—?*, took children of grades 3, 4, and 5 back to pilgrim times, where David, the imaginative hero, joins his father in a deer hunt. Next, David heads for the frontier with ancestors who built log cabins and hunted animals for meat and for pelts, which were trade goods. Hunting is presented as a natural, necessary event in the lives of the pioneers. Other realities of the frontier become object lessons. Along the way, David's great-grandfather tells David that the pioneers cut down too many trees, caught too many fish, killed too many birds, buffalo, and other animals, and plowed too much land. "More trees, more wild animals, and better ways of farming!" David's great-grandfather says. "That's what we need."

Raindrops and Muddy Rivers, for grades 4, 5, and 6, has Sally sighing because rain cancels a trip. "Rain always spoils everything," she complains. Not so, says Jack. "Rain," he insists, "does a lot of good." The book then tells the reader about floods and droughts, about beaver dams and hydroelectric dams, and about the need for plant cover to prevent erosion. An experiment compared the runoff on a bare plot of land ("112,000 pounds of soil were lost, or enough to load 28 big two-ton trucks") and the runoff on a plot identical in size but covered with trees ("115 pounds . . . as much soil as you could put into a large potato sack").

Plants and Animals Live Together, for grades 5, 6, and 7, explains complex plant-animal relationships, from the pollination of flowers by bees to the burying of seeds by squirrels. The book also tells about game farms, fish hatcheries, wildlife refuges, and laws protecting wildlife. "Perhaps," the book says, "you would like to do what Bob and George did to help plants and animals. They formed a club, just the two of them, and called it 'The Good Deed for Wildlife Club.' " That club is the ancestor of Ranger Rick's Nature Club.

Nature's Bank—the Soil, for grades 6, 7, and 8, puts its young readers on the front lines in the battle against erosion. The book looks at soil problems in every section of the country and concludes with a teacher telling the class, "It is important for all citizens of this country, whether they live in cities, in villages, or in farmlands, to work together to conserve the wealth in America's land-bank."

The books may have helped teach children about the environment, but they certainly did not help to solve the financial problems of an organization struggling to stay alive. Because of flaws in the marketing program, the sales of the books did not cover the expense of producing them, and unsold books piled high in warehouses.

Another early venture into education took flight on the wings of a forlorn bird hovering over a desolate land, "as if," someone said, "looking in vain for a place to light." The bird, on the poster proclaiming the third week of March 1938 as the nation's first National Wildlife Restoration Week, carried a plaintive message: *Where to Now?* The question could have come from the fledgling National Wildlife Federation as well as from the forlorn bird. The Federation, financially tottering and struggling to garner support, was counting on publicity produced by Wildlife Week—and revenue from the concurrent distribution of wildlife stamps—to save the organization.

National Wildlife Restoration Week, a week set aside each year to alert the public to the needs of wildlife, did not accomplish all that its originator, advertising man Fred Jordan, had hoped. It did not become a phenomenal money-raiser and it was not taken over by the federal government, as he had predicted. Under continued Federation sponsorship, however, Wildlife Week became a popular educational event that annually replenished the cause of conservation.

Soon after the annual Wildlife Week was inaugurated it became an important vehicle for achieving the Federation's educational goals. The week carried the conservation message beyond the Federation's membership to school teachers, to lawmakers, to journalists, and to as many Americans as would take notice.

Each year, National Wildlife Week (the word "Restoration" was dropped in 1952) is devoted to a specific theme, such as saving wildlife habitats or campaigning for clean water. The themes have changed with the needs of the nation's wildlife and environment, but some themes have been persistent. Calls for clean water appeared on Wildlife Week posters in 1954, 1960, 1965, 1977, and 1984. Habitat has also been frequently stressed: "Make a Place for Wildlife" was the theme in 1957, "Provide Habitat" in 1969, and "Save a Place for Wildlife" in 1980. The soil erosion of the 1930s, an early concern of the Federation, became a theme in 1985, coinciding with the fiftieth anniversary of the U.S. Department of Agriculture's Soil Conservation Service.

Wildlife Week themes are not always broad. In some years, the week has focused attention on the plight of a single species, such as the Key deer. This small subspecies of the white-tailed deer got its name from its only habitat: the Florida Keys. In 1952, when "Save the Key Deer" was the Wildlife Week slogan, the deer were severely endangered, their numbers down to between twenty-five and fifty. The publicity about the Key deer helped generate national interest in the creation of a Key deer refuge.

Although still considered endangered, the deer have inched back from the brink of extinction; the Key deer population is now estimated to be around 300. The Federation's latest focus on a single species came in 1982, with a warning about the future of the eagle, under the theme "We Care About Eagles"—inspiring a presidential proclamation of 1982 as "The Year of the Eagle."

National Wildlife Week has continued to carry out its role as an educational public service campaign. As Hopalong Cassidy, the 1951 chairman, put it, "The primary purpose of National Wildlife Week is to make people aware of the steady drain on our resources—soil, forests, waters, and wildlife."

First, newspapers, magazines, and radio—then, later, television—seized on the week for an annual look at what was happening in America's great outdoors. In the early years, the week drew rapturous commentaries on wildlife from such legendary radio personalities as Graham McNamee, Grantland Rice, Fulton Lewis Jr., John Kieran, Raymond Gram Swing, and Lowell Thomas. The radio publicity for Wildlife Week led to a radio series that broadcast a conservation message—"Save America"—over 365 stations in forty-five states. (The scripts of the shows, which included "The Problem of Erosion" and "Wildlife and the Farmer," became some of the Federation's earliest publications. They were sold as a set for 25 cents.)

Child movie star Shirley Temple helped to publicize the week in 1940. (And thirty years later, as Shirley Temple Black, she became a member of the Federation's board of directors.) As television sets began to appear in American homes, media celebrities became honorary chairpersons for Wildlife Week. Besides movie and TV cowboy star Hopalong Cassidy there were many others, including Bing Crosby, Walt Disney, Walter Cronkite, Robert Redford, and "chair-amphibian" Kermit the Frog, a popular television puppet. Kermit's public-service announcement resulted in an avalanche of 20,000 requests to the Federation for more information.

In the beginning, 1938, Wildlife Week marked the launching of the annual, ever-hopeful fund-raising campaign based on wildlife stamps, which in their early years lost money and fostered irritation among affiliates. That the stamps endured and became a year-round promotional tool is testimony of faith and promise.

The stamp sheets have always been designed to have the widest possible appeal in terms of both the subject matter and the regions of the country that are represented: birds, butterflies, reptiles, amphibians, and wildflowers as well as big game and small mammals from the American deserts to the woodlands of New England.

Each painting, usually five inches by eight inches, must be highly accurate, but not too detailed. It must remain clear when reduced to stamp size. Errors have been rare, but keen-eyed stamp collectors have always spotted them. Above the hooves of a galloping pronghorn, for instance, Darling had painted dewclaws, an anatomical feature of deer but not of pronghorns. Other rarities included a bird with the wrong number of primary feathers and an over-stylized petal formation on a flower. One year, the mail brought a few complaints about too much accuracy. That was the year the stamps illustrated animal courtship behavior, and some parents complained that they had to explain what was going to happen after the animals went through their courtship.

Roger Tory Peterson, already a well-known painter and ornithologist when he was recruited as a wildlife stamp artist, painted sixteen birds for the 1939 issue. He later became the Federation's art director for the stamp program. Skilled and eminent artists like Peterson have submitted paintings every year, though they are paid only a very small honorarium compared to the artists' usual commissions.

The artists have been eager to participate, Peterson said in an interview, because there was a double attraction: "It was exposure of their work and belief in the cause. I think some of the strongest stamp paintings were done by Leslie Regan, a commercial artist known for railroad and commercial posters that were excellent. For the Federation he did trees and flowers, all that sort of thing. I did songbirds, and [Fred] Everett did mostly fish, and some mammals and birds.

"Then there was Lynn Bogue Hunt, who at that time would have been dean of sporting artists. I say sporting artists because he did mostly ducks and geese, so that sort of thing was given him to do. He was particularly good on waterfowl and grouse. And Francis Lee Jacques, who was with the American museum of Natural History and did the big backgrounds for the Museum dioramas, had a superb sense of design and did a great many of the stamps. Jacques did nongame birds as well as game birds and some fish and mammals."

When Walter A. Weber began painting birds for the 1940 issue of stamps, he too already had become a renowned wildlife artist. Weber painted *all* of the stamps for 1948, 1949, and 1950.

During World War II, Peterson served in the Army Corps of Engineers, working on technical manuals. When the war ended, he returned to the Federation, but soon was offered the position of art director on the staff of the *National Geographic* magazine. Peterson decided to discuss the offer with Richard Borden, then an associate of Federation President David Aylward. "Although I had decided to accept the Geographic's offer," Peterson reports, "I made the comment that 'If anything ever happens to Walt Weber [as NWF art director], would you consider me?' Then the *National Geographic* made Walt an offer. I hadn't anticipated that. Nor had Walt, I suppose.

"Weber was doing a large percentage of the paintings for the Federation, and he'd been employed by the National Geographic Society at the same time," said Peterson. "The Society wanted to have exclusive control of his name and work, so they offered him, I was told, a thousand dollars if he would stop painting for the Federation. Dick Borden called me up and said, 'How would you like to be the Federation's art director?'"

And so Walter Weber went to work exclusively for the *National Geographic* in the position that had been offered to Peterson, and Peterson, in 1952, took over the job that since 1947 had been Weber's— art director for the Federation. Weber's only regret was that he sorely wanted to continue painting for the Federation stamp program, to which he felt deeply committed. Now, Peterson said, it can do no harm to reveal that an artist named "Al Kremel," whose paintings were among the wildlife stamps issued in 1956, 1959, 1960, and 1961, was in reality Walter A. Weber.

As art director, Peterson has had the responsibility for planning the stamp sheets and, sometimes, of producing the albums sold along with the stamps. For years, Peterson also wrote the albums' short descriptions of the species portrayed in the stamps.

The albums give stamp collectors more than beautiful paintings. People learn that the Montana grayling is a fish that "takes artificial flies readily, indeed too readily for its own well being," that in cold areas the tamarack furnishes "fuel and wood where all other trees are missing," that paper wasps look like hornets but seldom sting, that newborn opossums are "so tiny that 20 will fit easily into a teaspoon." In essence, the albums are small textbooks about wildlife.

In recent years, Peterson has restricted his stamp work to selecting paintings and planning the layout of the sheets, in an informal partnership with Federation senior vice president Jim Davis. Each year Davis visits Peterson at his Connecticut home, where they review hundreds of paintings, make the selections, and lay out the sheets.

"During the year," Peterson said, "Jim Davis and I talk over whether we need a lot more fish, or perhaps we need some butterflies, or whatever. Then Jim and I get together. Criteria? Good design, color, movement in space. We tend to be realists. Variety is part of it. We don't like to repeat cardinals every year, and you can't always have a brook trout."

Since 1938, more than one thousand species and subspecies have been portrayed on the stamps. Down the years, the stamp producers have learned that collectors' favorite color is red, their favorite bird is the cardinal, and their favorite mammal is the whitetail deer. Snakes and spiders seem to be the least popular, but it has always been an article of faith that all forms of life have some inherent beauty and interest, and so no general category has been excluded. "No form of wildlife is taboo," Peterson said.

Stamp designers have experimented with variations. In 1941, two bird photographs by Dr. Arthur A. Allen appeared among a total of forty stamps. The color photographs are excellent for their time, but photographs, apparently because they jarred what had already become a tradition, were never used again.

An interesting sidelight to the stamp story appeared in the late 1950s and early 1960s. The Brooke-Bond Tea Corporation commissioned wildlife art, printed it on cards, and inserted the cards in the packets of tea, coffee, and baking powder it distributed in Canada. Each card bore a painting on one side and a descriptive legend in English—and, for French-Canadian readers, French on the other. For each complete set of forty-eight cards, a small album was provided. Like the cards, the album was bilingual. Although the art was commissioned by Brooke-Bond, the rights to the art were secured for the Federation to use in its stamp program.

By the end of the 1940s, Wildlife Conservation Stamps were becoming as familiar to many Americans as Easter Seals or Christmas Seals. Many of them were published in a 1951 book, *Wildlife in Color*, which itself became a star. The book was visible in Jimmy Stewart's bookcase in the classic Alfred Hitchcock film *Rear Window*.

To Peterson, the stamps symbolized an organization "I very, very much believed in [when I first started painting stamps]. And I still do. Some of the other conservation organizations have become so diffuse, they've gone away from wildlife, which is my passion. I've seen the Federation get stronger and stronger. If I were to evaluate the Federation, I would now rank it as Number One—with the finest history of accomplishment for conservation."

Some of the Federation's most important accomplishments have been in education. The stamps, like Wildlife Week, took on the role of conservation teacher. By showing both children and adults the beauty of nature, the stamps foster a sense of stewardship over the land and its wildlife. And they do more. As Peterson expresses it, "The stamps are an extraordinary educational tool, because most of us are visual, and a good picture does bring home what a thing looks like. That's the first step, for a child or an adult. The next step is naming things and what they do—the concepts come later."

This use of illustrations linked to names forms part of the Federation's educational concept. As one Federation staffer put it, "The educational philosophy of NWF might be described as a pyramid, with the naming being the first step. The material at the first step is useful for fund-raising as well as for education on the most basic level. The stamps, the Christmas cards, all the merchandise offered in our direct mail catalogs include pictures or silhouettes of wildlife, along with the names of the animals and a brief paragraph of information about them. The materials at the top of the pyramid, our specialized bibliographies, for example, are used for educating educators, with no expectation for fund-raising."

In the late 1960s, Wildlife Week began to become an even more important link between the Federation and the nation's schools. In 1968, for the first time, the Federation included something for youngsters—a standup figure of Ranger Rick holding his conservation pledge—in the package distributed to affiliates for use during Wildlife Week. By the early 1970s, schools across the nation were marking Wildlife Week with education kits the Federation developed expressly for teachers. In 1973, the Federation distributed 56,000 of these education kits.

Federation affiliates have always handled state-by-state distribution of the kits, making sure the kits reached schools, local nature centers, libraries, and museums. Through this grass-roots effort, by 1986 an estimated 20 million Americans were taking part in Wildlife Week and more than half a million free education kits were being passed out. Although kits are not identical from year to year, each kit usually contains two posters, thirty-six mini-poster stamps, and a sixteen-page teacher's guide that gives information about the theme of Wildlife Week and suggestions for classroom activities for all grades. Augmenting the kits are Wildlife Week audiovisual programs that are sold to schools.

Kits are formed around the year's theme. In 1984, when the theme was "Water, We Can't Live Without It," the education kit gave the students a fundamental lesson about water: it "was needed to produce or grow the lumber in your house, the furniture you use, the clothes you're wearing, the eggs you may have had for breakfast, and even the poster you're reading!" The lesson then got personal: "Now pinch yourself. You may feel fairly solid, but about 65% of you is made of water."

Next, the lesson radiated out from the student to the student's world: the water of rain and ocean, the water that flows through household plumbing, the water of lakes and ponds. And the problems of water: "Each year, several billion tons of soil are washed into our waterways. Added to this are untold amounts of untreated sewage, industrial wastes, pesticides, and fertilizers. They pollute our waterways, kill wildlife, close beaches, and contaminate our surface and underground drinking water supplies."

Another poster told, in English and Spanish, about aspects of water ranging from the types of wetlands and the animals that live in them to facts about canoeing and whitewater rafting. The teacher's guide, organized into four grade-level sections, provided a glossary and information about water. Suggested activities linked knowledge about water to lessons in mathematics, reading, science, art, and social studies. Students in grades 9 through 12 were asked to act out parts in trying to solve problems produced by the scenario of "The Wild River Dam Dilemma":

> The Wild River runs through the center of Big Valley County where the city of Bandell and the small town of Olsenville are located. Bandell, the county seat, has a modest amount of industry and a growing population. Olsenville recently celebrated its two hundredth anniversary and has many historical residences. It is the site of a major archaeological dig of an Indian settlement. The dig is responsible for a steady tourist industry. The Wild River also contributes to the tourist trade. The river is known for its white water rafting, kayaking rapids, and excellent trout fishing. Several small businesses in Olsenville have been built up around these activities.
>
> A three mile stretch of river near Olsenville passes through a heavily forested area where bald eagles roost during the winter. The rest of the county land surrounding the river is used for farming. Water is diverted from the river for irrigation.
>
> The Municipal Water District has released a study stating that at current usage rates, the city of Bandell will require additional water supplies and electricity within the next ten years. The Municipal Water Department has suggested a plan to dam the Wild River at Olsenville for water supply storage and hydroelectric power generation.

Students played the roles of the director of the Municipal Water District, a representative of a farmers' group, a builder, the president of the Wild River Kayaking Outdoor Club, a wildlife management professor, and other people who would be affected by decisions made about the dam. They were asked to sift through the conflicting demands for water and make decisions, many of which were difficult: "How do you make decisions about things with a price, like electric power, and things with no dollar value, such as eagles?"

Teachers' reactions to the education kits have helped Federation specialists add improvements. These informal, unsolicited reactions were augmented by more solid information in 1979, when Wildlife

Week kits contained questionnaires asking teachers what kind of conservation curriculum they wanted. The following year, the Federation tested whether Wildlife Week materials had any effect on students' understanding of conservation issues. The results of these tests convinced some analysts that students do learn from the Wildlife Week materials.

From the educational experience associated with Wildlife Week came new ideas about teaching and renewed commitment to providing materials for teachers. The result was the launching of the kind of ambitious education program the founders of the Federation had envisioned. The Federation's longtime concern about the need to put conservation in the classroom coincided in the 1970s with heightened national interest in the environment. Congress had started off the so-called Environmental Decade in 1970 by passing the Environmental Education Act, which the U.S. Office of Education had enthusiastically supported, saying the Act would lead to an "understanding of the environment, our relationship to it, and the concern and responsible action necessary to assure our survival."

The stirring words were not followed by much federal money. But state departments of education, local school districts, and—perhaps most of all—individual teachers did begin casting around for more ways to get environmental education into their curriculums. Many teachers seeking information and ideas turned to inexpensive, often free, materials published by the Federation. Though some of these publications were created especially for use in schools, most of them were reprints from Federation magazines (including *Ranger Rick*) and brochures and pamphlets used by the Federation and its affiliates to answer requests for information, to distribute at meetings, and for a variety of other purposes. But, because they presented complex information in easy-to-understand language, these publications were popular with teachers, who found them useful as background material for themselves or as handouts for their students.

In 1980 alone, the Federation handled 173,621 requests for these conservation materials. Nearly 1.5 million free publications were mailed out and more than 100,000 informational booklets were sold for nominal prices. In that year, the Federation had 111 educational publications in print. These showed the wide span of the Federation's interests—from "Pesticides and Your Environment," "Birdwatching with Roger Tory Peterson," and "Endangered Species of the United States" to "Trapping and Conservation" and "Advanced Hunter Education and Shooting Sports Responsibility."

Through the 1970s and 1980s—especially after the debut of *Ranger*

Rick magazine in 1967—the Federation began again to publish an array of materials created especially for use in formal education. Steps had been taken in this direction before: The four booklets in the My Land and Your Land Conservation Series; the controversial *Foundations of Conservation Education*, which had been published by the Federation in 1942. And in 1948 Vernon Carter's *Man on the Landscape* and A. C. Martin's *Botany and Our Social Economy* appeared. But these efforts had been sporadic. The Federation now wanted to provide teachers and school libraries with a steady supply of high quality, practical educational materials. It has made headway, producing enough educational materials by 1986 to fill a teacher's classroom shelves. There are filmstrips and slide programs, books, and a unique series of workbooks that show teachers imaginative ways to teach a wide range of science subjects.

One obstacle to creating educational materials suitable for the entire United States had been the problem of telling the wildlife story to students living in varied environments. The Federation's early education committee had unsuccessfully grappled with the problem of creating a single textbook that gave helpful information both to a pupil in the Southwest and to one in New England. How could a child in a Rocky Mountain mining town understand seashore erosion in North Carolina? The answer came when the Federation began publishing *National Wildlife, International Wildlife,* and *Ranger Rick* magazines. These richly illustrated materials opened the Federation's eye to the importance of color photographs. In these magazines people could *see* the animals and their habitats, no matter where in the world the animals lived. And so the Federation began to emphasize richly illustrated educational media, so that every place in the nation or on the globe was only a photograph away.

The "Discover Wildlife in Your World" filmstrip illustrates the usefulness of color photographs. The program begins with a series of photographs that quickly establishes the variety of the nation's wildlife habitats: "You might startle a bald eagle in a remote area of Alaska . . . or *be* startled by the tail of a huge whale while kayaking along the coast of Washington. . . . In the wilderness of northern Maine, you could see a magnificent moose, or, in a warm, Florida swamp, spot an alligator—up close." But, the filmstrip script continues, "it's not necessary to go far from home to find wildlife. No matter where you live—in the middle of a big city, in the suburbs, or in a quiet, rural town, you can discover all sorts of fascinating animals—from tiny insects to birds and mammals—right around you." And every place mentioned in the script is shown in a vivid photograph.

The viewer has no trouble comprehending the educational message, regardless of where he lives.

The Federation's educational publications go far beyond the first steps of showing and naming wildlife, but most of them are based on a similar theory about education. The theory is that people learn better if they become involved in the learning process. In most of these publications, *you* are always the person to whom the wildlife message is addressed. *You* are the discoverer. Typical of the approach is the message in the educator's guide to the filmstrip "Discover Wildlife in Your World": "Stop, look, and listen—and you will be surprised by how many animals are around. At first you may recognize only the familiar sights and sounds of robins or crickets. But the more you learn about animals, the more animals you will see." And the closer the Federation gets to achieving its goals in education.

Around the time the Environmental Decade ended, interest in environmental education began to wane in public schools. There had never been much federal money allocated to environmental education, and, in 1982, even the scant funding of the Environmental Education Act ended.

The dwindling of interest could not be explained away by budget cuts alone. Studies showed that the ideas conveyed through most environmental education methods were not getting through. Textbook-oriented, classroom-directed environmental education was not producing informed or, more importantly, *involved* students. "Ninety per cent of teachers teach more than ninety per cent of the time right out of a textbook," Robert Yager of the University of Iowa Science Education Center said in a 1982 *Audubon* magazine report on environmental education. "We miss all the basic elements of science. We never encourage puzzlement or exploration." Federation educational materials do.

Back in 1979, as an experiment tied to Wildlife Week, the Federation gathered together an assortment of teaching aids, worked them into a set of activities for kindergarten to eighth grade, and introduced the concept of the Conservation Classroom. Classes that participated in the program by completing two environmental education projects earned certificates attesting to the classes' ecological knowledge. Many of the projects were recycled back into the Conservation Classroom activity guides as examples of what classes could do and learn. By 1984, the Federation had sent out more than 6,800 kits and 550 classrooms had been certified.

The Conservation Classroom program was gradually replaced by the CLASS Project. CLASS (Conservation Learning Activities for Science and Social Studies) was set up to solve a basic problem in environmental education: some of the educational materials of the past did not work in a classroom and therefore didn't fit easily into existing public school curricula. They were square projects trying to be fit into round holes. The CLASS Project provided one avenue for getting environmental concepts incorporated into the standard curricula.

Designed for teachers of grades 6 through 9 who wanted their students to participate in community action projects and study local environmental issues, CLASS picks up where an activity like the one described in "Wild River" leaves off. There is no role-playing here. Students deal with real problems and with solutions that are workable and ethical.

CLASS, designed to help students develop what educators called an environmental ethic, covers six content areas: energy use, environmental issues, forest and watershed management, hazardous substances, wetlands, and wildlife habitat management. "The CLASS Project," says the introduction to the CLASS materials, "reflects our belief that many students do not feel like effective members of our culture and too rarely see academic disciplines as related and relevant to the world around them. . . . Through our program, students learn environmental and natural resource management concepts by conducting activities and investigations in the classrooms and on the school grounds. The skills students acquire through these activities will lead them toward involvement in community action projects."

One part of the program, "You Can Make It Happen," describes class projects that teachers have carried out. After attending a CLASS Project workshop, for example, a seventh-grade teacher in North Carolina developed a habitat project. "My students really got interested in wildlife, and particularly ducks, after we visited a local man who raises ducks," she said. "He gave us some duck eggs to hatch and raise. We didn't know what kind of ducks they were, but we hatched the eggs in an incubator in our classroom, and then moved the little ducks to a brooder pen right in the school. Finally, when they were big enough, one of the boys moved them to a pond on his family's farm."

The project went beyond raising and releasing ducks. "We built and erected bird feeders and bird nesting boxes all around the community," the teacher said, "and the students really began to see their role as stewards of wildlife for the future."

The CLASS Project, which was developed by the Federation under a $286,200 National Science Foundation grant awarded in 1979, offers more than just an innovative curriculum for teaching environmental concepts. It solves one of the biggest problems facing teachers who want to bring environmental education into the classroom: lack of teacher training. Standard certification requirements for teachers of intermediate school include a broad array of college courses, but rarely are more than one or two of these in the sciences. Such science courses are often narrowly focused—biology, geology, chemistry—and are seldom interdisciplinary. They usually don't include lessons on the management of environments or on environmental ethics.

To overcome this problem of inadequate exposure to environmental education programs, the Federation's Conservation Education Department set up CLASS teacher workshops. By 1985, the Federation had trained more than 3,000 people in the use of CLASS materials, and by the end of 1986 the project had been extended to thirty states. Sometimes students sat alongside teachers at the workshops and, in the words of one educator, "jumped right into it, grasping the concepts immediately. In many cases, they were instrumental in explaining the activities to the teachers."

Ranger Rick, meanwhile, had been doing its part for conservation education by publishing teacher's activity guides. These guides, one for each issue of *Ranger Rick* and free for the asking, provided tips like: "Spider webs can be fascinating. . . . Why not collect some webs and study them?" Teachers were encouraged to copy games, puzzles, and other activities so that entire classes could share them. Some of Rick's ideas helped teach arithmetic: "When Betsy Bee and her two sisters became adults, each of them laid four eggs. How many eggs did they lay in all?" Some ideas helped the art teacher: "Save the seeds from apples, pumpkins, watermelons, squash and other fruits and vegetables. Draw an outline of an owl, bat, jack-o-lantern or autumn scene on a piece of heavy cardboard. Glue seeds in different patterns and create artistic mosaics."

In 1984, after a survey of 30,000 educators and after discussions with teachers, science supervisors, elementary school principals, and other experts, the Federation replaced Ranger Rick Teacher's Guide with a unique series named *NatureScope*. Each sixty-four page *NatureScope* features a different subject in the sciences. Issues have been devoted to mammals, insects, dinosaurs, weather, birds, deserts, trees, and astronomy, for example. Specialists review the text and illustrations for accuracy, and editors make sure the copy is written in a light, easy-to-understand style. Each unit, as a Federation report says, "ties the background together for teachers and gives them the confidence they need to teach subjects that they were not previously comfortable with. This gives all teachers the same science foundation—whether they teach second grade or sixth grade."

An examination of the *Birds, Birds, Birds!* issue gives a good idea of what the series is like. The issue is divided into six chapters, each of which provides background material and classroom activities, starting with ones suitable for preschool or primary grades and ending with ones suitable for advanced grades. The "Family Life" chapter, for example, suggests that the younger children learn some bird songs by singing them or imitating the songs played on a bird record. Older children are asked to write a paragraph about some chosen bird, using new words—such as fledge, incubate, migrate—associated with bird life. Another group is asked to make a model of an egg out of plastic, egg-shaped pantyhose containers or out of balloons, plastic bags, tissue paper, or clay.

Teachers are encouraged to ask students to set up feeding stations and to take a bird's-eye view of the world: "What does a mallard duck do when the marsh where it's been living is filled with dirt and becomes an apartment complex? Or what happens to a pileated woodpecker when its forest home is bulldozed and becomes a shopping center?"

Another idea is to have students talk to their grandparents or older neighbors to find out how the community has changed—and how these changes have affected birds. "Many people don't understand the needs of wildlife and why it is important to protect habitat," the *NatureScope* students are told. "People ignorant of the issues often make decisions without knowing all the facts."

That is undoubtedly the most important lesson taught, and it appears in varied, enticing ways in every issue of *NatureScope*.

In this and other modern forms of conservation education, students learn a new way to see and understand the world. They discover that the environment, unlike such classroom subjects as history or mathematics, is alive, and the students live in it. Learning about the environment is learning about living. The lesson goes beyond the classroom.

For preschoolers, the educational program included the production of early-childhood educational materials in *Your Big Backyard*. A magazinelike nature-oriented series for children three to five, *Your Big Backyard* includes picture-based stories and activities that can be used in nursery school or the home. The series provides "an excellent means to introduce pre-school and elementary children to science and animal life," said *Science Books & Films*, a critical review of educational materials that is published by the American Association for the Advancement of Science.

"Invite Wildlife to Your Backyard," an article written by an architectural artist, an urban wildlife specialist, and a landscape architect, explained that a little bit of land—from "a quarter-acre of crabgrass" to a window box—"can become a wildlife refuge-in-miniature." The article gave readers ideas on how and what to plant to provide animals their four basic needs: food, water, protective cover, and reproductive cover. This article, in the April-May 1973 issue of *National Wildlife*, inspired the Backyard Wildlife Habitat Program.

The first wave of participants in the habitat program came from the ranks of gardeners who have always been among the Federation's most enthusiastic members. The habitat program particularly appeals to them because it helps them make their backyard more inviting to wildlife, enhancing gardens with flashes of life. As an added bonus for certain unpopular animals, the program clears up misconceptions about such beneficial creatures as bats, spiders, and snakes. People who modify their backyards to attract animals receive a Backyard Wildlife Habitat certificate. More than 4,600 properties, both residential and commercial, have been certified.

Word about the program has been spread through the Federation's book *Gardening with Wildlife;* a Gardening with Wildlife Kit that includes landscaping templates and other planning aids; the Public Broadcasting System's weekly show, "Victory Garden"; and "The Backyard Naturalist," a column distributed to newspapers. In his writing, the Backyard Naturalist, Craig Tufts, concentrates on the 9,000 square feet in his own yard. The buttonbushes there attract butterflies and hummingbirds. The lady bird beetles ("ladybugs") are cherished because they eat the aphids. And the bird feeders—a perennially favorite subject of Federation birdwatchers—are all filled with seeds recommended by Dr. Al Geis, former urban biologist for the U.S. Fish and Wildlife Service, and listed in "Wild Bird Feeding Preferences," a pamphlet published by the Federation.

Another educational venture in 1970 was the launching of the first Federation camp for children. Camp Energy was located at the Land Between the Lakes camping area on the Kentucky-Tennessee border. Besides the standard summer-camp fare of hiking, swimming, and nature craft, Camp Energy gave special attention to the role the campers could play in conserving the environment.

The successor to Camp Energy was the Ranger Rick Wildlife Camp in the Blue Ridge Mountains near Hendersonville, North Carolina. Children nine to thirteen attend the camp, and the Federation and other organizations provide "camperships" for needy children. (For teenagers there was the Earth Trek program, a twelve-day backpack into the wilderness in North Carolina or Colorado.) Daily activities at the camp revolve around environmental themes. Each camper selects a "quest," an environmental study area—such as small creatures or lakes and streams—and specializes in it while at camp. As the campers gain experience, they move up the ranks through a counselor-in-training program.

The camp program has been successful by all standards. "Ilenia was very excited about her camp experience," a parent wrote. "She sleeps in her sleeping bag on the floor, she talks about birds, pollution, and waste, she sings camp songs and misses you all." President Carter gave the Ranger Rick camps a special President's Environmental Youth award in 1979.

Ironically, the success of these camps was a source of frustration for the Federation. Eager to be helping young people understand their environment, NWF wanted to do more, but didn't think it was practical to set up and operate camps all over the country. Out of this frustration was born the concept of NatureQuest, a Federation work-shop program that teaches people who run summer camps how to introduce environmental activities at their own camps. NatureQuest multiplies the educational activities of Federation camps by passing along to counselors the ideas and ideals of environmentally-rooted camping experiences.

Conservation Summits are also part of the Federation's educational mission. Begun in 1970, the Summits are week-long summer vacations for families. Each of the Summits offers day care for preschoolers, Ranger Rick activities for younger children, backpacking for teen-agers, and a wide array of programs for adults, including hikes, eve-ning "owl prowls," workshops in mountain ecology and edible plants, and even a "nature creep" where participants crawl on hands and knees to get a closeup look at a small area. Locales have varied: Nova Scotia, Utah, the Adirondacks, Colorado, California, even Banff, Canada. A three-time camper called it a "fresh-air camp for grown-ups." In a critique of the Summits, she reported, "The food isn't fancy . . . but the accommodations—Bowdoin College housing (Maine) or YMCA conference center buildings—sure beat a tent and sleeping bags. . . ."

The Summits are more than vacations. They inform, they transform theories about the environment into practical experiences, and they increase the ranks of advocates for the environment. Many teachers attend and obtain college credits for courses in ecology and natural history. Indeed, most of the instructors at the Summits are college faculty members specially recruited for their expertise and teaching abilities.

The Summit idea came to Jim Davis one day when he was thinking about the associate members, who never get to meet each other. Davis ran an advertisement in *National Wildlife* asking readers if they would be interested in a National Wildlife Federation vacation. He asked interested readers to write to "Wild Idea" (which is what some unenthusiastic Federation officials had labeled it). Members wrote and telephoned in such numbers that the Wild Idea quickly became a reality that summer at Estes Park, Colorado, near Rocky Mountain National Park.

The idea of making contact with Federation members was carried farther afield when Davis saw a *Life* magazine story on travel to exotic places. He believed that people interested in conservation would want to visit places like the Galapagos Islands, the Amazon River, even Antarctica. All of the adventures described in *Life* had been orchestrated by travel entrepreneur Lars Lindblad. It sounded like a good idea to Davis, so he picked up the phone and called Lindblad. Beginning in 1968, the Federation offered exotic trips called Conservation Safaris as another way to educate members. The Safaris included trips to the Galapagos Islands, India's natural areas, and Africa. The safari program, however, ran aground on management problems and was phased out in the late 1970s.

All the while it was developing specialized educational programs, the Federation, through publications, continued to maintain its traditional links to the greater conservation community.

The annual *Conservation Directory*'s thirty-first edition was published in 1986. Begun in 1955 as a small pamphlet listing in simple alphabetical order about 3,400 individuals, the *Directory* now lists some 2,000 governmental and nongovernmental organizations and agencies, and almost 12,000 names of professionals associated with the use and management of natural resources. Included in the entry for each agency or organization is a brief description of its goals and activities, publications, membership, and founding date. Names, addresses, and phone numbers for officers and officials are also included.

A partial list of contents indicates the span of coverage: fish and game commissioners, state citizens groups (from the Alabama Wildlife Federation to the Wyoming Outdoor Council) and international, national, and interstate organizations (from Accord Associates to Zero Population Growth), U.S. and Canadian federal agencies, Canadian national citizens' groups (from the Atlantic Salmon Association to the Pollution Probe Foundation). State listings in the *Directory* give the names and addresses of Federation affiliates.

The *Directory* is a handy reference for professionals and volunteers in the conservation movement. Of narrower but extremely valuable interest to professionals is the Federation's periodically published *Sur-*

vey of Compensation in the Fields of Fish and Wildlife Management. This publication, usually simply called "the salary survey," gives wildlife managers a reliable guide to salary range and helps them map their careers. The periodical, which includes information on retirement as well as hospitalization and leave benefits, is especially used by state personnel departments to set competitive compensation scales. The twenty-fourth edition, published in 1985, surveyed the federal job outlook ("bleak") and employment trends in state fish and game agencies (gains in average salary ranges, in salary increases, and in the number of women employed in professional posts).

Conservation '86, begun in 1982 as *Conservation '82,* is published twice a month. It is the successor to two venerable publications, *Conservation News,* first published in 1936 as a regular news bulletin, and *Conservation Report,* a newsletter that began in 1946. *Conservation News* went to as many as 60,000 people concerned with conservation. *Conservation Report,* reaching a circulation of 25,000, presented information about federal natural resources legislation and was published weekly when Congress was in session. Both of these publications were mailed to leaders in federal and state agencies concerned with natural resources, to members of Congress, to conservationists in other organizations, to members of the media, and to leaders of clubs affiliated with NWF.

Conservation '86, distributed on request to associate members of NWF, condenses conservation and environmental news into reports that tell readers what has happened and what is likely to happen. It keeps watch over such environmental concerns as public lands and energy, pollution and toxics, legislative affairs, water resources, fisheries and wildlife, and international matters. It also reports on legislation, analyzes bills, covers hearings, and notes congressional activities that pertain to conservation. Topics in an issue of *Conservation '86* might range from how the huge national debts of Third World countries affect wildlife to how the Senate voted on the U.S. Forest Service budget.

The newest Federation publication is *Conservation Exchange.* A quarterly publication, it is an outgrowth of NWF's Corporate Conservation Council. The Corporate Council, whose members include corporate senior executives and NWF leaders, meets regularly to explore ways to balance the nation's need for economic growth with the need to protect national resources. The *Exchange* goes not only to corporate members of the council, but also to the chief executive officers of the nation's major corporations—the "Fortune 500"—to other industrial leaders, environmental groups, congressional staff members, business schools, and major foundations.

The quarterly reports on such topics as the lack of environmental training in the nation's business schools and the need to educate corporations about ways to save money and avoid trouble in ventures affecting the environment. The business community is told that wetlands can remove toxic iron and manganese compounds from acid mine drainage, that controlling pollution costs far less than cleaning up hazardous wastes, and that banks can lose federal support if they approve environmentally destructive projects in developing countries.

For many years, before many conservation organizations established offices in Washington, D.C., and communication among them became easier and more frequent, the Federation hosted meetings where the activities of the different conservation groups were discussed and sometimes coordinated. The Federation maintained a close relationship with such organizations as the now defunct Citizens Committee on Natural Resources and the American Committee for International Conservation, and still keeps in close touch with the Natural Resources Council of America and the International Association of Fish and Wildlife Agencies, of which it is a charter member. The premiere coordinating activity was the annual Conservation Conference, which from 1953 to 1985 drew representatives from numerous organizations to the Federation's Washington headquarters every December. The Federation arranged and conducted the conference. The Federation also sponsors smaller conferences on such subjects as federal grazing policies, the MX missile, and acid rain. From some conferences come publications that the Federation produces and helps to distribute.

Each year, at its annual meeting, the Federation recognizes conservation achievements with awards, the chief one being the National Conservation Achievement Award. Begun in 1965 with funds donated by Sears Roebuck and Co., the award program singles out individuals and organizations that have been paramount in spreading the conservation message and in mustering support for the environment. Some of the categories for awards are Conservationist of the Year, Communications, Education, Legislative, Organization, and Science. The recipient of the award in each category receives a small sculpture of a whooping crane, the "embodiment of wildlife preservation," as the board of directors called it. Recipients of these "Connie" awards have included Lady Bird Johnson, Nelson Rockefeller, The Nature Conservancy, and WGBH-TV, Boston, for NOVA. Affiliates also give awards on the state level as well as nominate people for national awards. (A list of national winners appears in appendix 5.

Educating people about the environment is a full-time occupation for Federation staffers, from top executives to the people who answer

Federation phones and field such questions as the one about jacka-lopes. The librarian got that one. She convinced the caller that the Federation had not produced the documentary he thought he had seen about the mythical beast. "I offered to send him a *Ranger Rick* issue that contains a piece about tall tales of the West, including the jackalope," she later reported, "and he agreed to suspend judgment about its authenticity until reading the article." Then there are the letters and calls for information on toxic wastes, acid rain, hunting, and yes—even cookies. A frantic mother who had agreed to make Bird Nest Cookies for her daughter's nursery school called for help. The recipe was in a lost copy of *Your Big Backyard*. The recipe was read to her, and the cookies were delivered on time.

Thus do the questions come in and the answers go out. In the beginning no one knew that environmental education would be so complicated and wide ranging. Now the Federation knows that whether the student is a preschooler or a member of Congress, and whether the teacher is a day-care-center storyteller or a Federation lobbyist, environmental education makes special demands upon teacher and pupil.

The National Wildlife Federation hopes that children or adults who are taught about the environment will learn more than mere facts. It also hopes that people will develop a positive attitude toward the environment, that they will embrace the idea that maintaining a pol-lution-free, life-sustaining world is ethically imperative, that they will work to bring it about. For arithmetic or spelling, no such ethical attitude is expected.

Both advantages and problems stem from this extraordinary de-mand. Dedication to the need for a healthy environment inspires many teachers. But the demands for teaching the ethics behind the environmental movement so alienate other teachers that they try to trim environmental education down to mere facts, ignoring ethical principles and consequences.

The Federation's long experience with this special subject has af-fected the lives of thousands of people—the Boy Scouts at a jamboree, seeing their first golden eagle; the families who are transforming their backyard into a habitat; the little boy who learns not to be afraid of bats. And for all the human lives affected, numerous wildlife species and their habitats have been conserved. They are the ultimate be-neficiaries of a sound environmental education.

6

Saving Species,
Preserving Habitat

Before the turn of the nineteenth century, hunting in the United States was virtually unregulated. The slaughter of animals by market hunters and wanton shooters was taking a devastating toll. Incensed sportsmen began lobbying for county and state laws and, eventually, for national laws to control hunting.

One early national law was the 1894 Yellowstone Park Protection Act. By shielding animals in Yellowstone from hunters and fishermen, the law established the precedent of setting aside habitat to ensure that wildlife had places to live. About the same time, several western states acted to conserve game animals. California established closed hunting seasons for antelope and tule elk. Nevada did the same for mountain goats and bighorn sheep.

In 1905 a much-publicized murder galvanized the conservation movement. By the early 1900s, milliners were paying as much as $32 an ounce—nearly twice the price of gold—for the wispy feathers of egrets. Men would kill for wealth like that. And in 1905, someone did. Guy Bradley, a warden hired by the National Audubon Society to protect egrets from poachers, was shot in his boat off Oyster Key, Florida, by the skipper of a boat with a cargo of dead egrets. New state laws against poachers and plume hunters and a federal law banning importation of wild-bird plumage were passed and hailed as monuments to Bradley's martyrdom.

The 1918 Federal Migratory Bird Treaty Act banned spring hunting and gave the federal government the right to set limits on the killing of migratory birds. The 1934 Migratory Bird Hunting Stamp Act raised funds to acquire, restore, and maintain habitat. And, by compelling duck hunters to buy "duck stamps," the act, in effect, created a federal duck hunting license.

The fact that Ding Darling not only had created the first duck stamp but also was sounding the call for establishing the National Wildlife Federation gave the new organization credence with old-line conservationists. A representative of the National Association of Audubon Societies, the doyen of conservation organizations, blessed the Federation by attending its founding meeting. Also at that meeting were delegates who knew extinction of animals as more than a theory, for they could remember the deaths of the last passenger pigeon in 1914 and the last Carolina parakeet in 1918, both in the Cincinnati Zoo.

The sportsmen's concern over endangerd animals and besieged habitats, which had inspired the creation of the National Wildlife Federation itself, was transformed into resolutions passed at the Federation's first annual meeting in 1937. Resolution Number Three endorsed the expansion of a wilderness system. Resolution Number Five extended concern over the ecosystem into the future: "Wildlife research should be expanded through the use of federal and state funds, in the manner of the Agricultural Extension Service." Resolution Number Seven called for the tightening of restrictions on the trapping of furbearing animals.

That resolution touched off vigorous debate among the strong-minded members. The controversy centered on whether the trapping of furbearing varmints—predators of game animals and livestock—should be restricted so that a balanced ecosystem would survive. The conclusion was "yes." The actual words of the resolution were: "There must be greater restrictions on the trapping of furbearing animals, and more attention to their preservation." By agreeing with that ecological concept, NWF sportsmen were going against the commonly accepted notion that predators ought to be eliminated because they reduced the number of game animals.

With such resolutions, delegates demonstrated that the National Wildlife Federation had been founded not only to protect the interests of hunters and fishermen, but also to protect the needs of animals.

Hunters and fishermen dominated the affiliates of the Federation. This fact was underlined when Remington Arms made a contribution that helped the struggling new Federation get through its early days. But, in its formative years, while it was finding its own identity, the Federation was also emphasizing a new identity for the hunter, who no longer was a man of the frontier. The Federation represented the American sportsman, the responsible, law-abiding enemy of the greedy market hunter and the criminal hunter who shot what and where he wanted, regardless of conservation laws. The sportsman saw conservation as an issue concerned not merely with game animals. The environment was where all animals lived, game and nongame, predator and prey, and the environment did not discriminate. If it disappeared, so did all the animals.

One of the Federation's earliest endeavors was to prevent the extinction of Florida's diminutive Key deer. And in working to save the Key deer, the Federation discovered that spotlighting a single endangered animal was one way to focus public attention on conservation. The young organization also learned just how much time and resourcefulness can be required to succeed.

Ding Darling had first heard about the plight of the Key deer around the late 1920s, when, aboard a boat off the Florida Keys, he spotted smoke rising from a key. The smoke, he was told, came from fires set by hunters to drive the tiny deer out of the mangroves and onto the beach, where they were shot for meat. Darling drew a cartoon of hunters gunning down the animals and captioned it, "The Last of the 'Toy' Deer of the Florida Keys."

The cartoon was widely circulated by conservationists concerned about the Key deer, and Darling tried to get officials in Florida to stop the slaughter. But nothing happened. Then, sometime in the late 1940s, James Silver, southeastern regional director for the U.S. Fish and Wildlife Service, and Bud Jackson, the field representative of the National Wildlife Federation, met and discussed the Key deer's plight.

Jackson alerted the Florida Wildlife Federation, which began working to find a sanctuary for the deer. At the same time, in Washington, the Federation started the kind of multifaceted campaign that was to become a pattern: testifying before congressional committees and lobbying among federal agencies; alerting affiliates; canvassing other organizations for support.

Richard Borden, executive director of the Federation and chairman of the Boone and Crockett Club's conservation committee, kept watch on the lobbying effort for the Key deer. In March 1950, Congressman Charles E. Bennett of Florida introduced legislation calling for the creation of a federal refuge for the Key deer. Bennett's bill was endorsed by the National Wildlife Federation, the Florida Wildlife Federation, the National Audubon Society, and the Wildlife Management Institute. But, primarily because of the opposition of Florida land developers, the bill was defeated.

Borden knew that a few months could mean survival or extinction to the deer, so he urged the Boone and Crocket Club to step in until a new legislative effort was mounted. The B and C contributed $5,000 to a Key deer fund and, as the Audubon Society had done in Florida some forty years before to protect egrets from plume collectors, decided to hire a private warden to protect the deer. The club commissioned Borden "to obtain, without delay, the services of a competent warden, suitably equipped."

Borden, meanwhile, had been holding urgent talks with Dr. Clarence Cottam, assistant director of the U.S. Fish and Wildlife Service. Through his man Silver, Cottam encouraged Coleman Newman, director of the Florida Game and Fresh Water Fish Commission, to back the idea of a Key deer warden. Newman did, even suggesting that the warden be deputized as a federal and state lawman to strengthen his authority. The Boone and Crockett Club promptly hired Jack C. Watson, a biologist who in addition to guarding the deer from poachers took a census and recorded invaluable observations about the deer's habits. Borden also received help from "Pink" Gutermuth, vice president of the Wildlife Management Institute and secretary of the North American Wildlife Foundation, who on behalf of the institute offered $5,000 to the fund to save the deer. The National Wildlife Federation raised and contributed $10,000 to the Key deer effort and assumed the cost of the warden's salary for a year.

In Washington, the Federation and other conservation organizations renewed their efforts to get a refuge bill through Congress. This time, late in 1951, the bill was introduced by Congressman Bill Lantaff, also of Florida. The Federation, meanwhile, stepped up the campaign by making the deer the first species to be featured as a National Wildlife Week theme. With "Save the Key Deer" reverberating through the media early in 1952, the bill seemed very likely to pass.

But the Florida land developers had geared up, too. And the battle came during the administration of Secretary of the Interior Douglas McKay, who once characterized conservationists as "punks" and who was leasing away thousands of acres of wildlife refuge land.

Lantaff's bill never even reached the floor. But in 1954 the Department of the Interior's appropriations contained authorization for leasing land for a refuge. The leasing had a built-in threat, however, because it provided that landowners could cancel the leases if they decided to sell the land or use it themselves.

The deer obviously needed something better than tentative leases to ensure permanent protection. As Silver put it in a report on the eve of his retirement, "Somewhere, somehow . . . a small area of land must be acquired under some form of ownership that will guarantee permanent and safe use by the Key deer for all time to come."

Primarily through the work of Gutermuth, the North American Wildlife Foundation bought a 17.5-acre tract and deeded it to the U.S. Fish and Wildlife Service. Congressman Bennett then introduced a new Key deer bill authorizing the acquisition of a thousand acres of additional land around the beachhead obtained by nonfederal efforts. The bill passed in 1957 and was signed by President Eisenhower (who in 1956 had replaced McKay with Fred A. Seaton, a secretary more amiable to conservationists). The bill, however, did not provide any federal money for buying refuge land. So Gutermuth again was forced to get commitments from private sources. Money was found for the purchase of enough land to support the deer. Since then, the Key deer population has slowly increased from fewer than fifty to approximately three hundred.

During the time it was working to help the Key deer, the Federation was asked to save another animal from heedless hunting. The appeal came in 1951 from Alf Madsen, a hunting guide and outfitter in Kodiak, Alaska. Madsen had written to Ted Wegener in Idaho, who took the letter with him to the Federation's 1951 annual meeting. Madsen warned that the Kodiak Livestock Growers Association— "about a dozen men who own less than a thousand cattle"—was campaigning, with apparent success, for an open season on the Kodiak bear, a race of the grizzly that lives on Kodiak and two nearby islands in the Gulf of Alaska. The bear had almost been wiped out at the turn of the century, hunted mercilessly because it killed salmon, livestock, and occasionally a hunter. A small, stable population of bears, however, still lived on the islands.

In 1951, Alaska was a territory full of mavericks, still eight years away from what some independent-minded sourdoughs saw as the straitjacket of statehood. Feverish calls for political independence went hand in hand with demands for the grand old Alaskan custom of wide-open hunting. It was no accident that two of the supporters of the open season on Kodiak bears were simultaneously urging that Alaska become an independent republic instead of a state.

Frontier-style slaughter of wildlife may have had an appeal in Alaska, but conservationists in the territory's prospective sister states reviled Alaska as the continent's leading enemy of wildlife. When Wegener raised the issue of the Kodiak bear, Herbert C. Kelly, the delegate from Colorado, put the matter squarely before his fellow delegates: "I think it is the policy of the National Wildlife Federation to go to the defense of any species that is in any way endangered as to its existence.

"It was a farfetched thought a couple of years ago for some of us to appreciate when Ding Darling and Ralph Cooksey [a director from Florida] and some others brought to our attention the critical situation with reference to the Key deer. I think all of us fully appreciate now what that danger is. Maybe it is too late, but we understand it.

"Now we go clear up to the Northwest and to the Kodiak bear. All of you who are acquainted with that area know that the esthetic value of Kodiak Island is principally the wildlife contained therein. More specifically, the giant Kodiak bear. That bear itself is more valuable, as far as people of the United States are concerned, than all the cattle or sheep that could be raised on Kodiak Island. . . .

"I move that this convention go on record and instruct our executive secretary to prepare a proper letter for transmittal to the Fish and Wildlife Service and to the people in the legislature of Alaska, opposing a permanent open season on the Kodiak bear."

The action did not endear the Federation in Alaska, where the lines already were being drawn for a confrontation between the Alaskan affiliate, with its fervent belief in state's rights, and the national Federation, with its belief that, if states fail to protect their natural resources, the federal government has the obligation to step in.

The issue had to be delicately handled because of the attitude of some hunters toward the whole idea of giving animals federal protection beyond that provided by state game laws. To critics of federal intervention in state game management, the Federation looked like a partner of the bureaucrats in Washington; the feds and the Federation even lived in the same place. For the Federation, there was a natural affinity between its conservation aims and the rapidly evolving federal involvement in the preservation of endangered species.

The federal focus on threatened animals began in 1966 with the Endangered Species Preservation Act, which ordered the Secretary of the Interior to determine what American animals were rare and threatened with extinction and then to list them in the Federal Register, a publication that announces executive orders and regulations. In 1969 came the Endangered Species Conservation Act, which gave the secretary of the interior the authority to cooperate with the states to protect and restore endangered species (including endangered mollusks and crustaceans). The 1969 law replaced the old terms "rare" and "endangered" with the terms "threatened" and "endangered."

The Endangered Species Act of 1973 went a great deal further, giving the secretary of the interior the authority to intervene in a state's wildlife activities if there was reason to believe that the state was not adequately protecting an endangered species. The 1973 act also broadened coverage to plants as well as animals, to subspecies, and to "any smaller taxonomic unit of plant or animal, and also any viable population segment thereof." (By 1986 there were 392 plant and animal species listed as "endangered" or "threatened.")

Ever since its beginnings, the Federation has campaigned for the conservation of species that are in trouble. Beginning with its 1937 resolution in favor of restricting the trapping of varmints, it has backed legislation to protect individual species. Wildlife Week themes repeatedly have focused on the plight of endangered species and called for the preservation of habitat as an important means of ensuring their survival.

In the 1960s, Rachel Carson's *Silent Spring* alerted Americans to the deadly effects of synthetic pesticides, DDT in particular, and the Federation recognized the need for all concerned people and organizations to support legislation that tackled the whole problem of endangered species rather than the problems of individual species. NWF resolutions in 1964 and 1965 showed the Federation's support for a federal law to protect endangered species. At its 1969 annual meeting, the Federation again made endangered wildlife a priority issue. Many animals, it said, were being threatened with extinction because of the deterioration of habitat "and also demands for commercial uses, especially for fashionable clothing and accessories." The Federation endorsed proposals to protect endangered species by prohibiting the trafficking of them in interstate or international commerce.

At the 1970 annual meeting, the Federation backed efforts to save several species—the whooping crane, the grizzly bear, the mountain lion, and birds of prey.

The whooping crane had been considered a candidate for extinction since the nineteenth century, when the guns of hunters and the encroachment of civilization on its wilderness habitats nearly wiped it out. In 1926, fewer than a dozen nesting pairs were thought to be alive. The birds held on at that precarious population level until 1945, when the National Audubon Society and the U.S. Fish and Wildlife Service joined in a widely publicized project to save the cranes, which then were believed to number only seventeen.

By 1970, when the Federation officially enlisted in the whoopers' cause, the Audubon Society was disputing a controversial Fish and Wildlife Service "take and put" program. Fish and Wildlife Service

One of the century's most influential conservationists, Jay N. "Ding" Darling founded the National Wildlife Federation. (NWF Archives)

"The Conservation Interests Can Get What They Need If They Will Pull Together"—1936 cartoon by Ding Darling. (First appeared in the *Des Moines Register*, February 1, 1936.)

President Franklin Delano Roosevelt, Frederick Jordan, a New York advertising executive and originator of Wildlife Week, and Minor Hudson, president of the Junior Chamber of Commerce, inspect the 1938 wildlife stamps. (NWF Archives)

Shirley Temple helped raise public awareness of the Federation's wildlife stamp program in 1940. Thirty years later, she was elected to NWF's board of directors. (Underwood & Underwood)

The First National Wildlife Week poster, 1938. (NWF File)

Two of the many notables who have served as chairperson of National Wildlife Week: Hopalong Cassidy in 1951, and Walt Disney in 1963. (NWF Archives)

Thomas L. Kimball (left) and J. A. "Ash" Brownridge looking at first press run of National Wildlife magazine, 1962. (R. F. Hildebrand)

Lady Bird Johnson presents NWF's National Distinguished Service Award to Nelson Rockefeller, 1966. (Finnigan & Associates)

Pictured on the U. S. Capitol steps are Louis Clapper, NWF Conservation director, and his staff—the Federation's Congressional lobbying team in the late 1970s. (Courtesy of L. Clapper)

NWF Executive Vice President Jay D. Hair meets with President Ronald Reagan, 1984. (Pete Souza, White House)

Laurel Ridge Conservation Education Center, Vienna, Virginia, features nature trails, a Backyard Wildlife Habitat exhibit area, and conservation programs. (NWF File)

NWF Headquarters Building in Washington, D. C., from 1960 to 1986. Each carved marble panel depicts the wildlife found in one of the 13 regions of the Federation. A new building being errected on this site will be occupied by NWF in the fall of 1987. (NWF Archives)

NWF Magazines

NWF Books

NWF Newsletters

NWF Special Publications

personnel were taking whooping crane eggs from nests in the wild, hatching the eggs and raising the nestlings in captivity until they could fend for themselves, and then putting the birds back into their natural habitat. Under this program, the argument went, more whoopers would survive the most dangerous period of life and live to become adults. Audubon was on the side of "protectionists," who urged environmental protection of the endangered whoopers by improving the protection given the birds in their habitats, but leaving the birds themselves completely alone. In its 1970 resolution on whoopers, the Federation—showing its support for more traditional wildlife management—endorsed the take and put program.

As with those for the whooper, management programs for grizzly bears have been controversial. Except for populations in Alaska, most grizzlies are found in Yellowstone and Glacier National Parks. In the late 1960s, the National Park Service, wanting to keep bears and park visitors separated, contemplated closing some camping areas near garbage dump sites where bears had become accustomed to foraging for food. The Federation backed the proposal in 1970, little expecting that years later the matter would put the Federation in a courtroom fighting its traditional ally, the National Park Service. (See chapter 7.)

The mountain lion, long a colorful member of America's clan of mythologized animals, is variously known as the cougar, puma, panther, and catamount (cat of the mountain). Its roar is said to sound like a woman's wail. Its predations on game animals and livestock are said to be prodigious. Because of its reputation, in many areas the mountain lion has been a year-round target for hunters, a year-round meal ticket for guides, and a year-round condemned varmint to ranchers.

Its numbers, especially in California, were decreasing at an alarming rate, and the big cat had few friends outside the conservation movement. In a 1970 resolution, the Federation urged that the mountain lion be protected by being classified as a game animal. As a Federation spokesman explains, "A regulated hunting season was all that could be justified, and it served the purpose of protecting the animals." Without the status of a game animal, the cougar was in legal limbo and subject to year-round hunting, trapping, and poisoning. Regulating hunting greatly reduced the threat to the cat's populations and, in the long run, will benefit hunters and cats. It gave no comfort, however, to those ranchers who did not want to hear about the value of predators in maintaining an ecological balance.

Birds of prey had even more enemies than the mountain lion. But the 1970 resolution concerning raptors was sweeping, asking that all birds commonly called hawks and buzzards, along with eagles, kites, vultures, ospreys, owls, and falcons—more than fifty species in all—be placed on the list of protected birds. While admitting that some raptor species are responsible for some predation upon game and domestic animals, the resolution pointed out that "few individuals can distinguish between which birds of prey are beneficial and which are harmful," the result being that all species, including eagles, are shot by "undiscriminating and ill-informed individuals."

In 1972, a year after the resolutions to protect whooping cranes, grizzly bears, cougars, and birds of prey, the Federation went on record with a resolution that reaffirmed its longstanding endorsement of professional wildlife management. Several protectionist groups had been trying to use the courts to scuttle wildlife management programs, especially when the programs included sport or other hunting. As Ding Darling fought hard to get politics out of wildlife management and science in, the Federation was working to make sure politics didn't oust scientific management. The resolution endorsed reliance on the judgment of "professional wildlife managers"—and not court decisions—for the "management of wildlife, including the establishment of open hunting seasons when the harvesting of animals is both desirable and necessary in order to protect the habitat or for other purposes." The convention also endorsed the management of predators by the use of "trained governmental professionals" rather than by the widespread application of poisons.

Wildlife managers have traditionally focused their attention on the environmental needs of game animals, and nongame animals almost invariably prosper alongside the game species. So, from the viewpoint of conservationists, support of wildlife management is support for animals in general. Most state laws, in fact, provide that the state is responsible for the welfare of all wildlife, game and nongame animals alike. State legislatures once provided for wildlife management only the funds that came from hunting and fishing licenses and taxes on arms and ammunition. In more recent times, however, most states have developed separate nongame programs, particularly ones for endangered species.

The protection of animal habitat has always won support from the Federation. The same 1971 resolution that backed wildlife managers also called for logging practices that would preserve patches of land, especially along stream banks and steep slopes, "to promote 'edge' effect for wildlife values."

In keeping with the idea of vigilance over habitat, National Wildlife Week has often been devoted to ecological problems that imperil animals—the loss of wetlands, pollution of the oceans, the loss of wildlife habitats in general. The Federation's National Wildlife Week that spotlighted the Key deer was followed by "Save the Prairie Chicken" in 1953. But not until 1982, when Wildlife Week was devoted to the eagle, was a single species again featured. In between were many themes promoting habitat protection.

The Pittman-Robertson Act had called for the federal government to assist state governments in the acquisition, restoration, and maintenance of habitat, but the idea of the Federation itself conserving habitat to protect an endangered species did not become a major program until the 1970s. The trail leading to that program began with concern over an endangered species, the American bald eagle.

In 1782, the Continental Congress designated the bald eagle the national symbol—over the objections of Benjamin Franklin, who pointed out that the eagle is a bird of prey. Franklin was ornithologically correct. But he missed the point. Americans then and later were not interested in the bird's behavior. The eagle was a heroic symbol—a handsome guardian on the dollar bill, a fierce protector on the presidential seal, a brave comrade on military insignia, even a patriotic trademark on cigar bands.

But farmers and ranchers, seeing what Franklin had seen, killed eagles as birds that preyed on livestock. Most states offered bounties on eagles and other raptors. In Alaska alone, from 1923 to 1940, bounties were paid for the killing of 103,459 bald eagles. Not until 1940 was the killing of eagles outlawed—with the exclusion of those in Alaska. (The Alaska eagle bounty ended in 1953. In 1972, Alaska gave some protection to eagles by passing legislation to protect certain habitats, including a stretch of the Chilkat River where as many as 3,500 bald eagles wintered.)

The 1940 Bald Eagle Protection Act punished with a $500 fine (now $10,000 to $20,000) and/or six months in prison (now one to two years) anyone who would "take, possess, sell, purchase, barter, or offer to sell, purchase or barter, transport, export or import" any bald eagle, dead or alive. The law broadly defines "taking" to mean "to pursue, shoot, shoot at, poison, wound, kill, capture, trap, collect, molest, or disturb."

But the killing went on—deliberately and unlawfully by the eagle's old enemies and by poachers peddling trophies, carelessly and lawfully by people using pesticides or accidentally fouling eagle nesting sites. In 1971, the Federation made its first move toward giving the eagle special attention by offering a $500 reward for information leading to the conviction of eagle killers. (One reward went to Fred Hamilton, a duck-hunting guide in Tennessee. He was watching soaring eagles one day when he saw one shot by someone in a nearby duck blind. Hamilton helped to identify the man in the blind, who was fined $1,000.)

The public was slow to realize that the eagle was not just a national symbol but an embattled animal facing extinction. By the 1970s, only about 2,000 northern bald eagles and 600 southern bald eagles (whose nesting range is roughly south of the 40th parallel) still lived in the lower forty-eight states. According to a 1973 estimate, only eight states had more than twenty-five nests. (About 6,000 eagles were thought to live in Alaska.)

Federation officials, who with the Key deer had discovered the value of a single species as a symbol of wildlife in danger, saw in the bald eagle an even more appealing symbol. For the eagle was an animal that Americans recognized and cherished. A crusade to save the eagle would attract Americans who never ventured out of doors, Americans who neither hunted nor fished, Americans who had never heard of the National Wildlife Federation. By helping the eagle, the Federation could also help itself.

The eagle would take wing over an environmental revolution that blazed throughout the 1970s. Ecology had entered everyday speech. Pollution had become a political issue. People demanded clean air and water—and they were joining conservation organizations. Membership in the National Audubon Society, which had hovered at around 45,000, soared to 193,000 in 1972. The Sierra Club had 35,000 members in 1966—and 137,000 in 1972. By 1975, the circulation of *National Wildlife* had jumped to 605,000 and *Ranger Rick* to 256,000. The Federation, with more than three million members and supporters in all fifty states, the Virgin Islands, Puerto Rico, and Guam, was already the largest nongovernmental conservation organization in the world.

The save-the-eagle crusade was approached in a clearheaded, businesslike way. Administrative Vice President Ash Brownridge, at a board of directors meeting in March 1972, said many corporations wanted to get involved in conservation programs. "They are not interested in cleaning up rivers, putting books in schools," he told the board members, "but they do, however, want to do something that is going to catch the fancy of the public, and they felt the eagle would be one of them."

Executive Director Tom Kimball was frank about the value of the eagle as a symbol. "There have been attempts by some of our so-called friends in the conservation movement to establish the National Wildlife Federation as just a group of hunters and fishermen," he told the board, "and we think that a project that would involve attempting to do something for our national symbol has many advantages to offset that concept as well as to assist in our fund-raising activities."

Minutes of the 1972 board of directors meeting provide an insight into how the Federation had to balance concepts of mission with the realities of budget. Kimball knew that the Federation itself could not launch a major fund-raising project because there was no money for it. But he had a plan.

The Federation had been meeting with the U.S. Fish and Wildlife Service to see what could be done to save the eagle. The answer was the creation of a refuge. Fish and Wildlife Service experts particularly wanted a thousand-acre piece of Missouri River bottomland on the South Dakota-Nebraska border. Each year this bottomland served as a winter home for about three hundred eagles, approximately fifteen percent of the bald eagles found in the lower forty-eight states.

The tract (all but about nineteen acres of it in South Dakota) was located about two miles below the Fort Randall Dam, near Pickstown, South Dakota. Because water flowing from the dam kept a stretch of the Missouri from freezing, eagles there could get water and catch fish all winter. They roosted on tall cottonwood trees in a perfect winter habitat they shared with white-tailed deer, wild turkey, bob-white quail, Canada geese, mallards, foxes, beavers, muskrats, coyotes, opossums, raccoons, and an occasional bobcat.

The eagle-watchers knew that the site, like other places where bald eagles traditionally wintered, was threatened by poaching, pesticides, and commercial development. Purchase this land to make a refuge, Federation officials were told, and you will save generations of eagles. But the Federation did not have the necessary money—almost $300,000.

Federation officials, however, had a potential source for land-purchase money: corporations eager to benefit from association with a symbol such as the eagle. The board, under Kimball's direction, recommended that the Federation "develop a fund-raising program to buy land and to establish a Bald Eagle Refuge, such effort to include special educational materials to be distributed separately and in conjunction with other National Wildlife Federation promotional activities."

The board added one cautionary note: The program was to be conducted in such a way that the Federation's fund-raising expenses would be deducted from the gross proceeds—meaning the program would not cost the Federation any money. The board members also decided to keep secret the location of the proposed refuge so that property prices would not be driven up.

The plan became a reality only five months later when the Federation and the 7-Eleven food store chain launched a campaign to secure a refuge for the bald eagle. Southland Corporation of Dallas said that at its 5,000 7-Eleven stores each cup of Slurpee drink would be served in a "special endangered species collector cup" and a penny from the sale of each cup would be given to the Federation for its eagle refuge.

The plastic cups had on their sides an old Federation idea—natural-history drawings. The portraits of sixty endangered mammals, birds, amphibians, reptiles, and fishes were done by wildlife artist Charles Ripper. Slurpee sippers, who consumed 15 to 20 million cups of the flavored drinks a year, were urged to "Save 'Em All—Save a Living Thing," just as previous Slurpee promotions had urged collectors to drink their way through a set of cups portraying baseball players, football players, or comic-book characters.

Drink and save they did. The Slurpee fans consumed 20.4 million cups of the drink. That produced $204,000 for purchase of the land. Customers in 7-Eleven stores also dropped $37,785.96 (mostly in small coins) into "Save a Living Thing" donation boxes. The Federation received $6,600 in direct contributions.

On December 19, 1974, Kimball thanked 7-Eleven for a "fitting Christmas present to the nation"—the land for the Missouri River eagle refuge. Control of the land was turned over to the Department of the Interior in a ceremony at the Federation's Washington headquarters. The land included a deed to 818 acres and a conservation easement covering another 305 acres.

Undersecretary of the Interior John C. Whitaker, accepting the deed for the land, said that the new refuge would be named for the late Senator Karl E. Mundt of South Dakota, who had introduced the original endangered species act in 1966. Whitaker also presented Kimball with a letter from President Gerald Ford, who wrote, "This generous gift is an outstanding demonstration of cooperative volunteer action by all those involved. . . . On behalf of the American people, I thank all of you who have worked to make this donation. I hope that your action will serve as a model for others to follow."

The president's hope was fulfilled not long afterward, when the Federation worked out an agreement with the Pacific Gas and Electric Company to protect nine eagle nests in California. The experience led to discussions with six utility companies to find ways to stop the electrocution of eagles on high-tension wires. With the Federation's help, the utilities developed designs for power line structures that would be safer for eagles and other roosting birds.

The success of the eagle crusade stimulated the Federation's Land Heritage program, which had been set up in 1973 primarily to promote gifts to the Federation of land (and other assets) that would be used for the preservation of wildlife habitats. (This program has evolved into the Planned Giving program of today.) NWF board member Ray Nesbit, serving as volunteer head of the program, began scouting for other endangered eagle habitats.

In the Upper Mississippi River Valley, Nesbit talked to members of EVE, the Eagle Valley Environmentalists. They told him about a 150-acre spot along the Wisconsin River near Sauk City, Wisconsin, where eagles congregated. Nesbit then asked the Federation to find a corporate purchaser for the eagle habitat, known as Ferry Bluff Roost. Anheuser-Busch donated the $47,000 needed to purchase the land, the Federation named it Ferry Bluff Eagle Sanctuary, and called on EVE to run it.

The crusade was working, both for the bird and for the Federation, which was becoming recognized as the leader in the campaign to save the eagle. A National Wildlife Federation television spot about the bald eagle, for example, drew 2,400 responses, compared to 107 responses for a Bing Crosby "Save Our Wetlands" spot and 945 in reaction to a Lorne Greene spot on habitats. The Federation capitalized on the national interest in the eagle by underwriting a documentary film, "Everybody's Eagle," which was widely distributed and critically acclaimed.

The save-the-eagle campaign came as the nation prepared for its bicentennial celebration. As 1976 drew near, the interest in the bicentennial generated extensive research about eagles. Responding to the need for coordination among eagle researchers, the Federation set up a computerized "eagle data bank" for dissemination of information to libraries and laboratories across the nation. Exxon Company, U.S.A., contributed $85,000 to help launch the data bank, which was designated an official bicentennial program. The data bank quickly expanded into the NWF Raptor Information Center. What had begun in 1974 as an image-building, land-buying, save-the-eagle campaign was leading the Federation down other paths as well.

By the time of the bicentennial, *Save the eagle* became a rallying cry for those who would save the environment. Partly because of its campaign to help the eagle, the Federation became closely identified with all organizations that saw the saving of endangered animal species and their habitat as a continuing effort rather than as solitary conservation projects.

The tempo of the save-the-eagle crusade changed from a one-time fund-raising campaign to a permanent Federation program for eagles and their kin, collectively called raptors. Dr. Jeffrey L. Lincer, hired to start the eagle data bank, said that more than a bank was needed. In the course of discussing it with more than eighty scientists, agency personnel, and other individuals representing many different disciplines, he said, "it became obvious that the needs of our raptors far exceeded the original expectations." The bank expanded its charter so that it accepted entries not only on eagles but also on other raptors.

Raptors are fascinating birds especially equipped for their lives as birds of prey. All have sharp, powerful talons for grasping and killing prey and hooked beaks for tearing flesh. Their eyes, by some estimates, are eight times as sharp as human eyes. Modifications from the basic raptor design give species what they need for what they do: the osprey, which eats only fish, has an outer toe that rotates to aid in gripping a slippery catch; the falcon's upper beak is notched in such a way that the bird can break the neck of the prey it has seized.

Study of such a diverse group of birds involves "intensive research and free-flowing communications between researchers," Lincer said, adding that what was needed was a "clearinghouse"—an idea that harkened back to Ding Darling's earliest manifestos. Using at first the $37,785.96 from the 7-Eleven money boxes (some Federation staffers called the money a Slurpee-lus), the Federation transformed the relatively modest eagle data bank project into a major, wide-ranging program: the Raptor Information Center. The chief missions of the center were "to identify and protect critical raptor habitat; increase communications among raptor scientists and managers; monitor raptor populations; and identify and encourage the support of priority raptor research."

At first, eagles dominated the work of the center. Letters telling of the need to identify bald eagle habitats went out to all Federation affiliates. When a besieged habitat was found, the center passed the information on to the Land Heritage Committee with a recommendation that the land be leased or purchased. After helping to develop the Karl Mundt National Wildlife Refuge and the Ferry Bluff Eagle Sanctuary, the Federation was involved in the acquisition of two other winter roosting sites: the 105-acre Oak Valley Eagle Refuge on the Mississippi near East Moline, Illinois, and the 960-acre Three Sisters

Bald Eagle Preserve adjoining the Klamath National Forest in California.

With funding from the U.S. Fish and Wildlife Service and the states of Virginia and Maryland, the center launched a Chesapeake Bay bald eagle banding project and, in January 1979, a nationwide midwinter bald eagle survey. About 2,600 people helped to count 9,834 bald eagles in that first survey, which became an annual event. (In the 1986 continental survey, volunteers and state and federal wildlife officials in thirty-eight states counted more than 8,300 adult and immature eagles.)

The Chesapeake is the largest of the nation's 840 estuaries and, in terms of eagles and other wildlife, one of the most fertile. But bald eagles had been dying off there, as they had been dying at many other places in North America. Between 1936 and 1970, the number of eagles nesting around the bay dropped from an estimated 600 to fewer than 90.

"This decline," a National Wildlife Federation report said, "was caused by habitat destruction and a build-up of DDE, a form of the pesticide DDT, in the fish and birds the eagles feed on. As they consumed this contaminated prey, DDE accumulated in the eagles and caused them to lay thin-shelled eggs that would break before hatching. Another pesticide, dieldrin, also built up in the eagles' bodies and caused some to die." Adding to the problem was the predator's natural inclination to single out sick or wounded prey. Eagles—and other fish-eaters like falcons and osprey—sought out ailing fish, many of which were dying of poisoning, thus increasing the intake of poison into their own systems.

When the Raptor Information Center began making its annual surveys, DDT and dieldrin had been banned and bald eagles were making a comeback on their bay home grounds, the fourth largest eagle breeding ground in the lower forty-eight states. The centers first banding team found thirty-six nests and banded thirty-seven young eagles.

The banding operation begins each February when spotter planes make a series of flights over the vast bay to survey the extent of the eagles' nest-building and nest-repairing, which usually has started in December. Working from maps based on the nest-spotting overflights, the banding crews visit nests between May 1 and June 15 to band the nestlings, which by then are four to eight weeks old.

The nests are relatively easy to spot from the air because eagles invariably select nesting sites close to the water and high in towering trees—the height of nesting trees around the bay averages 90 feet.

The nests are big and bulky, a jumble of sticks sometimes five feet across and three or four feet deep. Some eagles choose the same nest year after year; others switch from one to another of several nests scattered about a breeding territory.

By 1985, the project had expanded into a complex operation for the study of the reproductive success of eagles in 126 nests. The operation had become more than a banding project. In 1985, for example, eagle banders participated in an attempt to restore the bald eagle in North Carolina. After receiving permission from state wildlife agencies in Maryland and Virginia, banders plucked six nestlings from their Chesapeake Bay nests and gave them to the North Carolina Wildlife Resources Commission, which, after fledging them, released them in the eastern part of the state. In another experiment, a researcher attached radio transmitters to seven nestlings for a study of bald eagle movements and habitat preference.

At one nest, three nestlings were lowered to the ground and a veterinarian from the U.S. Fish and Wildlife Service's Patuxent Wildlife Research Center took a blood sample from each bird to study the geographic gene flow among bald eagle populations. Two dead birds found at other locations were taken to Patuxent for autopsies. The species of trees holding nests were recorded. The remains of food found in some nests were removed and analyzed to determine the eagles' most likely prey. (Besides the basic diet of fish, the eagles' food included snow geese, herons, robins, squirrels, and, at nineteen nests, turtles.)

One heartening aspect of the annual banding report had to do with human beings. Although eighty-four percent of the occupied nests were on private land, "there was no evidence that human disturbance led to any nesting failures this season [1985]." Because eagles and people share the Bay, the Raptor Information Center published a guide for landowners who have eagles on their property. The guide explains that eagles are most sensitive to disturbance by people during the most crucial events of the reproduction cycle—nest-building, incubation, and the nestlings' first month.

Landowners are also advised on how best to establish "protection zones." One landowner, the vast U.S. Army Aberdeen Proving Ground, remarkably contains twenty or more of the Bay's eagle nests. The center advises the Army on how to fire weapons and detonate high explosives without disturbing the eagles that have chosen to nest where most people would fear to tread.

The center's work as a significant scientific publisher began not with a publication about the eagle, but with the *Working Bibliography of Owls of the World*. This publication had its start, according to its senior authors, "as an academic diversion for a couple of aspiring students of ornithology seeking escape from the intense pressures of graduate course work."

The students, Richard J. Clark and Dwight G. Smith, met for the first time at an ornithological conference in 1973 and discovered that each of them had been working separately on an owl bibliography. "As we talked," one of them recalled, "it became apparent that the only sensible thing to do was to pool our efforts." They later asked Leon H. Kelso, an expert on the owls of South America, to join them. They took their project to the newly formed Raptor Information Center, which agreed to publish the work.

The owl bibliography, which contains about 6,800 references, reaffirmed the concept of a clearinghouse for wildlife information. It became Number 1 of the National Wildlife Federation Scientific/Technical Series.

Publication Number 2 of the series was *Working Bibliography of the Bald Eagle*. Approximately 2,000 entries were codified, as in the owl bibliography, through a keyword system by subject and geographic area. The center has published similar bibliographies on the golden eagle, the genus Aquila, and the peregrine falcon.

Lincer, who signed on as the first director of the bald eagle data bank and saw that bank quickly become the center, left when, in his words, it was like an eyas—"still developing its muscles, not yet airborne, but occasionally lifting itself on new feathers not yet hard-penned." One of Lincer's legacies is the *Eyas*, which began as a newsletter and, evolving as swiftly as the center, became a fully fledged publication that appears three times a year. The *Eyas* is directed toward professional wildlife managers, biologists, and others whose responsibilities include the protection of birds of prey.

At center-run workshops, conservation law enforcement officers learn what they need to know to uphold laws protecting raptors, including how to handle injured raptors. Other workshops deal with the management of raptors in specific regions. The Southwest symposium and workshop in 1986, for example, gave information on endangered or threatened raptors found only in that region. Wildlife and land managers heard about the impact of mining and grazing on raptor survival and ways to offset habitat loss from these and other encroachments. And the losses of birds and habitats are serious. A 1982 study showed that forty of the fifty-three species of birds of prey living in the United States were considered by wildlife agencies to be endangered.

In 1984, the Federation showed its special feelings about raptors by helping to establish "National Birds of Prey Conservation Week." The roots for this week can be traced back to 1956 and researchers at Bake Oven Knob, Pennsylvania. There, in the words of one researcher and writer, Donald S. Heintzelman, "dozens of gunners frequented shooting blinds at this site and elsewhere along this ridge. Day after day I watched men in these blinds engaged in their deadly activities, watched then-unprotected hawks blasted from the sky or wounded birds glide into the forest to die in pain and misery."

Several researchers and hawk watchers, who called themselves "ridgerunners," darted among the gunners to gather evidence for the prosecution of people who shot osprey, peregrine falcons, and other species that were protected. "At times," Heintzelman said, "the visits were made at considerable risk. Indeed, on three separate occasions, hawk shooters peppered the trees overhead with pellets from their shotguns."

In 1957, all of the hawks migrating along the ridge were given state protection, and the shootout at Bake Oven Knob became history. In ensuing years, several states, from New Hampshire to Wisconsin, declared birds of prey weeks. Then, at the Federation's annual meeting in March 1984, the Pennsylvania Federation of Sportsmen's Clubs, a National Wildlife Federation affiliate, introduced a resolution calling for a National Birds of Prey Week. The resolution passed and the Federation went to work.

Pennsylvania's Senator Arlen Specter and Representative Donald Ritter introduced bills declaring the week. They found little support among colleagues, however, until one day Migisiwa, a bald eagle on loan to the Federation from the U.S. Fish and Wildlife Service, appeared with his handler on the steps of the Capitol. Members of Congress lined up to have their photographs taken with the nation's symbol.

Because of a broken wing that could not be repaired, Migisiwa could not return to the wild. Before his death in 1986, Migisiwa helped his kin by making educational public appearances like the one on the Capitol steps. And that day he earned his keep. Before Migisiwa's visit, 125 members of Congress supported the birds of prey week; after Migisiwa's visit, 223 supported it. National Birds of Prey Week was celebrated the second week of October, 1984.

This touch of showmanship momentarily brought public attention to birds of prey, but a far more significant measure of the success of NWF and its Raptor Information Center has been scientists' acceptance and use of the center's work and publications. Acceptance also was demonstrated by the Federation's board, which used the raptor center as a template for the establishment in 1981 of the Institute for Wildlife Research, which became the overseer of the Raptor Information Center, the Feline Research Center (founded in 1981), and the Bear Research Center (founded in 1984).

The paths to the research centers can be traced to concerns expressed at the 1970 annual meeting, when the resolutions about grizzlies, mountain lions, and birds of prey were passed. Few people at that meeting could have predicted that the Federation had taken its first steps down those paths. But, as often happens with the unexpected path, it appears logical and obvious when looked back on from a distance.

The early 1970s also saw NWF officials looking more closely at conservation issues beyond American borders. The launching of *International Wildlife* magazine in 1971 coincided with the new worldview. A year after the first issue was published, at the same time the United Nations "Conference on the Human Environment" was held, the Federation sponsored a separate, international symposium—also held in Stockholm, and called "Uniting Nations for Biosurvival." During the conference, NWF distributed a World Environmental Quality Index, the only nongovernment report officially passed out to all delegates of both conferences. This symposium gave the Federation credentials as an organization with scientific and international interests.

Also in 1972, and later in 1976, Executive Director Tom Kimball was a member of the U.S. delegation to annual meetings of the U.S.-USSR Joint Committee on Cooperation in the Field of Environmental Protection. He also participated in the International Whaling Conference and the World Energy Conference. The Federation, the National Audubon Society, and other conservation groups cooperated in the delivery of whale-protection petitions to the Soviet and Japanese embassies in Washington. The Federation's work expanded greatly in this decade and ranged from helping establish the Arctic National Wildlife Range to giving advice on establishing bird sanctuaries in India.

"The National Wildlife Federation," Kimball said in 1974, "is an organization that has successfully united birdwatcher and hunter; preservationist and conservationist; protectionist and consumptive user in the wildlife cause." It was not the definition that was new; it was the setting: a symposium sponsored by NWF at its annual meeting. The symposium examined what a distinguished scientist, Dr. A. Starker Leopold, called the current dilemma of hunting versus protectionism.

Though it did not settle the issue of hunter versus antihunter, the symposium showed that the Federation was managing to keep its divergent groups under one roof. The symposium also displayed the Federation in the role of scientific coordinator. To study the use of satellites to track wildlife, for example, who needed to be involved? Answer: The U.S. Geological Survey, the National Aeronautics and Space Administration, the U.S. Fish and Wildlife Service, the Canadian Wildlife Service, and the International Association of Fish and Wildlife Agencies. The Federation was the catalyst that brought them all together.

In the 1970s, the Federation began sponsoring sessions on wildlife topics at the annual meeting of the American Association for the Advancement of Science, which heard papers on such subjects as what species may become extinct in the next century and how environmental modification affects wildlife.

A fellowship program, set up in 1951 with a grant from the James Hopkins estate, encourages research and has enhanced the Federation's scientific reputation. An early fellowship sponsored a series of sophisticated studies of salmon, done in cooperation with Canadian and Danish scientists. Other fellowships have covered a wide range of interests, from studies of humpback whales to a survey of children's gardening in America.

From 1971 to 1985, matching grants from the Federation and the American Petroleum Institute bolstered the fellowship program. The joint fellowships funded important research on the problem of oil exploration and drilling in wildlife areas. One study concentrated on a potential oil field in Alaska, where ninety percent of the breeding population of the emperor goose nested; another study examined the effects of oil on the developing larvae of bivalve shellfish.

Not all wildlife habitats are as far away as Alaska, and not all of them require sophisticated, professional management programs to support populations of wild animals. A wildlife habitat can be as close as your city park, or even your yard. The Federation's Backyard Wildlife Habitat program, begun in 1973, instructs participants on how to use simple scientific principles in transforming a yard into an oasis for wildlife. But more than interest in science is involved in getting people to compensate for shrinking wildlife habitats by creating little refuges in their backyards. People become caught up in the magic of seeing wildlife outside the window. They learn how to provide water and nesting sites, how to build a birdhouse or feeding station. They get tips on birdwatching from Roger Tory Peterson. And many of them write it all down in a journal they hope someday will be a family treasure.

More than 4,600 lovingly developed little refuges are registered in the official Backyard Wildlife Habitat rolls. The habitats include gardens behind ordinary houses and tracts behind governor's mansions, ribbons of land alongside schools and shops, meticulously tended three-acre lots—even an eighty-square-foot plot outside an office condominium.

Thousands of requests for information pour into Federation headquarters every time the Backyard Wildlife Habitat program is mentioned on a television show—in particular, "The Victory Garden" on public television—or in print—*Time* one month, *Reader's Digest* or *Better Homes and Gardens* another. Backyard wildlife managers get tips all year long from "Backyard Naturalist" Craig Tufts, director of the Federation's urban wildlife programs; his column is distributed to hundreds of weekly and daily newspapers.

The National Wildlife Federation's own Backyard Wildlife Habitat blooms at its 43-acre Laurel Ridge Conservation Education Center in a northern Virginia suburb of Washington, D.C. The land, much of which has been set aside for nature programs, is one of scores of parcels acquired by the Federation as gifts, legacies, and purchases in what began as the Land Heritage program. Many of these properties are sold and the proceeds used for conservation. One farm donated to the Federation in 1975, for example, was sold in 1986 for $8.5 million. The proceeds were used to create an endangered species fund.

The work of the Federation's Institute for Wildlife Research, which manages the raptor, feline, and bear research centers, provides grants for a wide range of research. A 1985 report indicates the span of its activities:

- Funding to the University of Michigan School of Natural Resources to underwrite the cost of reprinting the *Endangered Species Technical Bulletin*. Federal budget slashes cut back distribution of this bulletin, the official source of information about federal work on endangered species.

- A grant to support research on the behavior of the margay and jaguarundi in Belize. Specialists studying these small cats believe they may still exist in the American Southwest. Anticipating possible management of them in the United States, researchers want to study them in Belize, where they are more easily found.

- Funding of a moose radio-telemetry study at Isle Royale National Park in Michigan. Researchers have been studying wolf-moose relationships for nearly three decades, but many questions about the management of a wolf-moose habitat remain controversial. The institute funded the moose research in the belief that continued studies "build upon past knowledge and postulate future consequences of management decisions."

- Funding of a Michigan School of Natural Resources workshop on minimum viable population size. As civilization encroaches on wildlife habitat, wildlife managers are continually asked to play God and use formulas derived from such studies to maintain enough of particular habitats so that all the individual species that normally inhabit them are able to survive. In recent years, species especially threatened by loss of habitat have included grizzly bears and birds such as owls and woodpeckers. "Most of the work in this area," the institute report said, "is highly theoretical and based upon mathematical models." The workshop was designed to "help bridge the gap between theory and reality."

- Continued funding of survey techniques to search out undiscovered populations of black-footed ferrets, often cited as North America's rarest and most endangered mammal.

- Partial funding of a project to study more than 6,000 nestling ospreys banded in the Chesapeake Bay area. The project—"an unprecedented opportunity" to study a large bird population— will also monitor the osprey as efforts continue to control pollution sources in the Bay.

The institute's Feline Research Center, unlike the Raptor Information Center, was an idea quickly transformed into reality. Dr. Maurice Hornocker, an internationally renowned biologist, is the Federation's senior scientific advisor to the feline center, which has focused on North American cats.

Hornocker is famous for his pioneering field studies of wild cats. Before him, no one had made extensive investigations of the behavior of cougars and other American wild cats. Hornocker began his career in Montana in 1963 when he hired hunters to find and tree cougars— the preferred local name for *Felis concolor*—at $50 per treed cat.

As soon as a cougar was up a tree, the hunters summoned Hornocker, who hiked to the spot, shot the cat with a tranquilizer gun, then climbed the tree and carried down the stunned but conscious cat—which sometimes was not quite tranquilized enough. His first cat groggily took a swipe at Hornocker, who grabbed it by the tail and flung it down into a snow drift.

Year after year, Hornocker went into the wilderness to capture cats, tag and tattoo them, and produce enough solid scientific information to dispel generations of myths. "I heard stories about cougars carrying yearling colts over ten-foot fences," he recalled. "Of course, that's impossible, but because there was no one to refute all the tall tales, cougar myths such as that one were common."

Hornocker's studies helped to change public opinion about the cougar, which, like the eagle, had long been a target of bounty hunters because they were accused of wanton, wasteful killing of livestock and game. "Maurice has demonstrated that the cougar is not the bloodthirsty cattle and big-game killer it was long thought to be," said S. Douglas Miller, vice president in charge of wildlife research for the National Wildlife Federation. "He has also shown other animal researchers the importance of presenting scientific data in popular, layman's terms. He has helped close some big information gaps—both for the public and for other scientists."

One of the information gaps Hornocker closed was the one about cougars depriving hunters of big game: From what he observed, "cougars killed deer or elk that were less fit either behaviorally or physically. The cats didn't really select their prey. The prey was selected for the cougars by other factors in the environment. Cougars certainly kill big-game animals, but the effect of that killing is often exaggerated. In our area, it was insignificant to the populations of deer and elk."

With a research grant from the Institute for Wildlife Research, Hornocker in 1986 began his twenty-sixth year studying cats in the wild. His research took him to the familiar isolation of Idaho's River of No Return Wilderness Area and to a new locale: Yellowstone National Park, for the first major study of the park's mountain lions.

Studies of bears in national parks were among the earliest projects of the Bear Research Center. Yellowstone and Glacier National Parks, in particular, contain prime bear habitat. In recent years, these popular parks also have had great difficulty in coping with an ever-increasing flow of visitors. The visitors, many of them campers, put pressures on park officials charged with maintaining a balance between the needs of visitors and the needs of wildlife. The most notorious problem has involved the clash for space between campers and bears, especially grizzly bears.

The grizzly bear's reputation as the most dangerous animal in North America, says the authoritative Walker's *Mammals of the World*, "may be true"—if "we disregard venomous insects, disease-spreading rodents, domestic animals, and people themselves." Rationally perceived, the bear is not a monster. But the primordial fear of grizzlies transcends all other dangers confronted in the outdoors.

Grizzly bears may not be monsters, but they can be dangerous. In Glacier, grizzlies killed two young women in a single night in 1967; they were the first such deaths since the park opened in 1910. In 1980, bears killed three people in the park and another person in Canada. Yellowstone's first recorded killing of a person by a bear came in 1972. Frightening encounters between bears and campers and hikers have become more commonplace in the parks.

The deaths and the scares inspired demands for more protection of people and less protection of bears. National Park Service authorities surrounded themselves with experts, each with a different solution. Hovering over the problem is the federal endangered species law. The grizzly has been declared threatened in the lower forty-eight states. Federal regulations about grizzlies are extremely complicated; the law allows the killing of threatening bears and even, under certain circumstances, the hunting of them, for sport, outside the parks. But grizzlies cannot be simply "managed" out of a park; under the law, they must be protected.

The issue of how to handle the bear problem at Yellowstone flared again in May 1986. As thousands of visitors poured into the park for its first big weekend of the season, the Park Service announced that the Fishing Bridge Camping Ground, where bears had frequently confronted campers, would be open to campers again that summer. The announcement had the effect of a challenge to environmentalists, especially the Federation, for years before the Park Service had agreed to close Fishing Bridge if doing so was necessary to keep bears and campers apart.

The Federation and other environmental organizations knew that Fishing Bridge was in a major grizzly habitat; bear-camper confrontations would be inevitable. And this meant that bears would be relocated or slain. Relocation does not always work, for often the bears return. To park managers, whose job it is to keep campers happy and bears alive, a prodigal bear is a serious problem, an uncooperative creature that does not understand good management techniques. Uncooperative bears do not have much of a future in Yellowstone.

Adding to the issue of how best to cope with bears that visit campgrounds were the business people in the communities around the park. The business people translated the proposed closing of the camping ground into a decrease in visitors and revenue. The business interests not only strongly opposed the closing, but also asked members of the Wyoming congressional delegation to put pressure on the Park Service. And Fishing Bridge Camping Ground was opened for the season.

The Federation has always understood that wildlife management often involves judgment that may ignite controversy. The Federation also understands how politics can influence management decisions; ever since its founding the Federation has been a broker between wildlife managers and competing outside interests. But when the Federation believes that political considerations threaten the welfare of wildlife, the Federation's role changes from broker to advocate.

As an advocate, the Federation can stay inside the controversy, working to get federal or state officials to stand up for wildlife. The Federation can also call on its members and the public to come to the aid of the animals threatened by a political decision. Finally, the Federation can go to court and seek a legal remedy.

When the National Wildlife Federation and its affiliate, the Wyoming Wildlife Federation, went to U.S. District Court in Cheyenne and sued the Park Service over the management of bears in Yellowstone,* the Federation was carrying on an old tradition. A courtroom can also be a place to protect wildlife habitat.

*As of March 1987, this case had not been decided.

7

Getting the Law on Our Side

The new National Wildlife Federation was struggling through the Depression and its own financial quicksand when its first milestone came into view. The milestone was called the Pittman-Robertson Act, and only an organization like the brash young Federation would have championed it at all. At a time when money was scarce and New Deal politicians' eyes were turned toward hard-pressed cities and farms, the Pittman-Robertson Act called for a new deal for wildlife. In an era of dust bowls and soup lines, aid to ducks and deer seemed far-fetched. But there it stood on the trail: milestone number one. It could not be ignored.

The Pittman-Robertson Act, formally known as the Federal Aid in Wildlife Restoration Act, earmarked revenues from a federal excise tax on firearms and ammunition for a "federal aid to wildlife restoration fund." In its founding days the Federation made passage of the act its prime mission. Largely through the letter-writing of the diversified members of the Federation's affiliates, national politicians saw for the first time the extent of grass-roots support for wildlife, and the act became law in 1937.

The law was a milestone for the Federation because here, at this early point, a decision had to be made. Congress had passed the law. But bureaucrats could divert the excise tax revenues from where the law directed them to go. The law needed a sentinel. NWF had to decide whether to take on this additional role, and it did. The decision to function as a wildlife sentinel resulted in a series of milestones, year after year, decade after decade, each one marking a time when the

Federation had to take a stand on other issues before federal and state agencies, before congressional committees, and ultimately in courtrooms. It all began here, with the Pittman-Robertson Act.

The gun and ammunition excise tax is the source of money for what has come to be known as state Pittman-Robertson projects. The revenue raised by the Pittman-Robertson Act goes into a fund that contributes seventy-five percent of the cost of such projects; the state contributes twenty-five percent. By 1939, forty-three states had passed the state laws necessary for receiving Pittman-Robertson project funds. Most of the early projects were for acquiring habitat and studying wildlife problems.

The year the Pittman-Robertson Act was passed, Congress appropriated $1 million as an advance that would be paid back when the tax money began coming in. The following fiscal year, $1 million again was appropriated. Carl Shoemaker, the Federation's watchdog in Washington, discovered that from July 1938 to January 1939 the U.S. Treasury had recorded more than $2 million brought in by the excise tax—more than enough to repay the initial seed money and beef up the Pittman-Robertson fund.

Shoemaker drummed out the news through the Federation newsletter, affiliates responded with letters and phone calls, and Shoemaker, a one-man lobbying organization, made his rounds of Capitol Hill offices. And he was successful. In March 1939, the newsletter reported that Congress had added $1.5 million to the $1 million originally appropriated.

Ironically, though, the watchdogging to keep one law on track was putting the Federation in legal jeopardy with a law on another track. As a nonprofit association organized for educational purposes, the Federation in October of 1938 had secured a 101(8) status, the equivalent of today's 501(C)(4) status, which meant that NWF paid no income tax. Federation officials also wanted to attain a 101(6) status, the equivalent of today's 501(C)(3) status. This designation would mean that all contributions to NWF would be tax-deductible, which would attract more and larger donations to the Federation.

But both the U.S. Treasury and the Unemployment Compensation Board of the District of Columbia rejected petitions for the new tax status in 1939. The reason given: the Federation's activities as "sponsor" of the Pittman-Robertson Act.

In July 1940, Federation President David Aylward revealed his worries about the 101(6) issue. In a memorandum to I. R. Watts, director of the Federation's still-new Servicing Division, Aylward quoted a provision of the law: efforts at propaganda or "otherwise attempting to

influence legislation" must constitute "no substantial part of the activities" of an association to which contributions were tax-deductible.
From now on, Aylward told Watts, "perhaps we shall have to do indirectly and more subtly some of the things we have been doing openly
in the past if we are to avoid these [101(6)] taxes."

Until the tax law changed in 1976, the Federation, like other nonprofit organizations, practiced being subtle and indirect. Officials
learned to deal with legislators discreetly. No representative of the
organization could boast, as Shoemaker had, that he had written a
law.

In 1940, the Income Tax Division of the Treasury Department, as
well as the Social Security Division and the District Unemployment
Compensation Board, "descended upon the Federation with a sort of
legal blitzkrieg," as Watts later described it. The Income Tax Division
ruled that the request for a 101(6) exemption must be reexamined;
the other agencies ruled against the exemption. During that year and
the next, Watts did considerable work preparing a brief and submit-
ting data to support the Federation's case.

In 1941, the tax authorities again ruled against the request for the
additional tax-exempt status. Early in 1942, Shoemaker himself—the
man who had written the Pittman-Robertson bill and had done much
to get support for it—petitioned the District Unemployment Compensation Board. In his letter, he stressed the Federation's educational
purpose, the encouragement of President Roosevelt and Secretary of
Agriculture Wallace, the Federation's unquestioned nonprofit status,
and the fact that he had prepared the Pittman-Robertson bill as part
of his duties as secretary of the Special Committee of the United States
Senate on the Conservation of Wildlife Resources. "The Federation,"
he wrote, "should not be charged with this responsibility."

The District Unemployment Compensation Board remained ada-
mant, as did the United States Treasury Department. On December
14, 1942, Aylward again applied to Internal Revenue for the additional tax-exempt status, this time arguing in effect that—by calling
the North American Wildlife Conference—the federal government
itself gave impetus to the formation and activities of the Federation.
"The Federation regards that whatever activities it carried on in connection with this bill . . . it did so under direction from the North
American Wildlife Conference, where it had its origin." What the
Federation did in connection with the Pittman-Robertson legislation,
he said, should not be regarded "as any substantial part of its activities
nor an attempt to influence legislation." Three and a half pages of
the fifteen-page affidavit were devoted to an enumeration of the edu-

cational work the Federation had already accomplished from 1937 through 1942.

Possibly because of the education work, the desired tax status was finally granted in 1943. The ruling, however, was couched in terms warning that the tax officials retained their original position against outright lobbying. The ruling strongly implied that the Federation had better watch its step in the future. As to the Pittman-Robertson activities, the letter stated: "After a careful review of all the evidence, the Bureau adheres to its position that exemption cannot be allowed . . . for the calendar years of 1936 and 1937 due to your activities intended to influence legislation. . . . You are exempt . . . for 1938 and subsequent years, as it is believed that you are organized and now operate for educational purposes. Accordingly, you will not be required to file returns of income for 1938 and subsequent years unless you change the character of your organization, the purposes for which you were organized, or your method of operation. Any such changes should be reported immediately to the Collector of Internal Revenue. . . ."

The Federation now had both types of tax-exempt status. But what enhanced its finances severely restricted its conservation activities. The ban on lobbying threatened both the Federation's new 101(6) status and its years of hard work on what would become its second milestone, a law that would do for fish what the Pittman-Robertson Act had done for other wildlife.

In September 1938, the Federation newsletter had announced that "Washington headquarters has begun sounding out those among its Capitol Hill friends" who would support legislation to assist state fisheries. "The procedure we are suggesting," the newsletter said, "is that an excise tax on sales of fishermen's equipment shall be earmarked for use in projects to safeguard and restore our vanishing fishing resources."

The following May the newsletter reported that Congressman Frank Buck of California had introduced in the House a bill "sponsored and prepared by your National Wildlife Federation." Members were urged to "immediately sit down, take your pen or pencil in hand and write a personal letter to your Congressmen and your Senators, urging them to support the bill. . . ." The newsletter also suggested that the members get civic clubs, garden clubs, women's groups, and other conservation organizations to write similar letters.

The fisherman's version of the Pittman-Robertson Act, however, was temporarily snagged. When the Pittman-Robertson Act was first proposed, an excise tax on guns and ammunition already existed. But no such tax existed for fishing tackle, and manufacturers did not support the new proposal. Soon, though, as part of a wartime revenue package in the early 1940s, an excise tax was imposed on fishing tackle, along with many other items considered "non-essential" in time of war.

Consequently, the Federation didn't have to continue its blatant lobbying on the fishing bill. And thus the Federation was spared the risk of losing its tax-exempt status because of such "lobbying" as that earnest newsletter urging action on the fishing bill. Not until after the war, when the question of eliminating the wartime taxes arose in Congress, would the issue of a fishing tax fund appear again.

As a result of its efforts to acquire 101(6) status, NWF realized how strict the Internal Revenue Service was in defining lobbying as activities aimed at influencing legislation. The Federation also learned that policy studies, research, and public education were not considered lobbying. Consequently, its officials more and more sought ways to stress ideas and research. And it took care about venturing into congressional offices. Instead, it attempted to influence the federal agencies that carried out the laws—and supplied Congress with information that was intended to be transformed into laws.

An insight into this person-to-person agency lobbying comes from a memo written in October 1940 to Aylward by Watts. He begins by saying that he "paid a visit to the Department of Agriculture" and met with an executive assistant in the office of the Soil Conservation Service. The man "happened to be a fraternity brother of mine, which made things considerably more simple." The fraternity brother set up an immediate appointment with another official, who talked to Watts about ways in which the Federation could cooperate with the Soil Conservation Service. Watts then spoke to the acting chief of the Service's biology division, who told Watts he wanted information about wildlife needs in Ohio. Watts suggested the name of the rod and gun editor of the *Cleveland Plain Dealer* and held out the possibility of an article on the Soil Conservation Service in *American Wildlife*, a journal NWF published in cooperation with the American Wildlife Institute, precursor of the Wildlife Management Institute. "When I left there around 4 o'clock," Watts wrote, "I was about as full of information as I could hold."

Federation officials, unable to lobby Congress, used publications distributed to NWF members to rally their support for some legislation and to warn them of problems. "The House Appropriations Committee cut the Pittman-Robertson budget from three to two and a half million in their report," Watts reported to Aylward in May 1941. "If it's not put back on the floor, we'll get out a Conservation Information Service letter so that the boys out on the firing line can start working on this situation and their Senators if they care to (of course, in no way influenced by anything said in the C.I.S.)." The funds were restored. "I don't believe any other agency is responsible except the Federation," Aylward wrote Watts.

The Federation hoped to skirt the tax issue by using the Conservation Information Service as a lobbying channel. When bills were introduced to permit mining in the Organ Pipe Cactus National Monument in Arizona, for example, Aylward instructed Watts to "have a notice go out" and to talk to an executive of the National Parks Association, cautioning Watts: "I think you know the formula as to the language we should use."

The Federation also distributed to affiliates "canned" press releases for use in local newspapers. Here is one sent out in 1942. It is headlined *Wildlife Administration Endangered by Appropriation Cuts in Congress:*

> "Sportsmen and other conservationists are alarmed at the cuts recently made by the Lower House of Congress in the appropriations for the Fish and Wildlife Service," said (*Insert your name as officer, director or State Representative of the National Wildlife Federation or State Wildlife Federation*).
>
> Continuing, Mr. (*Insert your name here*) called attention to the cut made in Pittman-Robertson funds which are made available for federal aid to state wildlife restoration projects in 46 states of the Union. These revenues arise from an excise tax of 10% on sporting arms and ammunition.
>
> "At the present time this fund has nearly eight million dollars in it, which represents an accumulated surplus over former appropriations. It is money paid in willingly by the sportsmen of (*Name Your State*) and the other states of our country for the purpose of building up and restoring our wildlife and its environment of field, forest and water," said Mr. (*Insert your name here*).
>
> "The National Budget Director recommended that $2,250,000 be appropriated for Pittman-Robertson projects. The House cut this to $1,250,000, a wholly inadequate sum to carry on this important work the country over," said Mr. (*Insert your name here*).
>
> "A nationwide drive is being made among the sportsmen to write their Senators, asking them to urge the members of the Senate Appropriations Committee to restore this item to the full amount of $2,250,000 recommended by the Budget Director," he concluded.

In 1944, when a senator introduced a bill allowing federal agencies to have supervision over all wildlife populations on public lands, Federation officials "lobbied" by writing letters. It was a typical move. The officials believed that overriding constitutional rights would prevent the federal government from inflicting a tax punishment upon the Federation because citizens, exercising their freedom of speech, wrote to their legislators. The letters stated facts—in this case, facts in opposition—and that was educational, or so the argument went.

The letters of protest went to every representative and every senator, including the one who had introduced the bill. Only one representative said he would vote for the proposal—and the senator who had introduced it let it die, with the vow that he would never try the idea again.

Some lobbying was also concealed in the Federation-sponsored annual Conservation Conference, begun in 1953, and in small conferences on such matters as stream pollution and the relationship between farmland and wild land. Annual Conservation Conferences brought together the leaders of national conservation organizations and the International Association of Fish and Wildlife Agencies. In these closed and candid gatherings, strategies to influence legislation could be worked out, contacts made, ideas traded.

The law that was to become the Federation's second milestone— the fisherman's version of the Pittman-Robertson Act—reappeared in the legislative mists in 1949, when Representative John Dingell of Michigan drafted a bill similar to the one that Representative Buck had drawn up a decade before. Dingell teamed up with Senator Edwin C. Johnson of Colorado. The Federal Aid in Sport Fish Restoration Act, better known as the Dingell-Johnson Act, sailed through both houses of Congress. But President Truman vetoed the bill, arguing that the bill's earmarking of federal tax revenues "constitutes undesirable tax and fiscal policy." The bill, with slight changes made to please Truman, was introduced in 1950 and signed into law in July.

As a token of Carl Shoemaker's lobbying efforts, President Truman sent Shoemaker one of the pens used to sign the bill. The president's action conceivably could have triggered an Internal Revenue Service reaction, for the nonlobbying restrictions still prevailed. Federation officials constantly navigated between bringing down the wrath of the IRS by lobbying too much and becoming ineffectual by lobbying too little—or by not lobbying at all. The course was hard to steer because interpretations of IRS rules changed with every lawyer the Federation consulted, including the inevitable lawyers on its board of directors and among the officials of affiliates.

Lawyers pointed gravely to what was happening to other organizations, such as the Federation of Western Outdoor Clubs, which lost its tax-exempt status because, among other offenses, it passed resolutions on conservation issues "then the subject of political controversy" and urged members to "drop a line to your representatives telling them of your support of the Wilderness Bill."

Because "the distinction between what is and what is not substantial legislative activities is one of degree," a lawyer told the Federation in 1958, "it is advisable . . . to limit as much as possible the activities designed to influence legislation. From what we have learned of your activities, we do not believe that your tax status is jeopardized by the present level of legislative efforts. Particularly in controversial areas, however, it would be well to minimize publicity as to the influence of the Federation. In other words, even though the Federation deems it necessary to take an active part in certain legislation, it would be safer not to take credit for successes."

This last bit of lawyerly advice was not particularly difficult for the Federation to follow in the 1950s because there were not many legislative victories to take credit for. The Federation, reflecting the nation's mood of quiescence, was not stirring up Congress. Ernie Swift, an assistant director of the U.S. Fish and Wildlife Service under President Eisenhower, became executive director of the Federation and quietly watched over its slow and steady growth in numbers, if not in legislative influence.

At times, concern surfaced over the amount of energy the Washington office should devote to national issues. The problem was defined by a Rhode Island delegate to an NWF annual meeting: "I admit that practically everything that happened throughout the country is of some interest to us, but the bulk of our work is getting down to the local problems. . . . I feel that there is an overemphasis on the national legislation in the service rendered to the state groups. It is desirable, but I think we need additional help on, say, the Pennsylvania problem of too many deer or the Rhode Island problem of too many oysters."

Hovering unseen, perhaps, was a growing anti-Washington bias stemming from an ongoing national controversy over state's rights. State officials—and many of the Federation's state affiliates—were suspicious of the idea that federal legislation was needed to solve local problems. But NWF continued to stress that many issues touched every American in every state.

The Federation bannered "Clean Waters for All America" as its Wildlife Week theme in 1954 and "Save America's Wetlands" in 1955. The emphasis was on a national problem that was felt locally. As a follow up to these themes, officials worked with representatives and senators on a proposed federal water-pollution control law. There was even talk that NWF would join in suits against polluters. But a member of the Federation's board warned in 1958 that if the Federation accepted the idea of suing to stop water projects, "there would be no end to it and we would be spending practically all of our budget for fighting law suits on water all over the United States."

Fears of losing the (by now) 501(C)(3) tax status, which continued to attract contributors, persisted in the 1960s. The question was the same—how much lobbying was permissible. The IRS code said that an organization with a 501(C)(3) exemption could not devote more than an "insubstantial" part of its activities to "carrying on propaganda, or otherwise attempting to influence legislation." The Federation, a board member delicately suggested, "must respect the law sufficiently," meaning just enough so that NWF would not lose the precious status.

The keep-your-head-down advice clashed with the activist plans of Thomas L. Kimball, who had become executive director in 1960. One influential board member warned Kimball that if the Federation lost its tax status, "we might as well fold our tents and have the bugler call for a general retreat." If the IRS wants to make a test case, he continued, "in all probability they would pick National Wildlife Federation as the first objective."

Federation administrators could not even be sure whether it was safe to say in NWF literature, "Wire or write your congressman or senator." As an interim move, the Federation diffused the lobby issue by setting up "National Affairs Committees" in all congressional districts, thus seemingly passing to state affiliates the task of handling political issues. Officially, said a 1962 annual meeting statement, NWF "does not maintain any control whatever over policies or activities of the independent state affiliates," which "may seek the attainment of conservation objectives through whatever manner and means they may deem desirable and appropriate." For years, several affiliates maintained a 501(C)(4) tax status for the express purpose of being able to lobby. But, in reality, the National Affairs Committees received a great deal of support—and direction—from NWF headquarters.

Kimball, bridling against the restrictions, continued to dispatch Federation officials to congressional committee hearings on conservation legislation. According to some recollections, Kimball became more discreet about *requesting* invitations to testify, but he did not cut back on NWF appearances before committees. In fact, the Federation had standing invitations to attend the meetings of certain committees. These invitations were kept on file and used whenever needed.

Kimball insisted that the Federation's activities revolved around conservation issues and the education of the public. The distribution of information, definitely an educational activity, included sending *Conservation News* and the *Conservation Report* to every member of Congress, leaders of pertinent federal and state agencies, officers of state affiliates and leaders of the local clubs, leaders of other conservation organizations, and members of the media.

In 1966, the IRS stripped the Sierra Club of its 501(C)(3) tax status because of the club's advocacy on controversial issues. (The club still retained its 501(C)(4) tax status.) The alarms went off again at Federation headquarters. But Kimball, while maintaining "protective measures," stepped up the "education" of Congress. In 1967, members of the Federation's Washington staff made forty-four "personal appearances" on bills and wrote sixty-six letters or statements to "guide" lawmakers.

"We *could* express NWF policies," Louis Clapper, a veteran Federation lobbyist, recalled, "as determined by resolutions adopted in annual meetings, communications with the executive branch, agencies, or when our people met with presidents, departmental secretaries, bureau directors, and lesser officials. Indeed, NWF employees served on official advisory groups to several departmental secretaries.

"We *could* report on and analyze congressional legislation, and did, through the weekly *Conservation Report,* the semi-monthly *Conservation News,* and later, through inserts in *National Wildlife* and *International Wildlife* magazines.

"When invited by committees of the Congress, we *could* testify on specific bills and often would present statements thirty to forty times per session. . . . [We] *could not,* and *did not,* urge our affiliates or others to contact their members of the Congress on specific legislation."

Such "protective measures," however, did not stop the Federation from engaging in some underground activity. Because of NWF's cautious, behind-the-scene methods of influencing legislation, the Federation was not publicly connected with early efforts to produce what would become one of the century's momentous conservation laws, the Wilderness Act.

Howard Zahniser, executive director of the Wilderness Society, began seeking support for his idea—federally designated wilderness areas—in the 1950s. A personal friend of the Federation's Ernie Swift, Zahniser asked Swift for help. But Zahniser was against hunting, and NWF wasn't. Swift told Zahniser that if he expected to get Federation help, he would have to accept hunting in wilderness areas. He did.

Later, as the Wilderness Act began to gain congressional support,

Kimball, then executive director, discreetly allowed the Federation's mailing list to be used by the Wilderness Society. "We were told by many members of Congress," Clapper recalled, "that, as a result of that mailing, they received more mail in favor of the Wilderness Act than any other issue they'd ever had."

As the act reached the floor of Congress, the Federation, risking loss of its special tax status, openly campaigned for the act. "FINAL PUSH," said the *Special Bulletin* sent out in July 1964 by H. L. "Hap" Powers, chairman of the NWF National Affairs Committee. He told state affiliate officers that "action" [unspecified] was needed at once on the Wilderness Act. Members of the Federation's board of directors not only endorsed the act; they applauded when they heard a report about NWF work on "the first order of business"—passage of the act.

When the historic Wilderness Act was signed into law in 1964, it designated nine million acres of wilderness and set up administrative machinery for adding other wilderness areas in the future. (By 1985, the National Wilderness Preservation System had grown to nearly 88 million acres.)

Three more environmental milestones were erected in the 1960s. The Clean Air Act of 1963 was supported by an annual-meeting resolution and Senate testimony by Kimball, who pointed out that air pollution, as with water pollution, in some ways results from interstate commerce and therefore the federal government could certainly do research on the problem. The final version of the act went beyond research to federal grants and control of pollutants. The Land and Water Conservation Fund Act of 1964 and the Scenic Rivers Act of 1968 also attracted Federation attention, primarily because of the organization's long-running participation in the "Clean Water Crusade," a coalition of several conservation groups. The crusade would frequently transcend all other issues in the coming years and decades. But not until the special tax status problem was alleviated would the Federation be able to unleash the full power of its huge and dedicated membership.

Some relief from lobbying restrictions came in the Tax Reform Act of 1976. The act was inspired, at least in part, by some behind-the-scenes work of environmental organizations. They pointed out to key congressmen that business and trade associations, reacting to the growing environmental movement, had been stepping up their legally recognized lobbying. But, the conservationists wryly pointed out, the business lobbying was, in effect, tax supported because the costs of Washington lobbying could be deducted as a business expense.

The reform act evened up the playing field for environmental organizations. Under a formula included in the act, the Federation and other organizations with 501(C)(3) tax status can spend a certain percentage of income in lobbying activities without losing the special status. For NWF, the amount is $1 million a year.

By then, however, the Federation had found another way to influence policy: direct legal action. Suddenly, in 1970, the Federation was on a new trail that led to courtrooms across the country.

The trail had begun at a board of directors meeting in August 1969, when Ernie Day, regional director of the vast western Region 13, passed around black-and-white photographs of the site of a proposed open-pit mine that would desecrate "a national treasure" in Idaho— the White Clouds mountains. According to Indian legend, the white limestone mountains were given the name White Clouds because that was what they looked like. To the American Smelting and Refining Company, the mountains looked more like an unopened treasure chest. In 1968, the company, working from old mining claims, began prospecting for molybdenum, which is primarily used to toughen and harden steel.

A year later, the company applied to the Forest Service for permission to build a road through a national forest that encompassed part of the mountains, to conduct more prospecting. The work presumably would lead to the open pit—the "monstrous thing that we are talking about," as Day told the board. Theoretically, under an old mining law, the Forest Service could not refuse a valid mining claim. The law did not acknowledge the new view of the environment, Day argued. "After all," he told the board, "the fact that anybody can go out and stake any kind of claim and . . . tear up the country, this does not fit in with the context of today's civilization and need for recreation."

Lawyers working with the Federation's Idaho affiliate, Day said, had made "a good case for the fact that the Forest Service does, in fact, have the horsepower to protect [White Clouds] and deny these claims for the road and mining permits. However, the Forest Service solicitors in Washington have seen fit to advise the chief that isn't the case." Day asked that the Federation join with the Idaho affiliate to stop the Forest Service with an injunction.

"The key issue, as I see it," said Tom Kimball, "is whether the Forest Service can, under its Multiple Use Act, consider all of the values, including recreation, aesthetic, fish and wildlife, in determining whether or not that permit should be issued in the public interest. . . . This is the whole fight. . . ."

A board member asked about Kimball's recommendation that the

National Wildlife Federation "join" the Idaho affiliate in the fight, for *join* had a special legal significance, providing, as Day put it, "the funds and backbone rather than legal counsel."

Stewart Udall, secretary of the interior during the Kennedy and Johnson administrations, spoke up, not only as a member of the Federation's board of directors but also as an expert on mining laws. Five days before leaving office in January 1969, in a letter to members of the Public Land Law Review Commission, he had said he believed that "the most important piece of unfinished business on the nation's natural resource agenda" is the replacement of the "obsolete and outdated" mining law of 1872.

"I think that Ernie is right," Udall said. "This is and should be a national issue."

As the cautious probing went on, director "Judge" Louis D. McGregor said, "The National Wildlife Federation, as such, has never instituted a legal action, at least in my memory. . . . This is what bothers me—not this one project, but the adoption of a principle. . . . Are we going to become a more activist organization? Are we going to participate in more of these things?" Then, speaking beyond his doubts, he added, "I hope so. I am in favor of it, but I want to be sure that we appreciate that this is a new departure from the policies of the Federation."

Udall had a special response for McGregor: "I join in your sentiments in feeling that if we are breaking new ground, it is good ground to break. I notice, for example, that the Audubon Society has become more militant, if you want to put it that way. . . . I would like to see this organization, both by legal actions and other actions, take part in some of these national issues, which others are going to be following and watching. I don't think you should always be the guy who is going along for the ride, but, actually, be the one carrying the ball."

Later in the discussion, Udall said, "I think that if we are going to get into the business of making some of these national fights on a legal basis, that this would be an excellent case to start with. . . . There may be some issues that are uniquely good issues for this organization, and, just as the Sierra Club takes the lead in some things, that we also take the lead. . . . You are not solely interested in glory, but, on the other hand, the more visibility there is of leadership, the better off we are."

After more discussion—less debating talk than cautious, clarifying talk—board member Walter L. Mims made what would be an historic motion: "that the National Wildlife Federation join with the Idaho Wildlife Federation in pursuing all of the administrative remedies available to them to prevent the construction of a road for mining purposes through the White Clouds area, and in the event that relief is not obtained, then to further consider legal action to prevent the construction of the subject road."

Ed Weinberg, former Solicitor of the Department of the Interior, handled the White Clouds case for the Federation. The case never actually reached litigation. The Federation convinced the Forest Service that it had the power to protect the treasure chest, and the road was not built. Now came another step along the activist path—a program to use legal action as an alternative to talking to Congress and lobbying in executive agencies.

A year later, when the board again took up the White Clouds, McGregor asked Kimball: "Did I not also hear you say last night at the meeting of the Budget and Finance Committee that we were going to hire an attorney and bring him in-house?"

"We are coming to that," Kimball responded.

"What is he going to be doing?" director Joseph Hughes asked.

Kimball first said something about contracts, such as those written for services. Then he mentioned "action programs."

"What do you mean by action programs?" Hughes asked. "Conservation?"

No, Kimball said, he is talking about litigation. The Federation, he said, has already spent $10,000 on the White Clouds case—another milestone, for it pitted the Federation against a federal agency in a legal confrontation. Now, for the first time, Federation officials and board members had to examine the idea of litigation "action programs," along with the potential triumphs and defeats that they could produce.

By 1970, White Clouds was not the only issue on the Federation's new litigation agenda. In Washington, D.C., NWF joined several other conservation groups in a legal battle to stop the construction of a bridge across the Potomac River. Supporting columns for the bridge would have obliterated a picturesque mid-river cluster of rocks known as the Three Sisters. Opposition to the Three Sisters Bridge was tied to Federation testimony before the District of Columbia City Council opposing freeways that would clutter the landscape around such national shrines as the Lincoln and Jefferson Memorials.

Demonstrations against the Three Sisters Bridge set off the largest mass arrest Washington had seen, foreshadowing the arrests that would later mark rallies against the Vietnam War. In the courtroom, Federation actions not only stopped the bridge and some other District of Columbia highway projects, but also set the stage for other highway battles. NWF litigation halted interstate highway construction not in compliance with National Environmental Policy Act regulations and resulted in court decisions that prohibited acquisition of highway rights-of-way before environmental impact statements had been approved. From then on, provisions of the environmental law restricted federal transportation policy.

Around the time the highway crusade began, the Federation was preparing for litigation to stop the Federal Power Commission from building a dam in the Middle Snake River in Idaho. And, in Maryland, the Federation appeared before the state's Department of Water Resources to protest the issuing of a permit allowing the use of Chesapeake Bay water to cool a nuclear power plant at Calvert Cliffs, which were renowned for the marine fossils they contained.

The Calvert Cliffs case would become a landmark in environmental law. Through a local activist group, the Federation sued Baltimore Gas & Electric and federal regulatory agencies, including the Atomic Energy Commission (predecessor to today's Nuclear Regulatory Commission), claiming that environmental concerns had been ignored. Because the Federation (unlike several of its affiliates) had never signed its name as a lead plaintiff in a lawsuit, officials hesitated. But they finally decided to join up with a local group of citizens, the Calvert Cliffs Coordinating Committee. The committee, which had been funded by NWF, did the actual suing. As a result, the case, which environmental lawyers hail as momentous, went into the law books as *Calvert Cliffs Coordinating Committee v. AEC.*

But it was, in reality, a Federation case, and an important one. It was the first case that interpreted the newly enacted National Environmental Policy Act (NEPA), which said that all federal agencies must prepare detailed environmental impact statements when planning projects that would significantly affect the quality of the environment. The AEC argued that the new law did not apply. The court said it did, and ordered the AEC to revise its procedures for licensing *all* nuclear power plants. The Federation followed up its victory with a handbook, *Nuclear Power Plants and You.*

In 1971, the Federation formed, within its Conservation Division, a Resources Defense Unit, whose legal staff received aid from Washington area law schools and private law firms. The unit tried to stay out of court, attempting first to settle issues "through personal contacts with executive branch decision-makers," then through publicity in Federation publications and other media.

The initial legal staff established two guidelines, which still define NWF's attitude toward litigation: Focus on cases that can set national precedents and improve decision-making about conservation issues;

keep watch over natural-resource problems that are of national importance, such as the use of environmentally threatening off-the-road vehicles on federal lands and administrative actions in large sites like Big Cypress Swamp and the Atchafalaya Basin.

Sometimes a seemingly local issue about wildlife can have lasting, nationwide implication. The Federation, for example, was notified by its Mississippi affiliate that a proposed interstate highway was threatening the last habitat of the Mississippi sandhill crane, an endangered species. The Federation, in conjunction with the Mississippi affiliate, started a federal court action against the Department of Transportation, the Federal Highway Administration, and the Mississippi Highway Department. The suit charged that plans for Interstate I-10 violated the Endangered Species Act and the Department of Transportation Act by bisecting the Mississippi Sandhill Crane National Wildlife Refuge. Because it would destroy or modify critical crane habitat, I-10 would jeopardize the existence of the crane.

In a 1975 court hearing, a judge ruled that the highway would not jeopardize the cranes. The Federation and the Mississippi affiliate appealed, and the circuit court reversed the judge's decision, directing the district court to issue an injunction preventing the Department of Transportation from starting work on the planned interchange. The Department of the Interior, acting under the Endangered Species Act, ruled that the Department of Transportation should purchase 1,960 acres of land adjacent to the interchange and along a nearby road to protect these lands from commercial and residential development. The interchange was built, and the Fish and Wildlife Service acquired the lands as part of the crane refuge.

During the appeals process, the case ultimately reached the Supreme Court, which, by refusing to hear the case, concurred with a lower court's ruling that recognized the Endangered Species Act as a statute with force.

Before a decision is made by NWF to file suit or to join in a lawsuit, certain criteria must be met and authorization must be given by the executive vice president. The criteria include the obvious one—likelihood of success. There are also others, tuned to Federation needs:

- Affiliate interest: Frequently, the Federation enters a case at the request of an affiliate. The issues at stake also should be "of a generic nature affecting the interests of a large number of affiliates." (Affiliates may also join a case initiated by the Federation.)

- Supporting resolutions: Authorization for litigation is based on one or more resolutions passed at an annual meeting. (The Federation cannot take any conservation action that is not supported by a resolution. Thus the affiliates, the source of resolutions, essentially direct the conservation policy of NWF.)

• Costs: Federation lawyers hold down costs by "shaping cases to present clean legal questions wherever possible," by getting free help from outside counsel, and by using volunteer experts rather than hired consultants.

• Jawboning: Talk is cheap. Before launching litigation, the Federation explores every other alternative, including negotiation, mediation, and administrative appeals. The opposition often accepts the negotiations route rather than go to court against an organization that has a high win average.

• Assessment of outside talent: Is the existing legal representation adequate? If not, the Federation shares the labor. Most such cases occurred in the early days of environmental litigation. A typical case involved a state or federal agency that was too timid or inexperienced to go it alone against a high-priced industry legal team. Federation lawyers joined with the litigant in need of help, sharing costs and investing only the time and talent necessary to help the partner achieve success.

• Legislative implications: A lawsuit can inspire a backlash in Congress or state legislatures. Federation lawyers may advise *against* a lawsuit, not because they have a bad case, but because winning the case could light a fuse and set off an uncontrollable political reaction. To be on the safe side, Federation lawyers develop a legislative strategy to follow through on the litigation. Litigation is a holding action, a last resort.

Typically, of seventy issues in which the Federation was involved in 1975, only eight were litigated. "When administrators discover that NWF is able to litigate," a Resources Conservation report said, "they often discover they can do something for wildlife."

The Federation's legal staff has passed its guidelines along to affiliates, many of which have paralleled the national Federation's move toward using lawyers *and* influencing legislators in achieving objectives. Requests for support from headquarters, said one report to the board, come from "all quarters—the Snake River is about to be drained, the Chesapeake is about to be paved." The actions are varied. While the Arizona affiliate is trying to stop the building of a dam that will wipe out a bald eagle habitat, the Georgia affiliate may be on the verge of suing over the water quality of a lake and the Massachusetts affiliate may be looking into legal action to stop the dumping of toxic chemicals into the ocean.

The Federation advises affiliates that it is a legal requirement that all administrative remedies be exhausted before a court will accept a lawsuit against a government. The affiliates are told that they can initiate legal actions and administrative appeals to executive agencies without losing their 501(C)(3) tax status. And the affiliates are advised to make lawsuits the focus for special fund raising campaigns and thus "use the issue to raise its own funding."

Legal action, the Federation says in its handbook for affiliates, "is a last resort. It indicates that you do not have the political muscle to bring your opponents to your point of view with cooperation and helpful comment." All lawsuits, the affiliates are told, "should be accompanied by a major effort to assure an eventual political victory whatever the result of the legal action."

To explain the Federation's decision to hire lawyers, one of the first lawyers, Oliver Houck, presented at the annual meeting in 1976 a panoramic view of the Resources Defense Unit (now combined with the legislative team and called the Resources Conservation Department). Houck, a former government prosecutor, selected the nation's wetlands as his example of an arena where Federation legal action was vitally needed.

Wetlands, which in 1900 covered 120 million acres, were down to 60 million acres, with about 15 million acres owned or somehow protected—"so that leaves 45 million acres naked . . . up for grabs."

Houck said the Federation was trying to protect those 45 million acres "from the activities of the United States government, because they have almost as many programs for dredging, developing, flooding, filling, polluting, and permitting no wetlands as they have for national defense—and the irony is they call them conservation programs."

He looked first at the U.S. Corps of Engineers, with some 850 projects—they "are either going to channelize something or they are going to flood." When the Corps was asked whether it was following the law that required it to replace habitat, the Corps said it could not follow the law because Congress had not appropriated funds for habitat replacement. So, Houck said, the Federation went into Tennessee, asked for legal relief, and got it.

"What do you have on your side now?" Houck asked his audience. "Well, it is a court order saying that when the Corps of Engineers goes to Congress, they had better have a mitigation plan authorized, and they do not move a drag line until they get money" for that mitigation plan.

In South Carolina and Minnesota, the Federation joined affiliates to force the Corps to abide by state laws—because states have a right to protect their fisheries, even against federal projects. Just by attending and testifying at a hearing on regulations, Houck said, "we saved some 7,000 acres of marsh."

If litigation had occurred in even half of the disputes the Federation waded into, he continued, "we would have gone home in a barrel a long time ago." But the mere threat of Federation action sometimes restrains the Corps, and relief often comes without going into court and beginning expensive litigation.

Moves to protect the wetlands, Houck said, must come before the bulldozer arrives, before someone looks out a window, picks up the phone, and calls the Federation to say, "My God! They are knocking down trees and have their drag lines in the water. They are starting to pave us!"

In 1977, a case almost as urgent as this hypothetical one confronted Pat Parenteau, a Nebraskan who had interned under Houck, gone off to teach law for a year, returned to the Federation, and eventually became one of its vice presidents. The landmark case involved a complex action against a series of projects threatening several species of migratory birds that needed the waters of the Platte River and its web of tributaries.

No single project threatened the birds, but the process of uncontrolled development was endangering critical habitat areas. "It's what I call the bologna syndrome," Parenteau said. "Keep taking a slice off the bologna, and pretty soon there's no bologna. People were wringing their hands because each one of these projects was being approved independently of the other and nobody was taking an overall look at what was happening. Nobody could figure out a way to do that legally."

The Federation decided to file suit against two projects, Grayrocks Dam to be erected in Wyoming by the Wheatland power plant, and the Narrows Dam in Colorado. (Later, the Little Blue River Diversion in Nebraska was drawn into what became known as the Grayrocks case.)

"Both of these projects . . . would take what would appear to be relatively a small amount of water from the river," Parenteau said. "But, again thinking of the cumulative effect of all these different diversions, they would eventually have a significant effect. . . . We were facing a situation where the river ceased to function in the habitat."

The Federation also used the Endangered Species Act for leverage, persuading the Department of the Interior to designate part of the

Platte River as a critical habitat for the whooping crane, an endangered species. Such special protection was not available for the other
birds that needed the habitat.

Parenteau, true to NWF litigation guidelines, tried to negotiate the
case to settlement. But the dispute with the power company "became
quite a hostile encounter." When, however, the Federation got an
injunction that stopped the $1.4 billion project, the power company
officials changed their minds. "So then began," Parenteau recalled, "a
new, interesting era in the case because both the states of Wyoming
and Nebraska were directly involved. We had shuttle diplomacy between the state capitals, with the personal intervention of both governors."

During the negotiations with the power company, no way could be
found to reach settlement until one day, as Parenteau described it,
the attorney for the power cooperative "said something about if there
was a way to pay you off, we'd pay you off. And I said, 'Well, maybe
there is. If you'd be willing to create a trust fund that would ensure
that the habitat was not adversely affected by the power plant, and
that the trust fund would have enough money in it so that it could
begin the job of acquiring the land and water rights necessary to
protect the habitat . . . then maybe we could settle it.' "

In a precedent-setting agreement, the power cooperative set up a
$7.5 million trust fund. "Some people call it a payoff," Parenteau said
ruefully. "Some people call it blackmail. In fact, what it was was a
pragmatic approach to a difficult problem." Similar trust-fund settle-
ments have been reached in Montana and Alaska.

Pragmatism like this kept the Federation *out* of a celebrated case:
a tiny, endangered fish called the snail darter versus the Tennessee
Valley Authority's proposed Tellico Dam on the Little Tennessee
River. "We were asked to be the ones to bring that case," Parenteau
said. "We declined because we saw it as a Pyrrhic victory. It was a
good *law case* for sure—but we saw very clearly there was going to be
a tremendous political and legislative backlash. And the statute, the
Endangered Species Act itself, might not survive it. It very nearly
didn't survive it.

"The people who did bring the lawsuit did not have the same appreciation for that connection and, as the Scripture says, they reaped
the whirlwind. . . . That dam nearly undid the Endangered Species
Act." The Federation did file an *amicus*—friend of the court—brief
when the case reached the Supreme Court because at that point the
Endangered Species Act needed as much support as it could get. The
Supreme Court upheld the snail darter and the act. But, as Parenteau

pointed out, "in symbolic terms, what happened was ridiculous: this big dam, a very important project, . . . was threatened by some silly little creature."

As a result of that famous case, Congress "was able to push through changes" in the Endangered Species Act that "we didn't want to see"— and Congress ultimately approved the dam. "I suppose candor compels us to also acknowledge that subsequent to the dam's being built, other populations of the snail darter were discovered. And, although the species is still threatened, its extinction, which was predicted by many, has not happened. So we all learned a lesson." (The snail darter experience inspired the "legislative backlash" warning in Federation criteria for deciding on litigation.)

Parenteau's pragmatism led him to build special resource teams within the Federation. Each team consisted of a lawyer, a lobbyist (often a professional, such as an economist), and a biologist or other scientist. Each team specializes on an issue, and the teams change as emphasis on issues changes. From 1979 to 1986, teams have worked on these issues: public lands and energy, legislative affairs, pollution and toxics, fisheries and wildlife, public works and transportation, and water resources. Sometimes a team will initiate a case when a "mole within an agency" calls a team member or sends a "plain brown envelope" to report a bad policy.

Most of the time decisions about strategy come from within the Resources Conservation Department, which had grown from two lawyers hired by Lou Clapper in the 1970s to a group of thirty-five professionals—fifteen of them lawyers—in the mid 1980s.

A memo Parenteau wrote to a team illustrates how the Resources Conservation Department develops strategy. Planning legislative actions on amendments to the Endangered Species Act and the Clean Water Act, he asked team members to "start talking among yourselves and with other lobbyists" about grass-roots lobbying, especially among affiliates. "We'll need to target some key people. . . . We'll also need some mailing lists for Action Alerts. . . ." He told them to dig up material to fight off opposition arguments, to think up amendments that would strengthen the laws, to decide whether to "spearhead a small 'c' coalition," and to set up a media campaign.

This multifaceted campaign characterizes the modern Federation's approach toward issues. Now more than ever, Parenteau said, NWF is "an advocate for conservation and not an apologist for what positions it takes—even those positions that will cause a sharp attack by forestry professionals who don't like the fact that we advocate wilderness, by pure hunting groups that don't like the fact that we support parks, by utility industries that don't like the idea that we have problems with nuclear power."

Out of the Resources Conservation Department came the idea of Natural Resources Centers, regional "branch offices" where people could be trained to respond to natural-resource issues not only by knowing environmental law, but also by knowing the issues and the bureaucratic complexes in which they live. The centers are designed to work closely with local affiliates.

"At these . . . centers, NWF lawyers, scientists, and resource specialists look at federal programs on the ground, where the rubber meets the road," said David Burwell, former director of a resource team in the Resources Conservation Department. "No press conferences, no courthouse interviews, no signing ceremonies. Just the hard work of reviewing Bureau of Land Management land-use plans; reading Environmental Protection Agency water quality monitoring reports; and analyzing U.S. Forest Service timber sale offerings. The hard work of watching to see if all the flowery language and good intentions flowing out of Congress and federal agencies on the importance of saving our natural heritage is being translated into effective action."

The first center, the Rocky Mountain Natural Resources Clinic, opened in Boulder, Colorado, in 1978. It drew students and faculty members from the University of Colorado School of Law and the College of Forestry and Natural Resources of Colorado State University at Fort Collins.

Soon after the clinic began work, it filed a lawsuit on behalf of the New Mexico Wildlife Federation, in defense of the National Park Service's decision to remove feral burros from Bandelier National Park. The burros, not a natural animal to the area, were being removed because they were harming the environment. Some animal rights groups opposed the move because they felt that the burros had a right to live in the park. The issue exemplified the conflict between protectionist groups and organizations, like the Federation, that support professional wildlife management action, including control of populations by hunting and other methods. The Federation won the suit.

Another center, the Northwest Natural Resources Center, opened in 1979 in Eugene, Oregon—and promptly took on the timber industry that strongly supported the center's home, the University of Oregon Law School. Two years later, the center moved to Portland— and took on that area's influential Bonneville Power Authority.

Since 1979, three other centers have opened, and another is on the drawing table. The Northern Rockies Natural Resources Center, in Missoula, Montana, in one of its first acts, intervened on behalf of the Fish and Wildlife Service's plan to make wildlife management—rather than livestock foraging—the primary purpose of a wildlife refuge. The Southeastern Natural Resources Center, in Raleigh, North Carolina, brought suit with the North Carolina Wildlife Federation when the Corps of Engineers failed to make a peat mining company obtain a permit before chopping up wetlands for the harvesting of peat logs. The Great Lakes Natural Resources Center, in Ann Arbor, Michigan, campaigned against toxic pollution of the lakes, which contain twenty percent of the world's fresh water. A sixth center, the Prairie Wetlands Natural Resource Center, is due to open in Bismarck, North Dakota, in the spring of 1987.

An attempt was made to establish a center in Alaska, but after a short time it was abandoned. For years the Federation had found the climate there ranging from chilling to frigid. The Federation's Alaskan ordeal began in the early 1970s, when the national leaders—and many of the members—found themselves moving toward a showdown with the Alaska affiliate. The issue involved the disposal of millions of acres of public lands in the 49th state.

The debate started with the Alaska Native Claims Settlement Act, signed into law by President Nixon in 1971. The act allotted 44 million acres to the state's native peoples and authorized the secretary of the interior to set aside up to 80 million acres as "national interest" lands devoted to national parks, national forests, wildlife refuges, and wild and scenic rivers. Millions of other acres were to be federally owned as "public interest" lands. These latter interests included mining, timbering, flood control, and recreation.

The Alaskan land rush began: native peoples complained about the size and location of the lands given to them; timber, mining, and oil interests set out stakes for what they wanted; conservationists launched extensive studies to determine the type and extent of protection that would best serve the habitats and wildlife of Alaska. The Department of the Interior, several Alaskan state agencies, and national conservation organizations began drawing lines on maps.

The lines became front lines on the battlefield of Alaska. In 1977, Congressman Morris Udall, advancing for the conservationists, introduced the first version of the Alaska National Interests Conservation Act (ANILCA), a bill that would give federal protection to more than 100 million acres of Alaska's wild lands. (Stewart Udall, once a member of the Federation's board of directors, is Morris' brother and his predecessor in the House.)

A familiar name in Federation annals was opposing ANILCA. The co-author of an opposing bill, incorporating the state of Alaska's positions, was John D. Dingell, son of the Michigan congressman who had been an author of the milestone fishing law that years before had won Federation support.

On one side of the Alaska land war were some fifty environmental organizations united in the Alaska Coalition. On the other side were the state and national lobbyists of the mining, oil, and timber industries; the National Rifle Association; the U.S. Chamber of Commerce; the AFL-CIO—and the Federation's Alaska affiliate.

The affiliate argued that the environmentalist-backed proposal violated states' rights and put an unwarranted economic burden on Alaska. The state wanted most of the public land assigned to the Bureau of Land Management, which would open it up for economic development. The Alaskan affiliate endorsed the state's plan, siding with most of its members and many of its fellow residents, including the powerful association of guides. The guides—they included among their supporters a former guide turned governor—resisted any conversion of land to national parks as a direct threat because of the restriction against hunting in national parks.

The Federation, although never formally part of the Alaska Coalition, worked with members of the coalition to develop a position. The coalition wanted a great swath of acreage earmarked for national parks. NWF believed that much of this acreage included areas containing large wildlife populations that, in the Federation's view, needed professional management, which could not be carried out under National Park Service policy.

But the coalition wanted the support of NWF, then over three million strong. The Federation's Tom Kimball suggested a compromise: shift some of the designated land from the status of national park to national wildlife refuge. In a wildlife refuge, hunting, logging, even mineral exploration is permitted, but wildlife conservation always takes priority. The U.S. Fish and Wildlife Service has the authority to block any other use determined to adversely affect wildlife.

Kimball met with Alaskan wildlife specialists, National Park Service officials, and experts on the habitats of big-game animals in Alaska. "The philosophy of the people of Alaska is different," Kimball said, recalling the dispute. "It's the last frontier. People go up there to make their millions. And they don't want any interference on what they can and can't do on those lands."

Most of all, Kimball said, Alaskans hated the rules: "You can't hunt there or you can't take your [hunting] client in there. Or you can't drill for oil and gas. You can't do this in our national parks. That was the case. So they all lined up together. The state of Alaska and all these special interest groups—commodities, forestry, minerals, the guides. They all lined up on the other side of the fence from the views held by the Alaska Coalition."

And they lined up behind two men who proved to be ANILCA's greatest obstacles—Alaska's two senators, Mike Gravel and Ted Stevens. Indeed, the first version of ANILCA, passed by the House, met defeat in the Senate under the leadership of Gravel and Stevens. Undaunted, Udall and Representative John Anderson of Illinois introduced another ANILCA early in 1979.

As the House vote on the new ANILCA neared, a classic confrontation began to build. The Alaska Coalition had the support of President Jimmy Carter and Secretary of the Interior Cecil D. Andrus. Jacques Cousteau added his name, as did Laurance Rockefeller and Theodore Roosevelt IV. On the other side, Alaskan industries formed the Citizens for Alaska Lands, and the state's own lobbying organization raised more than $2 million.

More than fifty lobbyists from environmental groups pounded on congressional doors and kept a constant head-count on supporters—and waverers. Pro-ANILCA committees were set up in every congressional district. Mailing lists containing more than three million names were merged and organized by congressional districts. "I'd say, 'So-and-so's wavering,'" Udall told the *Washington Post,* and "they could push a button and have 800 Mailgrams in to the guy the next day."

The House bill passed, 268 to 157. The battle in the Senate dragged on for another year and a half, with Gravel and Stevens again leading the skirmishes mounted by the opposition—to no avail. In the end, the conservationists won. The Alaska Lands Bill was signed by President Carter in December 1980.

The Alaska Lands Bill not only expanded the nation's federal wildlife refuge and park system by those millions of acres, it also established new management standards in Alaska. "We took on the timber industry. We took on the mining industry. And we took on all those special-interest resource groups," Kimball said. "And we cleaned their plow. . . . That's why I say that in my tenure of twenty-one years that was the greatest victory we ever had. It put into permanent status millions of acres of land which are protected for all the people of our country. It's a national resource."

The Alaska Lands Bill was signed less than a month before the inauguration of President Ronald Reagan, the arrival in Washington of Secretary of the Interior James D. Watt, and the beginning of new wars.

The Alaska land campaign also revivified the issue of hunting, which once again pitted sportsmen against anti-hunters. The controversy emerged this time because of the "united front" nature of the Alaska battle. Among the organizations with which the NWF cooperated during the battle were groups that usually would not find themselves associating with hunters. Such organizations are often labeled "protectionist" or "preservationist" (in contrast to "conservationist"). Like most labels, they paste over, rather than actually identify, complex disputes.

A representative flare-up between conservationists and preservationists occurred during a long-lasting struggle to repeal bounties. The traditional, pro-hunting organizations, including the Federation, had been quietly working for years to eliminate bounties. In 1940 and 1962, these organizations successfully campaigned for federal laws to protect bald and golden eagles. State by state, the traditional groups had also won adoption of the Audubon Society's Model Predatory Bird Protection law, which repealed bounties and extended protection already given to eagles, hawks, owls, and other predatory birds. These organizations endorsed the concept of managing wildlife to maintain the predator-prey balance. The motive for supporting anti-bounty legislation was *conservation* of hawks, wolves, and other predators as species—not the *protection* of all individual predators from hunters' guns.

But in the 1970s, such protectionist groups as the Fund for Animals and Friends of Animals allied with the traditional groups in their effort to repeal bounties on wolves. The motives behind the campaign became mixed in the public's view. The conservationist-protectionist alliance, though directed toward the bounty system or other specific issues, blurred the permanent boundary between the two approaches to wildlife stewardship.

"The entry of the ultraprotectionist into the folds of the conservation movement confused the public if it did nothing else," wrote James B. Trefethen, former publications director of the Wildlife Management Institute. "On some issues the newcomers allied themselves with the older organizations, but their opposition to wildlife management or population control in any form made it difficult or impossible for any group with experience and scientific knowledge to work with them." Trefethen expressed the extreme frustration of the established groups, which, of course, were not the only ones with "experience and scientific knowledge." But intemperate charges and language was inevitable when temporary, united-front alliances broke down between protectionists and traditional, pro-management organizations.

"Compounding the difficulty," Kimball said in 1976, "is the changing life-styles of many Americans. As more and more people grow up in urban areas, they become more and more isolated from the natural environment. As a result, they know less about the natural balance between wildlife and their habitats. Consequently they fall prey to protectionist appeals."

There were also disputes in the ranks of the traditional pro-management, pro-hunting groups. One dispute that produced a great deal of impassioned oratory involved objects weighed in grams: the shot in shotgun shells.

Each year, hunters fire millions of shots at various species of waterfowl. One of the results is several thousand tons of spent shot added to the bottoms of marshes, rivers, and ponds each year. As birds eat, they sometimes ingest pellets along with food and grist for their gizzards. From as far back as 1874, studies have shown that ingested lead shot poisons birds. Estimates of lead poisoning range around 2 to 3 percent of the population of all waterfowl species.

Dr. Louis N. Locke of the U.S. Fish and Wildlife Service once described how hundreds of geese had died in Maryland. "There is a muscular weakness" at the beginning, he said. "Next the bird loses the ability to fly. Frequently the esophagus is impacted—stuffed with sand, corn, and mud. The pectoral muscles waste away. Anemia sets in. Sometimes when you pick up one of these emaciated birds, it struggles, suffers an acute cardiac attack, and dies."

If hunters switched from lead to steel loads, the poisoning would greatly diminish and gradually cease as accumulating sediment covers up the spent lead pellets. But many hunters oppose steel shot because, they say, it has inferior ballistic properties and damages shotgun barrels. By the mid-1970s, however, the Federation was convinced that the needs of the birds transcended the concerns expressed by hunters. Besides, research was demonstrating that steel shot did no more appreciable damage to modern shotguns than lead shot did. And appropriate loads of steel shot were proving to be as effective as lead loads.

The U.S. Fish and Wildlife Service went to the NWF annual meeting in 1976 and asked for, and received, a Federation endorsement of steel shot. Armed with this endorsement and with studies confirming the perils of lead shot, Fish and Wildlife then began requiring the use of steel shot in areas of proven, extensive lead poisoning. The requirement infuriated many waterfowl hunters and heated up an issue that, to some hunters, lined up neatly as hunting (lead shot) versus anti-hunting (steel shot).

The principal proponent of the pro-lead-shot dogma was the National Rifle Association, which reacted to the U.S. Fish and Wildlife Service's anti-lead order by filing suit, charging that the order was arbitrary and capricious. A Federation brief endorsing the decision helped Fish and Wildlife win the case. When the National Rifle Association appealed, NWF again joined the fight on the side of Fish and Wildlife.

The National Rifle Association reacted by charging that the lead versus steel shot dispute was "a conflict between hunters and anti-hunters." Many outdoor writers took up the Rifle Association's argument. The Federation sent information packets to the writers, stressing that "this country's sportsmen/conservationists have enough real enemies to go around without picking fights with their friends (by questioning their aims and motives)." (See appendix 9 for a history of this litigation.)

The lead-or-steel controversy raged on, as did several other Federation battles. They included a crusade for a national law that would put a deposit on all beverage containers. Members were asked to mail "Cans to Carter" as part of the campaign to impress President Carter with the grass-roots support of the proposal. (Well over 35,000 cans were mailed to the White House, where staffers duly recycled them.) The Federation found itself up against one of the most powerful lobbies it had ever encountered—an alliance of soda and beer companies, aluminum and glass container manufacturers, and retail grocer associations.

The national bottle bill never even got a hearing. But it did add one more issue to the growing list of Federation interests pursued during Kimball's tenure. And it showed how NWF's activism had evolved from the days of the tax code's severe restrictions on lobbying to the direct, bold attempts to influence federal agencies and the White House in the 1970s and 1980s.

One of the most effective—but delicate—ways of swaying the minds of policy makers in the Executive Branch involves talking to people in the White House and, ultimately, to the president. Presidential-Federation talking went all the way back to Franklin D. Roosevelt. Kimball's experience with presidents went back to Eisenhower, who was never known as an environmentalist. In a recollection of his White House dealings, Kimball said that President Johnson had little interest in environmental issues, either. Luckily, though, Lady Bird Johnson made up for the president's lack of enthusiasm. When he signed the Wilderness Bill, Kimball recalled, Johnson picked up the pen, shook his head, and said, "I don't know what this is all about. But Lady Bird says it's good." Like Eisenhower, President Nixon recognized the political importance of the conservationist movement and met several times with its representatives, including Kimball. But it was not until the Ford administration that the Federation began aggressive, sustained lobbying of the White House.

During President Ford's first ten months in office, conservationists watched with mounting concern as Ford met with representatives of many groups that had little passion about environmental issues. Ford did veto a strip-mining bill. But many of his other conservation decisions were on the wrong track, in the opinion of Federation leaders and other environmentalists.

Through the conservationists' grapevine, word eventually reached Ford that his environmental record was bad and was doing him little good politically. He reacted by inviting a group of conservationists to meet with him. Kimball, as spokesman, told the president that the environment was losing out because of over-abundant concern with energy and the economy. Kimball said that it was not necessary to pollute air and water in order to have low employment rates and adequate energy resources. Kimball also asked that environmentalists get as much presidential attention as businessmen with special interests.

The Federation followed a similar script when, early in the Carter administration, conservationists again began worrying about presidential attitudes toward environmental issues. The White House was pressuring the Environmental Protection Agency to ease off on pollution-control enforcement activities, apparently in the belief that the activities were causing industrial production to slow down. Also, to cut house-building costs, the administration had ordered a "review" of federal timber sales; environmentalists saw this as the foreshadowing of heavier logging in national forests and on other public lands. There was also some sniping at the Endangered Species Act, which was accused of putting obscure animals in the path of major public works projects.

In May 1978, Kimball met with President Carter. A subsequent NWF board of directors report said that Kimball had come away impressed with Carter's genuine concern for natural resources. The report said Kimball "believes the president is a sincere and dedicated conservationist, despite disappointing shortcomings in his water project reform policy, opposition to nongame legislation, timber harvesting policies, etc." As a result of the meeting, "a mechanism has been set up whereby the conservationist viewpoint can be assured of direct presidential attention at periodic intervals."

The mechanism, publicly revealed during the fight over Alaska lands, was a guarantee that the president would meet with the leaders of conservation groups every six months. The conservationists were also to send to the president every two months a one-page memorandum that was to reach him without its being modified by anyone on his staff. Kimball would later rate Carter as the best environmental leader since Teddy Roosevelt.

When the Carter administration took office, Kimball felt that the time had come to push harder than ever for reform of federal water policies. The issue of clean water runs through the Federation's history like a clear mountain stream. From the first annual meeting's resolution warning about water pollution, down through the 1941 resolution condemning heedless dam building and later resolutions calling for a halt to widespread drainage of wetlands, the Federation has been a sentinel watching over this most vital natural resource.

Because free-flowing water knows no boundaries, water problems have usually been federal problems. But federal water policies, as a 1978 Federation report critically noted, "have traditionally been based on three principles—unlimited money to spend, unlimited water to distribute, and unlimited resources to destroy."

In contrast are the Federation's four principles, which have endured since Lou Clapper cited them in congressional testimony in 1969:

- Nobody has an inherent right to pollute public water resources.

- Those who use public water have a basic responsibility to return it at least as clean as they received it.

- Those who damage public waters should have the responsibility for repairing the damage.

- The cost of waste treatment must be considered an integral part of the operating cost of "doing business," one to be shared by users of the products or services rather than being passed along to everyone through desecration of the environment.

Now that the Carter administration was in office, Kimball felt that the best strategy for a reform of federal water policies was not confrontations in courtrooms, but moves aimed at influencing the Executive Branch, up to and including the president. Kimball and

Federation specialists, looking at the nation's water resources in the late 1970s, saw this:

- The Soil Conservation Service, created to "hold the raindrop where it falls," seemed instead to be dedicated to "getting rid of as many raindrops as possible," actually speeding up their journey to the ocean. A Federation lawsuit in the early 1970s had stopped an SCS project in North Carolina and forced the Service to put environmental guidelines into its plans. Subsequent negotiations between SCS and the Federation limited what NWF specialists saw as the most threatening projects—those involving the channelization of streams.

- Dams, which the Federation often had confronted on a case-by-case basis, were now being looked at by NWF as a generic source of problems. Discharges from hydroelectric dams can produce a "point source" of pollution, killing off fish by drastically reducing the oxygen content of the discharge water. The Federation petitioned the Environmental Protection Agency for a general rule about discharges from hydroelectric dams. Meanwhile, the Federation kept up the pressure on local dam issues, from West Virginia to Texas. The common denominator of these local cases: NWF confronted issues, not agencies.

- Water quality, which became a major federal responsibility when the Water Quality Act was passed in 1965, increasingly became a national-level issue for NWF. The Federation filed suit to force the U.S. Coast Guard to draw up regulations for the design and construction of oil tankers plying U.S. coastal waters. NWF workshops taught citizens groups about their rights to good water under both the Water Quality Act and the Clean Water Act. The text for the workshops—and for activist groups throughout the nation—was *Setting the Course for Clean Water,* a Federation handbook on citizens' water rights. The message: The major sources of pollution from coast to coast are such "nonpoint" villains as runoff from parking lots and farms, and the sources of this type of runoff are hard to track down and control.

- Although the federal government had made an enormous contribution toward new sewage treatment facilities, construction of these facilities threatened to create other environmental problems. NWF lawyers monitored Environmental Protection Agency construction grants, making sure that plants were not being built on wetlands or that the grants were not being used to foster environmentally unwise commercial or residential development.

• A Corps of Engineers channelization project to control floods threatened more than 500 square miles of wetlands in the Atchafalaya River Basin in Louisiana. When NWF, shoulder to shoulder with the Louisiana affiliate, took on the Corps, a ditch wider than the combined length of two football fields had already been dug through half of the Atchafalaya basin. Eventually, with the help of the new National Environmental Policy Act, the Federation hammered out an agreement with the Corps calling for a new plan. Other Corps projects threatened shrimp and oyster grounds in Florida, migratory waterfowl in Arkansas, and wetlands wildlife from Tennessee to Minnesota.

"It's hard to imagine the Atchafalaya," Oliver Houck said in the midst of the fight to save it. "It's bigger than some states we have up North—producing a harvest of over 10 million crawfish a year, more abundant in fisheries than the much more famous Everglades, twice more abundant in fact. And it's the linchpin of the Mississippi Flyway, . . . [used by] half of the continental waterfowl population of North America." After eight years of "banging my head against the Corps of Engineers" in the Atchafalaya and elsewhere, Houck said in 1979, "something is beginning to crack besides my head." By then Houck, a vice president of the Federation and a member of the Corps' environmental board, was seeing changes within the Corps. Because of the need for environmental impact statements, for example, "hundreds of biologists" entered the ranks of the Corps. At one hearing, Houck said, five Corps generals were "out-environmenting" each other "to save the Cape Fear wetlands." The regulators in the Corps, he said, "are rising in status, responsibility, and impact."

The long crusade for pure water may have inspired reformation in the Corps of Engineers. But the news on land was not good. One area the Federation especially focused on was highway planning and construction. The Federation quickly discovered that bureaucrats making highway decisions were not listening to the people who would be most affected by the highways.

The Federation pointed the way toward citizen resistance to bulldozer-style highway decision making. "The time has come," the Federation said in 1977, "to take control by taking part—to realize that in a democratic nation citizens have duties as well as rights, duties which extend far beyond the ballot box. Every day public officials—with the 'help' of special private interests—are making transportation decisions which affect the development patterns of our communities, open space, parks, air and water quality, noise level, and tax rates."

The call to arms was sounded in a booklet, *The End of the Road. A Citizens' Guide to Transportation Problemsolving,* the work of David Burwell and Mary Ann Wilner of the Federation. The booklet showed how to comment on environmental impact statements and how to sue the government—if necessary—under laws ranging from the National Environmental Policy Act to the Clean Air Act and the Safe Drinking Water Act.

The Federation had begun gathering experience in highway litigation in 1973, with a successful suit that forced the U.S. Department of Transportation to publish federal rules governing highway construction. A year later the Federation sued the Department of Transportation again, this time to force the department to apply federal environmental standards to the interstate highway program, particularly when highways were aimed at parks, wetlands, and other natural areas.

"The impact of highways on fish and wildlife has been murderous," the booklet said. "An average of four animals are killed per car, per year (or close to 500 million kills in 1976). Many highways intersect with migration routes, mating grounds, and wetlands refuge areas. Highway fences in the West in some winters are lined with starved and frozen antelope which died attempting to migrate to grazing grounds. Salt from roads runs into streams, reservoirs and lakes, killing plant and fish life."

The booklet told highway fighters what they are up against: the ten largest domestic corporations have a direct interest in automotive travel. General Motors, by producing most of the nation's buses and locomotives, essentially controls the modes of transportation that compete with cars. "The point is simply that our present transportation system is based more on manufacturer preference than it is on public policy or consumer choice."

Blunt words like those characterized the Federation's approach under Kimball and were carried over into other issues, old and new—acid rain and strip-mining, endangered species and toxic wastes. And what the highway booklet had said about fighting highways was true in other confrontations: "Politicians remember organizations better than individuals, as do planners, administrators, and the media."

The politicians were learning lessons. From seashore to highway, from marsh to factory, from woodland to housing tract, the Federation had shown the interdependence of the modern world, the web of life that links the natural world and the urban world, wildlife refuges and cattle ranches. The Federation was teaching politicians that attention must be paid to people, to their environment, to wildlife, and ultimately to all of nature. A road was no longer something a faceless bureaucrat built. A road was a political act that had to be examined. People had a right to look at what was planned for them. And to stop it if they did not like it.

As Kimball's long tenure neared an end, the legal-scientific-lobbyist teams were at work on issues from land use to the disposal of toxic substances. The teams were part of the Kimball legacy when, in March 1981, he stepped down after twenty-one years as head of the National Wildlife Federation. Kimball was uneasy about leaving the fight, for he was troubled by what he had already seen of the Reagan administration, which had "turned back the clock in responsible resource use and environmental protection." He could encapsule his worry in a single word: Watt. But, Kimball knew, the official worry was no longer his. It had been inherited by his successor.

The board of directors, after a two-year search in which 161 candidates had been screened, selected as Kimball's successor Jay D. Hair, an associate professor of zoology and forestry at North Carolina State University. He was thirty-five years old.

Although Hair had served as president of the South Carolina Wildlife Federation, he was of a new breed, drawn from a new environment for Federation leaders. He had not worked for a state fish and game commission. He had come up through a route that took him more often to scientific seminars than to wildlife management conferences. He taught and managed people. He had administered not a wildlife refuge, but the fisheries and wildlife sciences program at North Carolina State.

Much of Hair's work had been on paper—in scientific journals and in monographs on policy. As a special assistant at the Department of the Interior, for example, he had helped to develop a national fish and wildlife policy. He had become an authority on the relationship between state and federal wildlife agencies. But his job would go beyond policy papers. He could summarize his first task of national importance not in a single word, but in a single question: How does the Federation handle Watt?

When James G. Watt became secretary of the interior, he assumed management of more than 700 million acres of public lands—one third of the land mass of the United States. Spurred on by a fervid belief in his own vision, he was soon attacking that land. He withdrew regulations designed to protect farmlands from the consequences of strip mining. He began leasing federal lands at an unprecedented rate. He accelerated plans for oil and gas exploration in Alaskan wild-life refuges. He began giving private concessioners in national parks a greater role in managing the parks.

Not long after Hair became executive vice president of the Federation, he attended a "summit meeting" of Watt and conservation leaders. Watt and his aides were especially genial toward Hair. As Hair said later, "I had the impression that they were trying to separate me from the others on the grounds that I represented sportsmen, who in their minds were or should be in conflict with preservationists. I think this was a big mistake in judgment on the part of the administration.

"For the past twenty years our organization and most sportsmen had been concerned with general environmental issues—habitat protection, clean water and air, land use, endangered species, toxic waste, and the rest. We have no basic conflict with others who happen to be non-hunters, which is much different from being anti-hunting. Whether you are a hunter or a bird photographer, you have basically the same environmental interests."

Hair's reaction to Watt's cordiality was to order an "in-depth evaluation" of Watt's performance. Federation staff members pored over Watt's speeches, testimony, public actions, and statements to the media. Affiliates were asked for their opinions. Associate members were surveyed.

The opinion survey of 4,000 members, released in July 1981, showed that nearly eighty percent of them disliked Watt's policies. Watt scoffed at the survey as "hilariously funny," despite the survey's proving that NWF members were not the wild-eyed liberals Watt had claimed his critics to be. NWF members had voted about two to one for Reagan over Carter.

Meanwhile, the Federation's analysis of Watt's performance kept growing. It was 117 pages long when completed in July. Hair studied it and then wrote President Reagan a letter that said, "Evidence of Mr. Watt's unsuitability has become so overwhelming that the sooner he is relieved of his duties, the better it will be for the country and its resources."

The new man at the National Wildlife Federation had begun his tenure by calling for the removal of the secretary of the interior. James Baker, President Reagan's chief of staff, said the president had "absolute faith" in Watt.

The National Wildlife Federation, which had been born in 1936 with a presidential blessing, was nearing its half-century milestone on a collision course with another president of the United States.

Epilogue

The National Wildlife Federation's Laurel Ridge Education Center commands a knoll off a commuters' highway near Vienna, Virginia, a suburban town a few miles outside the beltway that surrounds Washington, D.C. On this crisp fall day, about eight kindergartners, convoyed by three mothers and led by a Federation volunteer guide, wander along one of the trails that wind through the meadow and woods around the center.

The trail, wide and paved to accommodate the handicapped, rounds a bend. The adults gently gather their flock to the ridge that gives the center its name. The laurels' thick, evergreen leaves glisten amid the muted clusters of reds and yellows. The children are quiet now, looking up at a chestnut oak, listening to a downy woodpecker at work.

Inside the center, where a lifesize wooden eagle guards the library door and a green canoe leans against a corridor wall, a staff naturalist prepares for a bird banding demonstration. The phone in the library rings and a desperate high schooler asks for some help on a wildlife paper that does not yet have a theme.

In Washington, at Federation headquarters, a staff biologist and a lawyer also contemplate a woodpecker. They are huddling over a report on the red-cockaded woodpecker, an endangered species that prefers pine woodlands. The woodpecker's populations have been decreasing in recent years. *That Florida case. A pine forest. Do they know down there that the red-cockaded woodpecker might be in trouble?*

Elsewhere in Washington, at the headquarters of the National Park Service, federal biologists pore over a Federation legal brief calling for the closing of the Fishing Bridge camp grounds in Yellowstone. Across the river, at the Pentagon, the general counsel to the secretary of defense anticipates a new battle on the horizon. House Resolution 1202 would force the Department of Defense to manage the 25 million acres of land on U.S. military bases so that fish and wildlife get equal consideration with forestry and agriculture. *Red-cockaded woodpeckers, says a report he is reading, are found in the longleaf pine forests of North Carolina's Fort Bragg and Camp Lejeune.*

From California to Maine, thirteen regional executives—eleven men and the two newest executives, both of them women—are either meeting with representatives of affiliates somewhere or on the way to meet them. A new officer of an affiliate is told why the Federation has taken a stand against off-road vehicles on public lands. *Well, a lot of the members have dune buggies and they're muttering about the Federation's high and mighty attitude . . . and what they want to say is . . .* The executive listens patiently and makes a note to get some more ORV literature to the affiliate.

Half a continent away, an affiliate seeks advice on the new plan the Forest Service has announced for the local national forest. *You have to have adequate reasons to oppose any part of a plan. Look at the roads, for instance. The runoff from those dirt roads might clog a stream and hurt the fish life. Now that's a reason. . . .*

James Watt has long since resigned his post. He no longer thinks the Federation's campaign against him was hilarious. One of his successors, Donald P. Hodel, has received a "Dear Don" letter from Jay Hair. The letter informs him that the Federation is about to sue the Department of the Interior to block the use of lead shot for waterfowl hunting in several states. . . .

Waterfowl season is open again. Soon, under a plan propounded by the U.S. Fish and Wildlife Service to resolve NWF lawsuits, the use of lead shot for waterfowl hunting will disappear. After a series of lawsuits spanning ten years, the U.S. Fish and Wildlife Service has agreed that nontoxic steel shot will be mandatory for hunting migratory waterfowl throught the nation by 1991. Any state that has not outlawed lead shot by then will not be allowed to have a waterfowl season.

Along the Atlantic and Gulf Coasts, the sun rises on barrier islands that will change now only under the whims of sand and sea. The islands, so fragile and so beautiful, will remain in their natural state, and no fewer than 4,500 people take credit. They are "Americans for the Coast," mobilized by the Federation and its affiliates from New England to the Gulf. The islands were saved by a law, the Coastal Barrier Resources Act, which made the undeveloped barrier islands along the two coasts ineligible for federal subsidies on sewers, roads, bridges, and other works that make paradises into tourist attractions. The novel law essentially seals off the islands from the woes of mainland progress.

Jay Hair, who at congressional hearings in 1982 had spoken for the future of the barrier islands, found himself speaking of the Federation's history three years later, when the Federation marked its half century.

"We have traveled a long distance," he said, looking back through his own years of leadership to the days when Ding Darling said there was no army to fight for the things that conservationists wanted.

"If there was a bridge or a series of power dams planned across the major rivers of the United States—perhaps choking one of our main arteries of fishways and fish production—all the chambers of commerce and real estate associations would be active," Darling had said then. "If I chose to oppose the dam and sent out word for help, only an echo of my own voice would come back."

Fifty years later, Hair said, the Federation is stopping dams and preserving wetlands throughout the nation. And the chambers of commerce and the real estate associations are paying more attention to the environment. They have to. It is the law, brought into being and watched over by sentinels in the Federation and other conservation groups.

But, as Hair wrote Federation members in 1986, "All the lobbyists in Washington . . . can't accomplish anything without *you*." Federation members, he continued, "have a track record of successfully influencing the nation's policy makers. They generated thousands of letters to Washington on the importance of protecting Alaskan lands. The result was impressive—today, 100 million acres of Alaska's wildlands are part of our national parks and wildlife refuges. . . . Remember—our job in Washington can't be done without you."

To better mobilize this power, Hair started the Resource Conservation Alliance, a select group of conservationists who work outside of Washington to augment the Federation's efforts "by staying current and being vocal on the crucial conservation decisions being made by our public officials."

Alliance members, who numbered 25,000 by the end of 1986, receive specially prepared NWF publications, such as "Watching the Watchdogs" on how to influence federal agencies and "Use the News to Protect Your Environment," a primer on the news media. "The next time an environmental problem rears its ugly head in your neighborhood," it advises, "don't just sit there. There is something you can do. Get the media involved and you just might win that fight!"

Just as Clean Sites, Inc., grew out of the Federation's experience with the Superfund, another venture into the private sector resulted in the creation of the Corporate Conservation Council, formed of representatives of chemical companies and power companies. The council got its start in 1982 when delegates from major corporations, which had often followed self-serving environmental policies attacked by conservation groups, met with staffers of the Federation to find a way to turn from confrontation to cooperation.

The council's primary task is to promote a continuing dialogue between the Federation and industrial leaders. Motivating the council is the belief that the corporate world and the Federation can work out ways to balance the need for economic growth with the need for protecting natural resources.

"We've had enough talk about 'dirty dozens' and 'filthy fives,' " said David Kuhn of Conoco, Inc., after the initial meeting of the council. "The current method of shouting at one another just isn't working."

Members of the council in the fall of 1986 were NWF; Atlantic Richfield Co.; E.I. du Pont de Nemours & Co., Inc.; Dow Chemical U.S.A.; Duke Power Co.; Exxon Co., U.S.A.; Miller Brewing Co.; Monsanto Co.; Tenneco Inc.; Tennessee Valley Authority; 3M Co.; USX; and Weyerhaeuser Co.

In 1986 the council chose a project on which to focus its resources: the conservation of our wetlands.

"Although we recognize that agreement will not always be easy," the corporation delegates said in a statement, "we are committed to seeking out those areas in which informed discussion between knowledgeable representatives can ease tension and move us toward greater understanding."

At a meeting between Federation officials and members of the council, a specialist on wetlands presses for the next step. We need more than words, he says. And as they begin to plan, they know that behind the Federation lie fifty years of experience and millions of loyal members and supporters who, year after year, have renewed their support for the Federation and swelled the chorus of conservationists in the land.

Affiliates of the National Wildlife Federation

(December 1986)

Alabama Wildlife Federation
Wildlife Federation of Alaska
Arizona Wildlife Federation
Arkansas Wildlife Federation
California Natural Resources Federation
Colorado Wildlife Federation
Connecticut Wildlife Federation
Wildlife Federation of Delaware
Florida Wildlife Federation
Georgia Wildlife Federation
Conservation Council for Hawaii
Idaho Wildlife Federation
Illinois Wildlife Federation
Indiana Wildlife Federation
Iowa Wildlife Federation
Kansas Wildlife Federation, Inc.
League of Kentucky Sportsmen, Inc.
Louisiana Wildlife Federation, Inc.
Natural Resources Council of Maine
Maryland*
Massachusetts Wildlife Federation
Michigan United Conservation Clubs, Inc.
Minnesota Conservation Federation
Mississippi Wildlife Federation
Conservation Federation of Missouri
Montana Wildlife Federation
Nebraska Wildlife Federation, Inc.
Nevada Wildlife Federation, Inc.
New Hampshire Wildlife Federation
New Jersey State Federation of Sportsmen's Clubs
New Mexico Wildlife Federation
New York State Conservation Council, Inc.
North Carolina Wildlife Federation
North Dakota Wildlife Federation

*Maryland has no state affiliate in 1986.

League of Ohio Sportsmen
Oklahoma Wildlife Federation
Oregon Wildlife Federation
Pennsylvania Federation of Sportsmen's Clubs, Inc.
Natural History Society of Puerto Rico, Inc.
Environment Council of Rhode Island, Inc.
South Carolina Wildlife Federation
South Dakota Wildlife Federation
Tennessee Conservation League
Sportsmen's Clubs of Texas, Inc.
Utah Wildlife Federation
Vermont Natural Resources Council
Virginia Wildlife Federation
Virgin Islands Conservation Society, Inc.
Washington State Sportsmen's Council
West Virginia Wildlife Federation, Inc.
Wisconsin Wildlife Federation, Inc.
Wyoming Wildlife Federation

For the address and phone number of any state affiliate, consult the most recent edition of the *Conservation Directory* (published annually by the National Wildlife Federation), available in many libraries, or write: National Wildlife Federation, Affiliate Services, 1412 16th Street, N.W., Washington, D.C. 20036.

APPENDIX 2

National Wildlife Week

Year	Theme	Chairperson
1938	National Wildlife Restoration Week	
1939	National Wildlife Restoration Week	
1940	National Wildlife Restoration Week	
1941	National Wildlife Restoration Week	
1942	National Wildlife Restoration Week	
1943	National Wildlife Restoration Week	
1944	National Wildlife Restoration Week	
1945	National Wildlife Restoration Week	
1946	National Wildlife Restoration Week	
1947	National Wildlife Restoration Week	
1948	National Wildlife Restoration Week	
1949	This Is Your Land—Conserve It	
1950	National Wildlife Restoration Week	Bing Crosby
1951	National Wildlife Restoration Week	Hopalong Cassidy
1952	Save the Key Deer	Ed Dodd
1953	Save the Prairie Chicken	Ed Dodd
1954	Clean Waters for All America	Ed Dodd
1955	Save America's Wetlands	Ed Dodd
1956	Save Endangered Wildlife	Walt Disney
1957	Make a Place for Wildlife	Walt Disney
1958	Protect Our Public Lands	Walt Disney
1959	Conservation in the Schools	Walt Disney
1960	Water: Key to Your Survival	Walt Disney
1961	Multiple Use of Our Natural Resources	Walt Disney
1962	Waterfowl for the Future	J. N. Darling & Walt Disney
1963	Chemical Pesticides Are Poison	Walt Disney
1964	America Needs Outdoor Recreation	Walt Disney
1965	Fight Dirty Water	Walt Disney
1966	Protect Natural Beauty	Walt Disney
1967	This Is Your Land	
1968	Learn to Live with Nature	Dick van Dyke
1969	Provide Habitat	
1970	Seen Any Wildlife Lately?	Arthur Godfrey
1971	Wildlife: Who Needs It?	Robert Redford

1972	Ecology: A Wild Idea	Robert Redford
1973	Discover Wildlife: It's Too Good to Miss	Shirley Temple Black
1974	We Care About Endangered Wildlife	Shirley Temple Black
1975	We Care About Wildlife Habitat	Lorne Greene
1976	Save Our Wetlands	Bing Crosby
1977	We All Need Clean Water	Robert Redford
1978	Wildlife Needs You	Robert Redford
1979	Conserve Our Wildlife	Robert Redford
1980	Save a Place for Wildlife	Robert Redford
1981	We Care About Oceans	Walter Cronkite
1982	We Care About Eagles	Robert Redford
1983	This Is Your Land—Public Lands Belong To All Of Us	Loretta Lynn
1984	Water: We Can't Live without It	Kermit the Frog
1985	Soil: We Can't Grow without It	Eddie Albert & Rowlf the Dog
1986	Discover Wildlife in Your World	Roger Tory Peterson

The Original
Wildlife Week Proclamation

by President Roosevelt, 1938

WHEREAS, one of the most important phases of the conservation of our natural resources is the protection and preservation of our wildlife; and

WHEREAS, this is a work in which virtually our entire citizenship can participate whole-heartedly and enthusiastically whether resident in the large metropolitan centers with limited access to the great outdoors or permitted to enjoy at first hand the wonders of nature; and

WHEREAS, the carrying into effect of any program for the consideration of our hereditary wildlife—in the past seriously diminished and depleted by destructive exploitation and lack of proper understanding and sympathy—must enlist the support of all our citizens if the mistakes of the past are to be avoided in the future in dealing with these important resources of incalculable social, economic, esthetic and recreational value:

Now, therefore, I, Franklin D. Roosevelt, President of the United States of America, do hereby proclaim and designate the week beginning March 20th, first to recognize the importance of the problem of conservation of these assets in wildlife and then to work with one accord for their proper protection and preservation. To this end I call upon all citizens in every community to give thought during this period to the needs of the denizens of field, forest and water and intelligent consideration of the best means for translating the intentions into practical action in behalf of these invaluable but inarticulate values. Only through the full cooperation of all can wildlife be restored for the present generation and perpetuated for posterity.

In Witness Whereof I have heretofore set my hand and caused the seal of the United States to be affixed.

Done at the City of Washington this 14th day of February in the year of our Lord 1938 and of the Independence of the United States of America the 162nd.

FRANKLIN D. ROOSEVELT

APPENDIX 4

NWF Presidents

Jay Norwood "Ding" Darling	1936–1939
David Archer Aylward	1939–1950
Claude D. Kelley	1950–1961
Dr. Paul A. Herbert	1961–1963
Ross L. Leffler	1963–1964
Judge Louis D. McGregor	1964–1967
Dr. Donald J. Zinn	1967–1970
Dr. James H. Shaeffer	1970–1972
N. A. "Bill" Winter, Jr.	1972–1974
Walter L. Mims	1974–1976
G. Ray Arnett	1976–1978
Dr. Frederick R. Scroggin	1978–1981
C. Clifton Young	1981–1983
Dr. Benjamin Clay Dysart, III	1983–1985
Carl N. Crouse	1985–

APPENDIX 5

Past Winners of the NWF
National Conservation Achievement Awards

JAY N. "DING" DARLING MEDAL /
    CONSERVATIONIST OF THE YEAR

1986   C. R. Gutermuth
1985   Morris K. Udall

CONSERVATIONIST OF THE YEAR

1984   William D. Ruckelshaus
1983   National Academy of Sciences and
           National Academy of Engineering
1982   S. David Freeman
1981   Glenn L. Bowers
           Thomas L. Kimball (Conservationist
              of the Decade)
1980   Cecil D. Andrus
           Richard K. Yancey
1979   Frank C. Bellrose
1978   Jimmy Carter
           Fred G. Evenden
1977   Butler Derrick
1976   William E. Towell
1975   Warren G. Magnuson
1974   Russell E. Train
1973   Tom McCall
1972   Jack C. Watson
1971   Russell W. Peterson
1970   H. James Morrison, Jr.
1969   David R. Strickland
1968   Howard Tanner
1967   Ed Dodd
1966   Guido R. Rahr
1965   Marvin B. Durning

COMMUNICATIONS

1986   Edward Flattau
1985   Thomas W. Horton, Baltimore Sunpapers

1984	The Louisville Courier-Journal
1983	Martin Crutsinger, Associated Press
1982	Lawrence Mosher, National Journal
1981	Robert H. Boyle, Sports Illustrated
1980	Walter Cronkite
1979	WGBH-TV, Boston, NOVA
1978	The Boston Globe
1977	Arkansas Gazette
	George Fisher
1976	Brian Kelley
1975	The Detroit News
1974	Ernest B. Furguson
1972	Lupi Saldana
	The Providence Journal-Bulletin
1970	Jacques Cousteau
	Patrick R. Cullen
1969	Bill Mauldin
	Pat Oliphant
1968	Christian Science Monitor
1967	NBC News
1966	National Association of Broadcasters
1965	Outdoor Writers Association of America

CORPORATE LEADERSHIP

1986	L.L. Bean, Inc.
1985	David M. Roderick, USX
1984	Duke Power Company
1983	Tenneco Inc.

EDUCATION

1986	Marge Hagerty
1985	The Alliance for Environmental Education
1984	Yosemite Institute
1983	Western Regional Environmental Education Council
1982	Eugene Odum
1981	Clay Schoenfeld
1980	John H. Reeves, Jr.

GOVERNMENT

1985	Governor Lamar Alexander (TN)
1984	Governor Bob Graham (FL)
1983	Governor James B. Hunt, Jr. (NC)

INTERNATIONAL

1986	David A. Munro
1983	HRH Prince Philip, Duke of Edinburgh
1982	Salim Ali
1978	Ian McTaggart Cowen
1977	Ruth C. Clusen
1976	Robert M. White
1975	Peter Markham Scott
1972	Maurice F. Strong

LEGISLATIVE

1986	John F. Seiberling
1985	Patrick Leahy
1984	Silvio O. Conte
1983	John Breaux
1982	Dale Bumpers
1981	John H. Chafee
	George Mitchell
1980	Edwin B. Forsythe
1978	Phillip Burton
1977	Gary Hart
1976	Richard L. Ottinger
1975	(Warren G. Magnuson)
1974	Ernest Hollings
1973	Morris K. Udall
1972	Clinton P. Anderson
1971	Henry S. Reuss
1970	Philip A. Hart
1969	Henry M. Jackson
1968	Gaylord Nelson
1967	John D. Dingell
1966	Edmund S. Muskie
1965	Frank Church

ORGANIZATION

1985	Natural Resources Defense Council
1984	The Conservation Foundation
1983	The Wildlife Society
1981	The Nature Conservancy
1980	American Fisheries Society
1979	The Izaak Walton League of America
1978	Environmental Study Conference
1977	Wildlife Management Institute
1976	Rachel Carson Trust for the Living Environment
	Conservation Federation of Missouri

1975	Gulf States Paper Corporation
1974	Society for the Protection of New Hampshire Forests
1973	The United States Jaycees Environmental Improvement Program
1972	The Scouting Movement of America
1971	Douglas MacArthur High School Anti-Pollution Committee
1969	Save Our Bay Action Committee
1968	League of Women Voters
1967	Ford Motor Company
1966	General Electric Company

SCIENCE

1986	Earnest F. Gloyna
1985	Dr. Gilbert White
1984	George Schaller
1983	Durward Allen

RESOURCES DEFENCE

1981	Terris and Sunderland
1980	Joseph L. Sax
1979	Bruce H. Anderson
1978	James Goetz
	William Madden
1977	Michael Osborne
1976	Gus Speth

SPECIAL ACHIEVEMENT

1986	H. Albert Hochbaum
	Celia Hunter
1985	Elliot Barker
	Marjory Stoneman Douglas
	Maurice K. Goddard
	Ken McLeod
	Mardy Murie
1984	Chesapeake Bay Foundation
	Louis Fernandez
	National Geographic Society
	Merrill Petoskey
	Tracks Magazine
	Reuben Trippensee
	John Turner
1983	Ansel Adams
	Robert Northshield
1982	Bruce Babbitt

J. A. Brownridge
Joseph J. Hickey
Robert L. Morris
Pennzoil Company
Remington Farms
John E. Vogt
Henry Waxman
John G. Wellman
1981   Lester R. Brown
Kenneth A. Brynaert
Louis S. Clapper
William S. Huey
Stephen Kellert
Garry B. Trudeau
The World Bank
1980   Richard W. Riley
Southern California Edison Company
Robert T. Stafford
Lucille F. Stickel
Keith Wright
1979   J. Clark Akers
Norman A. Berg
The Conservation Law Foundation
     of New England, Inc.
Lynn Ludlow
George Reiger
1978   Luther J. Carter
Florida Wildlife Federation
High Country News
William G. Milliken
Ted S. Petit
South Carolina Wildlife Magazine
Elvis J. Stahr
Jane Hurt Yarn
1977   Steve Gallizioli
Seth Gordon
Henry Herrmann
John E. Murphy
Laurence Pringle
1976   Barbara Blum
Lewis E. Carpenter
Henry E. Clepper
William J. Hargis, Jr.
1975   Carl N. Crouse
Ray C. Erickson
Joseph M. Long
Arthur R. Marshall
Lily Peter
Richard H. Stroud

1974	E. Budd Marter, III
	Roger Tory Peterson
	Mrs. Lewis E. Smoot
1973	John S. Gottschalk
1972	Ralph A. MacMullan
1970	Frederick N. and Frances
	Hamerstrom
	Joseph Paul
	John Esposito
1969	Joseph W. Penfold
	Philip Vaughan
	Victor John Yannacone, Jr.
1968	Orville L. Freeman
	George A. Selke
1967	Alan Bible
	Thomas H. Kuchel
	Mr. and Mrs. J. Meredith
	Tatton
1966	Dorothy R. Buell
	Paul H. Douglas
1965	Mrs. Lyndon B. Johnson
	Nelson A. Rockefeller

OUTSTANDING NWF STATE AFFILIATE

1986	Minnesota Conservation Federation
1985	Mississippi Wildlife Federation
1984	Colorado Wildlife Federation
1983	Wyoming Wildlife Federation
1982	Natural Resources Council of Maine
1981	Pennsylvania Federation of Sportsmen's Clubs
1980	Wisconsin Wildlife Federation
1979	Tennessee Conservation League
1978	Iowa Wildlife Federation
	Virginia Wildlife Federation
1977	South Carolina Wildlife Federation
1976	Michigan United Conservation Clubs
1975	North Carolina Wildlife Federation
	North Dakota Wildlife Federation
1974	Georgia Wildlife Federation
	Oklahoma Wildlife Federation
1973	Kansas Wildlife Federation
	Montana Wildlife Federation
1972	Alabama Wildlife Federation
1971	Vermont Natural Resources Council
1970	Arkansas Wildlife Federation
1969	Natural Resources Council of Maine
	North Carolina Wildlife Federation
1968	Indiana Conservation Council

1967	Federated Sportsmen's Clubs of New Hampshire
1966	Virginia Wildlife Federation
1965	Minnesota Conservation Federation

APPENDIX 6

The National
Wildlife Federation
Creed . . .

I pledge myself, as a responsible human, to assume my share of the stewardship of our natural resources.

I will use my share with gratitude, without greed, or waste.

I will respect the rights of others and abide by the law.

I will support sound management of the resources we use, the restoration of the resources we have despoiled, and the safekeeping of significant resources for posterity.

I will never forget that life and beauty, wealth and progress, depend on how wisely we use these gifts . . . the soil, the water, the air, the minerals, the plant life, and the wildlife.

APPENDIX 7

Purposes of the National Wildlife Federation as Expressed in Its Articles of Incorporation

● To coordinate all agencies, societies, clubs and individuals which are or should be interested in the restoration, wise use, conservation and scientific management of wildlife and other natural resources into a permanent, unified, active agency for the purpose of securing adequate public recognition of the needs and values of wildlife resources and other natural resources.

● To develop, promote and support a comprehensive educational program based upon scientific study and technical research for the advancement, restoration, wise use, management and conservation of wildlife and other natural resources.

● To inform and educate the public through the dissemination of pertinent facts, scientific and research discoveries and information that may contribute to the solution of the problem involved in the restoration, wise use and conservation of wildlife and other natural resources.

● To stimulate a proper public attitude and appreciation regarding the use and management of all natural resources, enabling our people to appraise the aesthetic value and importance of all resources.

● To cooperate with other conservation and wildlife organizations and to promote improved educational methods by encouraging the training of teachers and providing educational materials for the enlightened understanding of resource management.

● To do all such acts as are necessary or proper for carrying out the purposes set forth above.

NWF Legislation Timeline

By testifying before congressional committees, by working closely with the executive branch, and—after the Tax Reform Act of 1976—by lobbying, the National Wildlife Federation has influenced the fate of many bills concerning wildlife and the environment. Listed below are the most important of these laws which the Federation and its affiliates, working with numerous senators and representatives, helped secure. (Popular name of legislation appears in parentheses following official name.)

1937. Federal Aid in Wildlife Restoration Act (Pittman-Robertson). This act created a federal excise tax on firearms and provides matching funds to states for the acquisition, restoration, and maintenance of habitat for the management of wildlife and for research concerning wildlife management.

1947. Federal Insecticide, Fungicide, and Rodenticide Act (FIFRA). Landmark legislation addressing toxic chemicals in the environment, FIFRA defines "economic poisons" to be any product "intended for preventing, destroying, repelling, or mitigating any insects, rodents, nematodes, fungi, weeds" or other forms of life declared to be a pest. Plant regulators, defoliants, and desiccants are also included as economic poisons. This act requires that all such poisons be registered and labeled with a warning and instructions for use to prevent injury to nontarget organisms. This was the first time a federal law considered the effects of certain poisons on nontarget wildlife.

1948. Transfer of Certain Real Property for Wildlife Conservation Purposes Act. Under this legislation, if a federal agency possesses land it no longer needs but which has particular value for migratory birds, the agency can be reimbursed for transferring the land to the secretary of the interior or to a state agency for wildlife conservation.

1950. Federal Aid in Fish Restoration Act (Dingell-Johnson). An extension of the concept of the Pittman-Robertson Act, this act uses a general tax on sport fishing equipment to raise funds which are made available to states for the restoration and management of sport fisheries.

1956. Water Pollution Control Act. This landmark legislation stipulates that federal grants may be given for the construction of water treatment plants. Originally limited to interstate waters, this act was extended in 1975 to include navigable waters.

1956. Fish and Wildlife Reorganization Act. This act split the Fish and Wildlife Service into two bureaus: Sport Fisheries and Wildlife, and Commercial Fisheries. In addition, the act authorizes the secretary of the interior to take steps "required for the development, advancement, management, conservation and protection of fishery and wildlife resources" through research, acquisition of refuge lands, and development of existing facilities.

1958. Pesticide Research Act. This act directs the U.S. Fish and Wildlife Service to investigate wildlife losses possibly caused by the application of pesticides and to research ways to reduce damage and loss.

1960. Sikes Act. This act requires all U.S. military reservations to develop, maintain, and coordinate conservation programs for wildlife, fish, and game.

1961. Wetlands Loan Act. An advanced, interest-free appropriation to the Migratory Bird Hunting Stamp Fund (to acquire refuges and waterfowl production areas) of up to $105 million for a 7-year period was authorized.

1963. Clean Air Act. Acting on its own or at the request of a state, the Department of Health, Education, and Welfare (and now the Environmental Protection Agency) can initiate public hearings, conferences, and court proceedings to effect compliance with air pollution regulations.

1964. Wilderness Act. The National Wilderness System was created out of wilderness, wild, and canoe areas of the national forests and provision was made for a review system for the inclusion of additional wilderness areas.

1964. Land and Water Conservation Fund Act. Monies collected primarily from offshore oil and gas leases are used to fund a variety of state and federal recreational programs and to acquire recreational lands. Later amendments to the act increased the total annual expenditure, increased the proportion of the fund to be contributed by the federal government, and allowed the fund to be used to acquire areas needed for conserving endangered and threatened species of plants or animals.

1966. Endangered Species Preservation Act. The secretary of the nterior is directed to carry out a land acquisition program to "conserve, protect, restore, and propagate selected species of native fish and wildlife" in the Uniited States. Up to $15 million from the Land and Water Conservation Fund can be used for acquisition.

1968. Wild and Scenic Rivers Act. Segments of seven major rivers in their free-flowing state were set aside for recreational and conservation purposes; provision was made to add to the system.

1968. National Trails System Act. A national trail system was established, comprising National Recreation Trails and National Scenic Trails.

1969. National Environmental Policy Act (NEPA). All federal agencies must prepare, and make public, environmental impact statements with respect to any proposed legislation or other action that would significantly affect the quality of the environment.

1969. Endangered Species Conservation Act. Authority conferred on the secretary of the interior by the 1966 Endangered Species Act was expanded; types of wildlife under protection are defined. The secretary of the interior may promulgate a list of wildlife "threatened with worldwide extinction" and prohibit importation of any animal appearing on this list.

1969. Water Bank Act. The secretary of agriculture was given the authority to enter into agreements with private landowners to protect wetlands in areas important to the nesting and breeding of waterfowl.

1971. Alaska Native Claims Settlement Act. This legislation granted 44 million acres of federal land and a $1 million cash settlement to Alaskan natives, paving the way for the construction of the 800-mile Alyeska pipeline from Prudhoe Bay to the Gulf of Alaska. It also set the stage for the 1980 Alaska Lands Act by requiring the secretary of the interior to set aside over 80 million acres of Alaskan lands for Congress to designate as national parks, wildlife refuges, national forests, and wild and scenic rivers.

1972. Coastal Zone Management Act. This act was designed to "preserve, protect, develop, and, where possible, to restore or enhance the resources of the nation's coastal zone."

1972. Federal Water Pollution Control Act Amendments (Clean Water Act). With this legislation, the U.S. was provided with a new, comprehensive, and forceful strategy not only to stop the pollution but also to restore and maintain the chemical, physical, and biological integrity of lakes, streams, and surface waters. Under Section 404 of this act, the Army Corps of Engineers was given responsibility to oversee any discharge of dredged or fill material in navigable waters. (After a 1975 NWF lawsuit, this jurisdiction was extended to include wetlands and headwaters.)

1972. Marine Protection Research and Sanctuaries Act (Oceans Dumping Act). This act prevents and limits the dumping of specific waste materials at sea and authorizes the secretary of commerce, with presidential approval, to designate marine sanctuaries and preserve or restore these areas for their conservation, ecological, or esthetic values.

1972. Federal Environmental Pesticide Control Act. EPA was given much greater authority to control pesticide use, including a two-category system of registering pesticides as intended for "general" or "restricted" use, with the latter to be used only by certified applicators.

1972. Marine Mammals Protection Act. This act calls upon the federal government to establish a comprehensive, coordinated program to conserve ocean mammals and their products. It extends protection to individual population stocks as well as species or subspecies of marine mammals.

1973. Convention on International Trade in Endangered Species of Wild Fauna and Flora (CITES). Signed by 80 nations, including the United States, the convention established a system of import/export regulation to prevent the commercial overexploitation of endangered or threatened plants and animals. Different levels of trade regulations were provided depending on the threatened status of any particular species and the effect trade would have on that species.

1973. Endangered Species Act. This act created the endangered and threatened categories for species and extended the responsibility for conserving species to all federal agencies. The secretary of the interior was made responsible for updating and overseeing these efforts. In addition, the secretary was charged with insuring that federal activities neither jeopardize the continued existence of, nor destroy or modify critical habitat for, endangered or threatened species. With this act the United States ratified the CITES Treaty.

1974. Sikes Act Extension. With this act, the mandate to develop, maintain, and coordinate conservation programs for wildlife, fish, and game on military reservations is extended to include national forests, and public lands administered by the BLM and the Atomic Energy Commission. Such programs must include specific projects to improve habitat and must provide protection to threatened or endangered species.

1974. Forest and Rangelands Renewable Resources Planning Act. To facilitate long range planning for the use of renewable resources within the National Forest Systems, five-year plans must be prepared to outline the protection, management, and development of land in the system.

1976. Federal Land Policy and Management Act (BLM Organic Act). Signifying a major policy change, this act established management standards for federal lands under the jurisdiction of the BLM. The secretary of the interior is required to develop and maintain "land use plans which provide by tracts or areas for the use of public land" and for the protection of fish and wildlife habitat. In addition, "regulations and plans for the protection of public land areas of critical environmental concern" must be promptly developed.

1976. Toxic Substances Control Act. Designed to *prevent* environmental degradation, this law directed EPA to require testing of all existing and new substances which may present an unreasonable risk to public health or the environment and, if necessary, to step in with regulations.

1976. National Forest Management Act. An amendment to the 1974 Forest and Rangelands Renewable Resources Planning Act, this act prohibits clear-cutting in national forests and imposes detailed standards on Forest Service management. Public participation is required at every significant stage of administrative action.

1977. Surface Mining Control and Reclamation Act. This act prohibits surface mining on unsuitable land and sets strict standards for reclamation and restoration of land that is suitable for surface mining.

1978. National Parks and Recreation Act (Omnibus Parks Act). Eight new wilderness areas, covering almost 2 million acres, were added to the National Park System. Major additions were also made to the Wild and Scenic Rivers System and the National Scenic Trails System.

1980. Alaska National Interest Lands Conservation Act (Alaska Lands Act). With passage of this act, the country's federal wildlife refuge and park systems were expanded by nearly 100 million acres and new management standards were set for refuges in the 49th state.

1980. Fish and Wildlife Conservation Act (Nongame Act). This act authorizes federal funding to be made available for the conservation of *nongame* wildlife. In so doing, it strives to encourage comprehensive conservation planning, encompassing both non-game and other wildlife. Unlike Pittman-Robertson and Dingell-Johnson, funding for the Nongame Act comes not from an excise tax but from general appropriations from the U.S. Treasury. As of the end of 1986, Congress had appropriated no funds and the Nongame Act has had no opportunity to live up to its great potential.

1980. Comprehensive Environmental Response, Compensation and Liability Act (Superfund). In the event of any damaging release of a hazardous substance into the environment, the following parties may be held liable for any cleanup costs: the manufacturers and distributors of the substance, and the owners of waste disposal sites. If the responsible party refuses to cooperate, EPA may use the Superfund for immediate cleanup costs and later sue the responsible parties for recovery of expenses. This fund is maintained by federal allocations and taxes levied on the chemical industry.

1982. Coastal Barrier Resources Act. More than 600 miles of fragile beaches and barrier islands along the Atlantic and Gulf coast were designated as the Coastal Barrier Resource System. Federal subsidies are no longer granted for roads or bridges in these special areas.

1982. Endangered Species Act Amendments of 1982. Amendments to the Endangered Species Act in 1978 had a nearly crippling effect on the process of listing species as endangered or threatened. The amendments of 1982 speeded up the listing/delisting process by removing many of the burdensome requirements. They also removed economic or other extraneous considerations from the listing process, and extended the protection to include plants on federal land.

1985. Food Security Act (Farm Bill). Strong soil and water conservation provisions were included for the first time in a national farm bill that sets the country's agricultural policy. "Sodbuster" and "swampbuster" provisions deny federal benefits such as crop insurance, loans, and subsidies to farmers who plow, fill in, or otherwise destroy wetlands or grasslands, and make available federal funds to plant cover crops such as legumes and various grasses in fragile areas. In addition, a conservation reserve section was established, setting aside up to 40 million acres of highly erodible land.

1986. Water Resources Development Act. Before passage of this act, local beneficiaries of water projects did not contribute funds for their construction. By requiring that local as well as federal monies be used to fund construction, this legislation was intended to curb excessive spending as well as discourage environmentally damaging projects. The legislation also requires the Army Corps of Engineers to mitigate damages to fish and wildlife habitat and gives them authority to remedy damages to habitat caused by projects built in the past.

1986. Superfund Amendments and Reauthorization Act (Superfund Reauthorization). These amendments extended the 1980 Superfund legislation by setting standards and establishing a timetable for the cleanup process and by addressing the human predicaments associated with toxic contamination. The community-right-to-know provision requires chemical companies to report everyday releases of hazardous substances and devise emergency plans for the community. Assessments of hazards to human health from contamination must be made and communicated to people in the region. State laws that had prevented victims from seeking compensation were nullified. The Superfund itself, reauthorized at $8.5 billion, is maintained by federal allocations and taxes levied on the chemical and petroleum industry and producers of hazardous wastes.

NWF Litigation Timeline

In 1971, the National Wildlife Federation hired its first lawyers to help protect wildlife and its habitat by enforcing conservation legislation. From a handful of annual cases in the early 1970s, the Federation's involvement has expanded to encompass between 50 and 100 cases per year in the 1980s. A few of the most important of these cases are listed below. They are listed by their popular name or by the subject of the suit, rather than by the title on the court docket, because in several areas (e.g., highway and lead shot litigation) the Federation has been involved in several cases on the subject.

Calvert Cliffs. The Calvert Cliffs Coordinating Committee, with the urging and financial backing of NWF, sued to apply the newly enacted National Environmental Policy Act (NEPA) to the decision to locate a nuclear power plant on the Chesapeake Bay. In this first test of NEPA, a U.S. court of appeals ruled that the Atomic Energy Commission and all other federal agencies must submit environmental impact statements for any proposed project that will significantly affect the environment. This opinion has been widely cited as requiring a "careful balancing" between environmental and economic factors. (1970)

Highway Fights. NWF lawsuits opened highway planning to public scrutiny by forcing publication of federal highway regulations, by applying NEPA to ongoing highway projects and programs, and by requiring public hearings prior to acquisition of property for rights-of-way. (1970–1973)

Lead Shot. In 1972 NWF petitioned the secretary of the interior to regulate the use of lead shot in migratory waterfowl hunting. In response, Interior issued final regulations in 1976 calling for a gradual phase-in of nontoxic steel shot. The National Rifle Association (NRA) then sued Interior to enjoin the regulations; NWF intervened on the side of the government, defended the steel shot program, and won. NRA's appeal, in 1977, was unsuccessful. In 1985 NWF returned to court, this time filing suit *against* the Department of the Interior for its failure to set aside additional steel shot zones to protect the endangered bald eagle, which is protected by the Endangered Species Act. The federal court ordered Interior to require exclusive use of steel shot in 22 counties in 5 states that had refused to implement earlier regulations establishing the special zones. A year later, NWF protested that addressing the lead shot problem through special zones or "hot spots" where eagles are known to be particularly susceptible is inadequate, and it sought a court order requiring Interior to ban waterfowl hunters nationwide ("lower 48") from using lead shot beginning with the 1987–88 season. A U.S. district court judge dismissed the case as "premature," but made it clear that the Department of the Interior must live up to its commitment to phase out all use of lead shot for waterfowl hunting by 1991. (1972–1986)

Mississippi Sandhill Crane. An NWF lawsuit in 1975 challenged plans for a portion of federal highway I-10 that was to bisect habitat of the Mississippi Sandhill Crane, an endangered subspecies. NWF lost, but a favorable decision in an appeals court in 1976 prevented the most damaging aspects of construction. The U.S. Supreme Court, by denying review of this decision in 1976, upheld the lower court's decision. Meanwhile, the Department of Transportation and NWF had entered into negotiations over acquisition of lands adjacent to the proposed construction site to establish a crane refuge. In 1978 Congress authorized $4.5 million to acquire the crane refuge, allowing the highway to proceed without jeopardy to the species. (1975–1978)

Wetlands Protection. Section 404 of the Clean Water Act authorized the Army Corps of Engineers to regulate the discharge of dredged or fill materials into the waters of the United States. After a successful lawsuit in 1975 by NWF and the Natural Resources Defense Council, the Corps' jurisdiction was extended to include headwaters and wetlands, turning Section 404 into the nation's premier wetlands protection law.

With each successive lawsuit, the term *wetland* has been clarified and the domain of Section 404 has been expanded. In 1977 NWF sued to apply federal environmental laws to a private wetland drainage project in North Dakota; the project was stopped and thousands of acres of prairie potholes were protected. A successful NWF suit in 1978 resulted in protection for 20,000 acres of bottomland hardwoods in Louisiana and set a precedent for protecting an additional four million acres in Mississippi. Another lawsuit ended with a settlement in which the Corps agreed to: require individual permits for those activities that would destroy isolated wetlands 10 acres or more in size; follow EPA's "water dependency" test, which requires that projects under consideration for a 404 permit must be dependent on water to be granted the permit; and apply nationwide a federal appeals court's decision which concluded that discharges of fill material caused by land-clearing activities are subject to the Section 404 permit process.

In 1985 a Supreme Court ruling overturned a lower court decision which would have limited the types of wetlands protected under Section 404. NWF had earlier filed a legal brief supporting the Army Corps of Engineer's decision that all wetlands, not just those frequently flooded by adjacent surface waters, are covered under the law. The court ruling ensures continued protection of some four million acres of wetlands, including prairie potholes, pocosins, and tundra marshes. (1975–1983)

Ocean Dumping. In the late 1970s and early 1980s NWF filed a number of lawsuits over the federal government's handling of offshore waste disposal. In a 1978 case against the New York District of the Army Corps of Engineers, the court established an important precedent under NEPA: the Corps cannot treat each separate dumping activity at the same ocean site individually, but must address the impacts of, and alternatives to, ocean dumping in a comprehensive fashion. In another suit, NWF challenged EPA and the Corps of Engineers on their practice of routinely authorizing ocean dumping at 140 coastal sites given interim-approval not on the basis of prior study and evaluation, as required by law, but on the basis of historical usage. The government agreed to complete site-designation studies (supported by formal environmental impact statements) at specified dumpsites in 20 coastal areas—accounting for nearly 90 percent of U.S. ocean dumping—in accordance with a timetable that required the final site designations to be selected by March 1983. (1975–1986)

Endangered Species versus Hunting Rights of Native Americans. Several federal acts aimed at species protection (Walrus Protection Act of 1941, Fur Seal Act of 1966, Marine Mammals Act, and the Endangered Species Act) have recognized the need to exempt native Americans from the hunting restrictions so that they can meet their subsistence and/or handicraft needs. When the International Whaling Commission eliminated an exemption under which native Alaskans had been permitted to hunt bowhead whales, a highly endangered species, a group of Eskimos filed suit to seek what amounts to a mandatory injunction directing the secretary of state to file an objection. NWF entered the issue after a federal court order directed the secretary to file the objection. The secretary, supported by NWF, appealed the decision. The secretary argued that an objection by the United States would probably trigger objections by the Soviets, Japanese, and numerous other nations, leading to the killing off of entire herds of bowheads. The court ruled in favor of the secretary, and no objection was filed. (1977)

Trust Fund for an Endangered Species. In 1977 NWF filed suit to prevent the construction of the Grayrocks Dam in Wyoming because it, and several other similar proposed projects, threatened to degrade prime habitat of the endangered whooping crane along the Platte River in Wyoming and Nebraska. In 1978 NWF won the suit, entering a precedent-setting settlement that established a $7.5 million trust for the acquisition of water rights to protect crane habitat on the Platte for future generations. (1977–1978)

Water Resources Planning Panel. In 1979 NWF sued to stop the construction of a water treatment plant that would provide a major new water reservoir for Denver. The treatment plant, NWF asserted, was much larger than it need be for Denver's projected use of water, and its largeness would only promote unnecessary projects, such as diverting water across the Rocky Mountains, that might damage the environment. The settlement allowed the treatment plant to be constructed as planned, but, to NWF's satisfaction, forced city planners to look at the big picture of water resources in Denver: it established a panel to overhaul the area's water planning process, promote water conservation, and provide citizen participation in the planning process.

The National Environmental Policy Act (NEPA) in National Forests. NWF sued the U.S. Forest Service to apply NEPA to multiple-year timber harvest plans for national forests along coastal areas of the Pacific Northwest. The court stopped all timber sales there until the "worst-case analysis" of the effect of harvests on coastal fisheries was adequately assessed. (1983)

Nondevelopment Coal Lease on Vital Habitat. For the pronghorn antelope, the Red Rim area in Wyoming is a critical winter foraging ground. For Rocky

Mountain Energy, who owns the mineral right beneath Red Rim, it is a potential strip mine. In 1986, after more than three years of negotiations, the Wyoming Wildlife Federation and NWF reached a precedent-setting agreement with Rocky Mountain Energy: WWF and NWF were given a nondevelopment coal lease to the southern half of the region's subsurface coal. WWF and NWF will retain the lease until Rocky Mountain Energy, which retained the coal leases to the northern half of the Rim, has restored any mined areas to their original condition. (1981–1986)

Public Review of Public Land Protection. NWF discovered that the Bureau of Land Management (BLM), without prior public review or environmental analysis, had eliminated restrictions on development ("withdrawals") on over 170 million acres of federal land. NWF sued and obtained a preliminary injunction; the court restored public lands to their status in 1981 prior to the illegal elimination of development restrictions. (1981–)

Strip Mining. Soon after the 1977 Surface Mining and Reclamation Act passed, mining companies filed suit against the Office of Surface Mining (OSM) to contest the interim regulations written to enforce the Surface Mining Act. Entering the suit on the side of OSM, NWF helped to defend most of the interim regulations. Problems of enforcement still remained, however, and in 1979 NWF filed suit against OSM. Other conservation groups filed a similar suit in 1982. In 1984 an out-of-court settlement ended the two cases. OSM agreed to undertake a major initiative aimed at stopping repeated and flagrant violations of the strip mining laws. Among other things, OSM agreed to set up systems for denying new mining permits to coal operators found to be violating the law, issue penalties against individual corporate executives of coal companies in violation of the law, and secure court injunctions against dangerous operations.

Meanwhile, in the early 1980s, Secretary of the Interior James Watt made over 200 changes in the strip mining regulations that either weakened or repealed environmental protections mandated under the 1977 act. Nine lawsuits that had been filed by NWF and other conservation organizations were consolidated into one case in 1983. One part of the case was decided in 1984, with NWF winning on most of the issues it had raised: environmental impacts of coal processing plants must be regulated, mine operators preparing mining permit applications must supply information about fish and wildlife resources in the area to be mined, toxic ponds must be fenced or covered to prevent contamination to wildlife, and state-listed threatened and endangered species must be protected. The final decision, handed down in 1985, prohibited strip mining in national parks, federal wildlife refuges, national forests, and other protected areas.

NWF oversight of OSM continues. In May 1986 NWF filed an appeal with the D.C. Court of Appeals with respect to eight issues in its 1984 challenge of OSM regulations. In July NWF initiated a lawsuit against the federal OSM and the state of Kentucky over the failure of the agency to conduct adequate oversight of state programs and enforce the Surface Mining Act. (1979–)

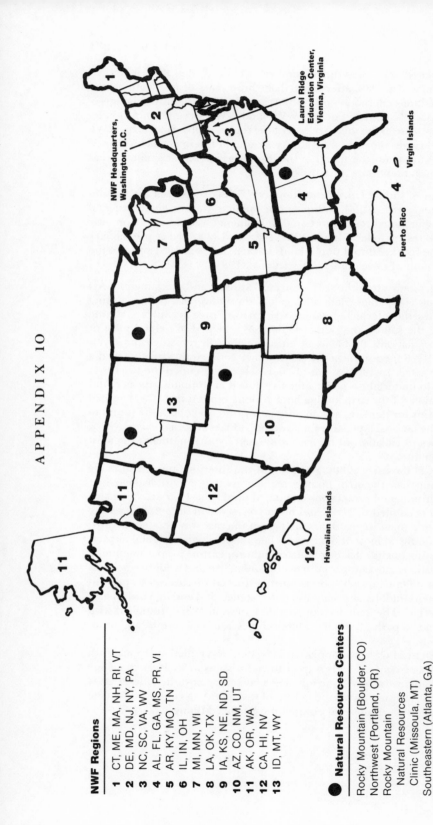

APPENDIX IO

NWF Regions

1 CT, ME, MA, NH, RI, VT
2 DE, MD, NJ, NY, PA
3 NC, SC, VA, WV
4 AL, FL, GA, MS, PR, VI
5 AR, KY, MO, TN
6 IL, IN, OH
7 MI, MN, WI
8 LA, OK, TX
9 IA, KS, NE, ND, SD
10 AZ, CO, NM, UT
11 AK, OR, WA
12 CA, HI, NV
13 ID, MT, WY

● **Natural Resources Centers**

Rocky Mountain (Boulder, CO)
Northwest (Portland, OR)
Rocky Mountain
  Natural Resources
  Clinic (Missoula, MT)
Southeastern (Atlanta, GA)
Great Lakes (Ann Arbor, MI)
Prairie Wetlands (Bismarck, ND)

NWF Headquarters,
Washington, D.C.

Laurel Ridge
Education Center,
Vienna, Virginia

Puerto Rico

Virgin Islands

Hawaiian Islands

**Regions of the National Wildlife Federation
(and location of its headquarters and Natural Resources Centers)**

SELECTED BIBLIOGRAPHY

Sources used to write *Guardian of the Wild* include: research and interviews with Federation leaders and officers conducted by Robert Elman; minutes from NWF annual meetings and board of directors' meetings; archival files of NWF officers and leaders; Federation publications; and personal communication with the staff of the National Wildlife Federation and several of its affiliates.

The sources relied on most consistently are the following:

Allen, Thomas B. *Vanishing Wildlife of North America.* New York: National Geographic Society, 1974.

Bean, Michael, J. *The Evolution of National Wildlife Law.* New York: Praeger Publishers, 1983.

Katlin, Steven. "History of Conservation." Unpublished manuscript.

Lendt, David L. *Ding: The Life of Jay Norwood Darling.* Iowa State University Press, Ames, Iowa, 1979.

Matthiessen, Peter. *Wildlife in America.* New York: The Viking Press, 1959.

"Mayflower Miracle." *Time.* 27 (17 February 1936):22.

Pack, Arthur N. "The Wildlife Conference." *Nature Magazine* 27 (April 1936):233–234.

Schoenfeld, Clay. "The Role of the Mass Media in Environmental Education." in *Environmental Education in Action—I: Case studies of selected public school and public action programs,* edited by Clay Schoenfeld and John Disinger, 296–306. 1977. Columbus, Ohio: Eric/Center for Science, Mathematics, and Environmental Education, College of Education, The Ohio State University; 343 pp.

Shoemaker, Carl. "Stories Behind the Federation." Washington, D.C.: (privately published—Shoemaker), 1960.

Steiner, Alan J. "U.S. History of Wildlife and Wildlife Law." Unpublished manuscript.

Trefethen, James B. *An American Crusade for Wildlife.* New York: Winchester Press and the Boone and Crocket Club, 1975.

"Wildlife Week." *Science* 87 (11 March 1938):229–230.

INDEX